RECOVERING BIBLICAL DISCIPLESHIP

RECOVERING BIBLICAL DISCIPLESHIP

*What Discipleship Was Supposed to Be,
and Maybe Christianity Too*

by

Brian Burson

XULON PRESS

Xulon Press
2301 Lucien Way #415
Maitland, FL 32751
407.339.4217
www.xulonpress.com

Due to the changing nature of the Internet, if there are any web addresses, links, or URLs included in this manuscript, these may have been altered and may no longer be accessible. The views and opinions shared in this book belong solely to the author and do not necessarily reflect those of the publisher. The publisher therefore disclaims responsibility for the views or opinions expressed within the work.

Unless otherwise indicated, Scripture quotations taken from the New American Standard Bible (NASB). Copyright © 1960, 1962, 1963, 1968, 1971, 1972, 1973, 1975, 1977, 1995, 1998, by The Lockman Foundation. Used by permission. All rights reserved.

Paperback ISBN-13: 978-1-6628-5718-8
Ebook ISBN-13: 978-1-6628-5719-5

ACKNOWLEDGEMENTS

I want to sincerely thank all those individuals who played a positive role in my Christian experience over many years. There have been many who were instruments of God's grace, from bringing me to personal faith in Christ and then nurturing me along the way of growing and developing. There have been more than can be listed by name. Many of them are already with the Lord in glory, enjoying their true reward.

Thanks to those who encouraged me to write this book, so I could share with a wider audience the insights that God has given me in this essential subject of the Christian experience. Thanks to Xulon Press for working with me in patience and encouragement to achieve completion of this book.

Special thanks goes to my loving wife for her constant and unwavering support and encouragement.

Thanks to all the following publishers who kindly granted me permission to quote text from the noted books:

David C. Cook
4050 Lee Vance View
Colorado Springs, CO 80918
Multiply, Disciples Making Disciples, by Francis Chan with Mark Beuving, 2012

Touchstone, Imprint of Simon & Schuster, Inc.
New York, NY
The Cost of Discipleship by Dietrich Bonhoeffer, 1995

Tyndale Publishers, Inc.
Wheaton, IL
Churchless, by Barna Group, George Barna and David Kinnaman
general editors, 2014
*He Is There and He Is Not Silent by Francis A. Schaffer, 1972

Fleming H. Revell Company
Old Tappan, New Jersey
An Expository Dictionary of New Testament Words by W.E.
Vine, M.A, 1966

Holman Bible Publishers
Nashville, TN
Ancient Faith Bible, 2007

Judson Press
Valley Forge, PA
$3.00 Worth of God by Wilbur E. Rees, 1971

William B. Eerdmans Publishing Co.
Grand Rapids, MI
Wuest's Word Studies From the Greek New Testament, Vol. 3. by
Kenneth S. Wuest, 1974

HarperCollins Publishers, Inc,
New York, New York
The Great Omission, by Dallas Willard, 2006
Dallas Willard, *The Divine Conspiracy* 1998

Baker Books
Grand Rapids, MI
The Creeds of Christendom, Vol. III, Phillip Schaff, editor, revised
by David S. Schaff, 2007

LifeWay Press
Nashville, TN
Experiencing God by Henry T. Blackaby, and Claude V. King, 1999

Zondervan
Grand Rapids, MI
Soul Keeping by John Ortberg, 2014

The University of Chicago Press
Chicago, USA
*A Greek-English Lexicon of the New Testament and Other Early
Christian Literature,* 1957 by Arndt and Gingrich

DEDICATION

This book is for everyone who has found themselves saying, "Is that all there is to Christianity?" This book is for everyone who has found themselves saying, "Why don't I experience a deep connection to God when I go to church?", or "Why don't I experience a deep connection with God in my faith?" This book is for everyone who has found themselves saying, "Why don't I find more Christlikeness amongst Christians?" This book is for everyone who has "tried Christianity…and found it wanting" or way short on delivery. This book is for everyone who feels like they have hit a stalemate in their Christian growth, and no one seems to have any guidance how to break through. In fact, they believe that only certain people have the right to break through. This book is for everyone who takes an interest in the Christian faith, from the casual observer to sincere seeker, to brand new Christian, to experienced and mature Christians. It was supposed to be different and can be still.

Epigraph

"...the governing assumption today, among professing Christians, is that we can be 'Christians' forever and never become disciples. That is the accepted teaching now....And this (with its various consequences) is the Great Omission from the "Great Commission" in which the Great Disparity is firmly rooted. As long as the Great Omission is permitted or sustained, the Great Disparity will flourish.... Conversely, if we cut the root in the Great Omission, the Great Disparity will wither, as it has repeatedly done in times past. No need to fight it. Just stop feeding it."[1]

— Dallas Willard

"Many people in the church have decided to take on the name of Christ and nothing else. This would be like Jesus walking up to those first disciples and saying, 'Hey, would you guys mind identifying yourselves with Me in some way? Don't worry, I don't actually care if you do anything I do, or change your lifestyle at all. I'm just looking for people who will be willing to say they believe in Me and call themselves Christians.' Seriously?"[2]

— Francis Chan

"What Jesus expects us to do is not complicated or obscure. In some cases, it will require that we change what we have been doing. But the Great Commission—His plan for spiritual formation, 'church growth' and world service—is pretty obvious. Let's just do it. He will provide all the teaching and support we need. Remember, when all else fails, follow the instructions."[3]

— Dallas Willard

TRUWAY
TABLE OF CONTENTS (5/19/22)

Section 4:   BIBLICAL DISCIPLESHIP

PREFACE

"Who told you that you needed all this stuff? I don't need it." This is the question that suddenly confronted me as I walked into the worship area of our church one Sunday morning. Not long afterwards, I was launched into a search for a truly authentic way of Christian discipleship—a discipleship that is based entirely on Scripture, not tradition or what is currently trending. This experience was like crossing a mountain stream on steppingstones. You can't see the whole crossing route until you take the next step onto each new stone. It can be a little scary at times. After many months of study, prayer, pondering, and discussing, a new picture began to develop that was so different that I struggled to take it in.

Through the centuries, Christianity has recognized the command of Christ known as the Great Commission. It directed His followers to go throughout the world and make disciples. The Church has believed this Great Commission, but it has been primarily devoted to sharing the gospel of Christ, not on true discipleship which Christ commanded. For centuries discipleship has been tragically ignored, misunderstood, misplaced, misguided and neglected. We still don't have discipleship correct, and yet discipleship is what is most lacking and most needed in today's Christian experience.

Recently, churches are talking more about discipleship, but there is little unity in what it means or how to go about it. Most approaches are simply warmed-over versions of what has failed in the past. It may be trendy, but if it doesn't work, it doesn't work. We are walking in circles which is the certain sign of being lost.

This book asserts and explains that true, Biblical discipleship can and must be recovered and reestablished, but we must correct the mistakes and take the right path. Fortunately, the instructions are indeed laid out in the Scriptures, but it will take courage and resolve by the Church to fix this. True discipleship is for every Christian, it is a function of grace-by-faith, and it does work! We must recover true Biblical discipleship! Only then will the Church become strong and healthy as we await the return of the King!

INTRODUCTION

I t was like a long drive through the Rockies or the Blue Ridge during peak fall leaves. Driving along roads lined by trees and shrubs in fall glory, suddenly a vast landscaped vista comes into view, bursting with beautiful colors and fascinating land features—stretching out as far as you can see. WOW!! AMAZING!! It almost takes your breath away. You drive on for a while, somewhat tunneled by the road, then another great vista opens to view. INCREDIBLE!! It was like looking through a kaleidoscope, gradually turning it until the last particle falls into place, and suddenly you see it is a masterpiece! SO BEAUTIFUL!! It was like looking at a faraway galaxy with a powerful, but originally faulty, Hubbell telescope, never quite able to see the image clearly, but knowing it was there and that it had to be discovered and understood. Gradually, steadily, the image becomes clear, and then it becomes astounding! AWESOME!! FANTASTIC!!

For several years now, Christ has been leading me on a spiritual journey that has been so wonderful as to be beyond words. It has been glorious! It seems that there is no end in sight yet. It has been a journey full of amazing and astounding discoveries and enlightenments. This book will tell you about this spiritual journey and invite you to join it as well, for it is like no other that you have ever been on, and you will never be the same.

I had been invited to participate in a study team to evaluate if a discipleship program would benefit our church. I had always been very interested in discipleship, so I gladly joined the effort. Along the way, the subjects of spiritual transformation, improving involvement and faithfulness, and reducing church turnover also arose. We read, studied, discussed, and prayed over these topics for months. We read and considered several books and curricula regarding all these subjects. After over a year of work, and reaching no real conclusion or clear direction, our effort ended to allow everyone to return to other priorities and activities of the church that seemed more pressing. However, I could not shake the feeling that we were on the edge of something very big and absolutely critical to further explore, discover, and understand. I could not let go. I pressed on, asking the Lord for continued guidance.

Reading many more books and prayerfully pouring over the Scriptures again and again, new understandings began to take shape. It began to become undeniably clear: We have simply missed some of the key truths from Scripture that make Christianity work together to fulfill what Jesus promised to those who follow Him. All true Christians have been devoted to the Lord, His message, His word and His Church; but something is clearly wrong. Something is missing, and all the fads and movements have not rediscovered or implemented it. It's like we have tried to build a bridge over a great river with critical components missing or constructed incorrectly. It's like we have tried to plant a great forest with half the trees required to make it thrive. It's like we have tried to assemble a complex jigsaw puzzle with several key pieces jammed into the wrong places to "make it work". The emperor is not naked in the parade, but he is missing several key parts of his wardrobe. He ought to be thoroughly embarrassed rather than smugly self-congratulatory. We all need to face and admit this, then humbly go to Christ and, "...buy from Him the glorious white garments..." that only He can provide. (Rev. 3:18)

I had complete, formal training in both pastoral studies and Biblical studies from a well-respected Bible college in the U.S. I had an unquestioned belief in the full inspiration and adequacy of the Scriptures. I had a strong commitment to teaching, discipleship and spiritual formation in the local church. I had a variety of adult ministry experiences, both vocational and non-vocational, in a variety of evangelical churches, both denominational and independent. Those had also allowed me to be on the receiving end of various church ministries, but from the viewpoint of the average pew-sitting Christian. This allowed me to be both inside and outside of the "ministry bubble" of the local church. My varied experiences allowed me to carefully observe what did and did not work in those churches, and in evangelical churches in general. What was clear was that the questions that our team had been wrestling with were all too common in a great many churches, and no one seemed to have any real answers.

However, what was now taking shape in my understanding was far different than I had ever read, seen, done or heard from any sources. As I observed and absorbed the new images, it became undeniably obvious that this was not just some new set of ideas, or ministry concepts. It was not merely a new philosophy of discipleship. This was a whole different way to understand Biblical discipleship. In fact, it was a whole new way to understand Biblical Christianity! But it was only new to the western mind that has controlled the church from early days, not new to the Cornerstone and Builder who is its source!

This went far beyond any normal study of God's word on any subject. This was Christ teaching me how to consistently obey all His commandments, without a cheat sheet of rules and without the sense of burden. This was Christ teaching me what it really means to be like Him. He was teaching me the joy of His love, not only as a theology, but as a very real daily experience. He was teaching me to love my Heavenly Father, just as He did. He was teaching me how to love others as they are, just as He loves them. He was teaching me how to relate to others warmly and genuinely, just as He did. He was teaching me how to forgive others, freely and joyfully, as He did. A whole new version of me was being created deep inside where He indwells by His Spirit. He was giving me insight into many parts of my life. I was beginning to understand who I was really supposed to be. I liked who He was remaking me to be and wished it had come far earlier.

I was beginning to understand what discipleship was supposed to be—but isn't. I was beginning to understand what Christianity was supposed to be—but isn't. Sometimes I wanted to dance in utter joy! Sometimes I wanted to crawl up in a corner and weep for how much we have missed and how it broke the heart of Christ! We are truly like the church at Laodicea described in Revelation 3: 17-18. It has profoundly expanded and deepened my understanding of, "…the faith once for all delivered to the saints" (Jude 3). It has answered many of the questions that so many of us have been asking for a long time. It has brought together numerous strands of theology and doctrine that often appear contradictory on the surface. Now I understood why it seems so prevalent for Christians to be so uninterested and unwilling to obey the word of their Lord. Honestly, I felt like I had discovered the Holy Grail, the secret entrance into Shangri-La, and the secret formula for warp speed all at once! Now, I feel compelled to tell others how to walk this path with God! If you decide to enter the journey, I believe God will change you too! I hope you will!

This is "the Way" which was owned exclusively by our Lord (John 14: 6) and alluded to by Luke (Acts 9:2; 16:19; 29:23) and the Apostle Paul (Acts 22:4, 24:14, 22). Even though this term did not continue into other portions of the New Testament documents, the same intention is clearly continued in all the gospels and letters written by the Apostles, and this is the only way to make any real sense of the instruction in these documents. The term has been claimed by certain churches throughout history; but it has been missed, mis-guided and mis-used in many ways, as will become clear as you read. However, it is still available, and can be, "…in your mouth and in your heart" (Romans 10:8), not just in your mind as an intellectual "belief", or just in your notebook stuffed in a drawer or stored on the shelf.

I will show you in this book that the reasons often stated by people for not wanting to attend church can be traced back to one primary reason—because God's people are not being discipled. I will show you in this book that the reasons usually stated by people for dropping out of church can be traced back to one primary reason—because God's people are not being discipled. I will show you in this book why, sooner or later, so many Christians feel like they have hit the glass ceiling and do not have a deeply satisfying relationship with God—because the people of God are not being discipled. I will show you in this book why the church has become a consumer organization, providing demanded services, rather than being a glorious supplier of truly met needs, and how this condition is traced back to one primary reason—because God's people are not being discipled. And it has been going on literally for centuries, mostly unnoticed and without much real concern!

No, I have not read every book in the world. No one has. I have not listened to every sermon or Bible lesson from every church and every teacher. No one has. If I had an exhaustive seminary library at hand, and unlimited time available, I may discover that some Christians have understood and practiced at least some of what I have now discovered. In fact, I know that such individuals and groups have been out there, but they have been only occasional, and for limited times. They were not able to affect the church in general in any age, and they left limited record or instruction that we might follow. I have now come to understand and experience that, once you put all the support pillars, all the trees, all the key pieces in place, only then does it all work together in powerful, wonderful and life-giving ways. It is Life, from the one in whom Life dwells!

I have endeavored to write this book in a manner that can be appreciated and embraced by the average reader. Therefore, I have not made any substantial effort to quote experts and scholars to prove or support the points that are made. It is my hope and prayer that each reader will discover for themselves that God's truth is self-authenticating. The Spirit of God bears witness of it Himself in your heart and spirit. It is the immediate response of the sheep who recognize the voice of their Shepherd (John 10: 4). It's called Truth!

As you read this book, you may find it completely new. You may find it reverses or substantially corrects what you thought you knew. You may find it confirms or strengthens what you already know. You may find it that it clarifies or deepens your understanding of things you already know in part.

Nothing in this book is based on any "secret new source of truth" that augments, replaces or supersedes the Scriptures. It is not based on any kind of secret ceremonies or experiences. It involves no Pentecostal or charismatic doctrines or practices. It is all simply taking the clear, original meaning of the Word of God at face value and learning to live in its ultimate reality. The words of the old hymn are still completely valid, "What more can He say than to you He has said."[4] I can almost guarantee that you will find it challenging, perhaps even a bit scary, because it may take you to places you've never been before.

Nothing you read here demands that you be really smart to understand. It does not require you to have a degree from a Bible college or seminary to understand, and you don't have to be a scholar. Nearly all first-generation Christians were simple people with little or no formal education, as we would think of it. In fact, many were slaves and likely could not read or write at all. Surprisingly enough, we discover that the limited places where true Christianity survived past the first century are little out of the way places with simple people. This is not because they were largely ignorant and unable to develop a more "sophisticated faith". It is because they had learned to fully and joyously function in all aspects of their normal daily life based on the ultimate, eternal truth of the True Living God—Father, Son, and Holy Spirit.

Nothing you read here requires you to have a certain personality or temperament. What we call personality and temperament are always a combination of natural and learned personality and temperament. You will discover that Christ frees you from all the unhealthy and unhappy elements of your learned personality and temperament and makes you joyously free to be who He intended you to be—who you really are! You will begin to understand that within who you were really supposed to be there is no real home for sin, because sin withers and destroys your soul. Without Christ, this can only end in the loss of your soul—both here and into eternity!

It is expressly not my intent in this book to unnecessarily or unfairly criticize or condemn any individuals, groups, or churches that have faithfully labored to know and walk in the truth as they knew it at the time and situation in which they lived. I write this in all humility as one who had to confront the issues myself, as God began to show them to me. I was falling woefully short as have many others, and I had to repent and surrender to the Lord. We all accepted what we were told because, "Surely those in teaching and leadership know what they are doing don't they?"

The trouble is that those in teaching and leadership across the centuries, up to, and including right now, were in the same boat for their training too. And those before them were also in that boat, and those before them, and those before them, etc. all the way back to the first century. No one can teach what they don't know. However, for the sake of us all, and for the glory of God in His Church, this must end. Someone has to declare to the emperor his embarrassing lack of garments and show him that only repentance and utter obedience can restore him. He has become like David's messengers in II Samuel 10: 1-5. At least they had the good sense to be embarrassed when half of their robes were cut off. The declaration must be made now before we reach the point of no return. Some would say we have already arrived!

You might rightly say, "How could God allow such past errors to persist in His church for so long? Surely that can't be." But the same question had to be faced by John Wycliffe, and by

Martin Luther, and by John Calvin, and by William Tyndale, and by the Anabaptists, and by the Puritans, etc. We've all been suffering from the same loss for a long time, and now that which has remained lost must be restored! The Reformation started by Martin Luther and others, but it isn't over because it was never truly completed. We must find our way back to true, full New Testament Christianity, as taught by our Lord Jesus Christ and His apostles, in the same way as those who went before us. May the Lord fully grant you this blessing!

I invite you to read this book—carefully, thoughtfully, prayerfully and courageously!

I urge you to read this book—carefully, thoughtfully, prayerfully and courageously!

I dare you to read this book—carefully, thoughtfully, prayerfully and courageously!

One word of caution and exhortation before you start. This book is not about simply knowing something new in your head, writing a lot of notes, and stuffing it into a drawer or binder. It is about learning TO DO, out of learning HOW TO BE A NEW YOU in Christ! Transformation drives discipleship, and discipleship drives transformation. They are inseparably symbiotic and there is no other way to do it. As you will see, this is how our Lord defined discipleship. (Matt. 28:19-20, Matt 10:24-25) Only He has the right to define discipleship—no one else! No one else, no matter how popular they are, no matter how big their church, no matter how many books they have written, no matter how high their elevation in the church or in the Christian community, has the right to change it, morph it, or "update it".

This book does not have ninety-five theses, but you should consider it the declaration nailed to the door of the church and the shot across the bow! Does anyone know the way to Wittenberg?

CHAPTER 1

I'M SORRY, BUT WE DON'T HAVE THAT ANYMORE

Most people have a favorite food. Many people have a favorite food in each main category—appetizer, soup, salad, main dish, side dish, dessert, etc. I subscribe to the view that dessert is the most important meal of the day, and my favorite dessert is Tiramisu. Now everyone who shares this passion knows that there is Tiramisu, and then there is TIRAMISU!! I mean, really great Tiramisu is not just to die for, it's to kill for!!

Imagine if you created the best recipe in the entire world for your favorite food. A complex combination of numerous ingredients. The ingredients have to be absolutely fresh, and it has to be made and served exactly right to be great. When it becomes so popular amongst your friends and family, you decide to bring it to market, and it quickly becomes a favorite all around the country. Now, let's suppose something calls you away to a part of the world that will not allow you to make or even enjoy your favorite food. To continue its popularity and sales, you entrust a very good friend to take charge of the secret recipe and run the company that makes it while you are away. You train him with great detail and obtain his solemn promise that he will be a completely dependable caretaker of it.

Several years later, you return, with your mouth watering for a taste of your favorite food. You stop at one of your favorite restaurants that had served your favorite food as you had created it. When you order it, your server responds with a mystified look and tells you that they have never heard of that dish. At your urging, they go to the kitchen to inquire if it can be provided. Then the manager gets involved. The manager steps to your table and says, "I'm sorry, but it has been a long time since we offered that, and I don't think the chef will even try. It's not considered very good, and no one orders it. I believe it is still sold at some of the gas stations in town if you wish to try that."

Astounded, and thinking there must be some terrible mistake, you leave the restaurant and head for the gas station out by the interstate. You rush into the station and start perusing the food shelves, confident that it will not be there. But then, to your utter shock and amazement, you spot it. It's offered in a sealed plastic wrapper with microwave heating instructions. You stare, confounded, at the list of ingredients and find that numerous essential ingredients have been left out and others have been replaced with artificial substitutes with chemical flavors and coloring. Now, almost in utter shock, you tear open the package, pop it in the microwave for the prescribed time, then carefully taste it. Ugh!! If this is what it has become, no wonder that no one likes it! Now, almost in tears and utter grief, you call your friend who was supposed to the dedicated guardian of the recipe and company. When he answers, you blurt out the story, demanding that he tell you what happened. He responds that, after a while, he decided a less expensive and simpler version would do better on the market and be more profitable, so he changed several things to better meet the market demands. Then he sold it to another buyer who changed it even more. But it's making a lot of money at the gas stations, and it was one of the best deals he has ever made!

Now, let's imagine the same story from the other end of the perspective. You decide to try a certain new dish because you have read that it was the favorite dish of a famous chef/restaurant chain owner. Much to your surprise you find it at the gas station. You unwrap it, warm it up and try a taste. Well, it's not terrible, but hardly great, and not stupendous for sure. It's certainly hard to understand how this was made by a famous chef or that it was once outrageously famous. However, you develop something of a taste for it and you sometimes eat it on long trips when you get hungry and don't have time to stop for a real meal.

One day, on one of your trips, you stop at a little diner in a small town and find that they actually serve it on the menu. You order it, assuming it will be much like what you are used to. While you are waiting for it to be served, you discover that the diner cook claims he is the creator of the original recipe, but he was cheated out of it by an unscrupulous friend. Then you have the first bite, and WOW! It is incredibly delicious! How many times after that do you think you will buy what is sold at the gas station? How many times do you think you will find an excuse to drive through this little town on most of your trips?

The Clammer of Voices

Numerous voices, both respected and new, have been calling out to the Church, urging us to recognize that we are rapidly losing our way. They urge us to correct our course immediately before it becomes uncorrectable. This chorus is becoming undeniable if you are listening. Most of the voices also propose what should be done to correct the course and get the church back on the proper Biblical pathway. In the meantime, many churches are not faring well at all in our current American culture. Many churches are closing their doors and scaling back their ministries and activities. They are reluctantly adjusting to be a smaller and smaller minority in the community and having a smaller and smaller voice. Others are closing their doors because most members have been drawn away to the big-box church across town where, "lots of exciting things are happening".

At the same time, other studies and surveys repeatedly tell us that there is less and less difference in the values, behavior and lifestyle of Christians compared with non-Christians. Sermons, books, songs and websites urge a revitalization and reawakening. They sing of visions that a great revival will happen, and they call for an array of bold changes to bring it about.

When I look closely at these suggestions, I find they fall into one of the following categories:

1. Keep working hard at what we are doing, and God will give the increase as He sees fit. This seems reasonable enough. The Scriptures certainly encourage faithful labor in the Lord and perseverance under trial. But it also fits into what has become a well-known definition of insanity: "Keep doing what we've always done but expect different results."

2. Go back to what we used to do. We all knew this new stuff wouldn't really work. The shrinking number of attendees do not seem to be particularly attracted by the fog machines and laser lights. Returning from

disobedience to faithfulness also seems reasonable and well supported in Scripture. Lots of good preaching passages to draw on for sure. It may apply in some cases, but normally what we used to do wasn't working very well either. That's why we left it! Didn't the last 50 members of the church vote to try something different? What were we thinking?

3. Radically alter the focus of the church to bring all resources to bear on some specialty ministry that is more likely to be recognized by the general community, like free food and lodging for the homeless or relief of suffering around the world. It radically changes and limits the historic purpose and message of the Church, but this would increase the opportunities for evangelism in church, and who can criticize that?

4. Give up and silently slip away into some form of isolation that will allow us to continue in our own version of faithfulness. We recognize that the end times are coming. Increase in disbelief, immorality and rebellion will continue to rise and there is nothing to be done except try to survive until the Rapture. After all, isn't this what some devoted ancient saints did when they lived in the deserts and caves to be alone with God and be more holy? And isn't this what the Puritans and other separatist groups did in the American colonies?

A few of these voices rightly identify, in one way or another, our need for discipleship as one of the primary purposes of the church and offer recommendations for how discipleship should be undertaken. Surely an energetic application of the Great Commission would have the blessing of God and lead us to success again.

As you will quickly discover in this book, I concur with this viewpoint, and have so for a long time, but with a very limited audience. However, most of the voices cannot seem to agree on what discipleship means or should be, nor how to pursue it in a local church setting (thus showing how confused we really are). Nevertheless, the number of books on discipleship is mushrooming, and it would already take a very long time to read and evaluate each one. While you were reading, many more would appear. How can we pursue a completely confused path? Granted a one-size-fits-all approach may not be the best thing, but at least we should be able agree on the core principles. Ask the Donner Party what happens when you strike out on a new path guided by someone who doesn't know for certain how to get to the desired destination. The number of churches and ministries that have already suffered various forms of this same fate is large indeed, and we don't need anymore. It is a sad and painful experience to watch a local church devour itself.

New or Old?

Thoughtfully and prayerfully read over the account of Jesus turning water into wine in John 2: 1-10 and His parable about old and new wine in Luke: 5: 39. Then compare it to the imaginary story above about the ruin of your favorite food. Listen for the voice of God in this imagery as you continue to read. (Yes, I want you to really do this.)

The parable of Luke 5 can be confusing at first. Is Jesus saying that old things should be abandoned in favor of new things? Is

He saying that new things cannot fit into old containers, as if form was the only issue? Or is He saying that we should go back to the old things because they are actually better? The answer is "all of the above and none of the above". Like understanding almost all of Jesus' parables, they usually contain a single, simple lesson and message. There is no need to make all parables have a uniform message, because they were not intended to be uniform. Truth is not so simple as that. Truth is like a beautiful jewel. It has many facets, and you don't have a jewel unless the facets are all present and in the proper relationship. When they are all present, it is absolutely beautiful and only then is it highly valued.

Overall, Jesus was simply saying that when something better is provided, anyone with any sense wants what is better, not what is inferior. Making yourself pretend to like something inferior when something better is available makes no sense at all—unless it's all you have. Sometimes the old is better and you should continue or go back to it. Sometimes what is new is better and you should sign up immediately. But being new doesn't automatically mean it is better. The issue is not age, but whether it is better; and we almost always recognize what is better very quickly. He was simply saying to these listeners that when He provides the way, the truth, and the life, (John 14: 6) nothing else can come close to matching it and you never want to go back or substitute.

There are two alarming elements popping up in the studies and surveys about church attendance and involvement. What they reveal is that there are two main groups dropping out of the church or showing less and less ongoing interest in the church:

- The seasoned veterans in the church who have kept the church functioning for many years.
- Next-Gen and Millennials who have watched, listened and experienced what the church has been, especially in the last fifty baby-boomer years.

The other alarming fact that is clearly emerging is that the Church is now splintering even more than ever, based on both the age and culture of those who attend. It appears obvious to me that this is the ultimate and predictable outcome of years of age-based ministries in churches, copying the secular school system. In the past, the age groups stayed within the same local church until young adult/college age. When young adults went off to college they typically disappeared into the oblivion of the world until they had experienced enough hard knocks to return. Next, we divided the church worship services into different versions to accommodate the preferences of different age groups = what is perceived as old and new. You could tell which service is about to commence by standing outside and observing the average age of those entering the worship area. Color and style of hair is also a sure giveaway. You didn't even need a watch.

But now, the distinct age groups are separating even further into become separate freestanding churches, based on age and societal sub-culture. Determining which church you are attending is as easy as observing what kind of technology is used, all the way from music, lighting, special effects and whether the Bible they are reading is a hard copy or on a streaming device. If the Bible is being preached at all, it is combined with a generous dose of something that resembles the opening of a stand-up comedy routine. All these results should, and do, cause great concern. After all, this is how the church operates now and how it will operate (or fail) in the immediate and not-so-distant future.

Quite frankly, it's a little hard for me to find fault with Next-Gen and Millennial Christians and seekers for wanting to "modernize" what the local church offers. They are the children and grandchildren of baby-boomers who did the same thing 50 years ago. Maybe this is simply "the chickens coming home to roost". We prompted the Jesus Freak movement, and for those who were too conservative to be Jesus Freaks, it led to "contemporary Christianity", complete with new music, new translations, and the independent Bible church movement. Everyone thought it was wonderful, but now it seems fewer are interested in staying the course. For one thing, it takes a lot of effort, structure, organization, coordination and money. All that seems to get in the way of kneeling at the feet of Jesus, hearing His word and worshiping with a joyful heart. Far too often, it seems like this takes way too much "production", and I'm not at all sure that is showing to be a good "Return on Investment" for the church. It also gets in the way of doing whatever you feel like at any moment.

What seems to escape our grasp is that both old and the new are not proving to be very satisfying, so both groups have diminishing faithfulness in attendance and involvement. This fact ought to shout to us about how the church is not offering what truly meets our deepest inner needs. But what else is there to try? Any new fads coming down the pike? The one thing we know about human behavior is that what we find to be truly rewarding gets repeated, and we quickly become devoted to it, sometimes almost addicted to it. Neither old nor new seems very addictive at this point, except for the devoted core group. Now how do you understand Jesus' parable about the old and new wine?

My Journey Begins

As usual, there is a backdrop to my journey and what prompted this book. It was like finding stepping-stones across a stream, a bit difficult to really discern until looking with hindsight. From where I am now, it seems quite clear, but as I was taking the first few steps it was rather tenuous. However, like crossing a stream by stepping-stones, with each step I knew I could not pivot and go back. It was too compelling and too wonderful!

Like most, upon graduation from my formal training in ministry, I was ready and anxious to charge the field. Get out there and grow local New Testament churches! In each church where we served, I did my best to teach, preach and implement what I understood to be New Testament Christianity at the local church level. Much to my shock and disappointment, I repeatedly discovered that most Christians do not know what a New Testament church is, and when it is taught to them, they respond with little real interest. Except for the few individuals, they simply can't get their arms around it. Its mystifying to them. It was almost like I was speaking in a foreign language. Even worse, existing leadership often resisted it as well. Over time, this began to wear very heavily on me. I was gradually becoming more and more dissatisfied with the current offering of churches and nearly at a point of giving up on all organized versions of Christianity. It was beyond my ability to grasp why

Christians would have so little interest and willingness to obey the word of their Lord, despite claiming to the contrary. Then, my path brought me to the first stone

One day I was perusing the Bibles offered at the local Bible bookstore and found one that I did not know. The cover, back and intermediate pages were printed like an ancient hand-scripted Bible. The cover was printed to mimic an ancient Celtic Bible with beautiful gold geometric shapes and scrolling vines all around a single, centered cross. It was called the "Ancient Faith Bible", a version of the Holman Christian Standard Bible. [5] It did not include many of the references and study tools that are included in many modern Bibles. Instead, it provided a number of pages regarding some of the ancient Church Fathers and Martyrs. It had been a long while since I had read this information in church history classes and for some reason it caught my attention in a new and fresh way. But what captured my imagination more strongly than ever before was the possible link to understanding New Testament Christianity in a better way. Somehow it opened a small new avenue of inquiry for further searching out New Testament Christianity. It stoked into a small flame an old ember of wishing to find a more authentic version of Christianity. Then I came to the second stone......

While I was serving as part of our worship team, I arrived one Sunday at church a little early for scheduled warm-up with the team. At this particular time, our church was meeting in a school auditorium. Like usual, this meant that the entire sound system had to be carried in, set up, adjusted and balanced before use. As I arrived, the sound team was busy doing just that. As I strolled down the aisle toward the stage, a profound thought suddenly struck me, as if a voice had spoken to me. It came to me as a question, "If the Apostle Paul walked in here this Sunday would he say to us, 'Who told you that you needed all this stuff'?" Of course, the next thought was, "If Jesus walked in here today, fresh off a teaching session on the beach at Capernaum, would He say, 'Who told you that you needed all this stuff? I certainly don't need it.'" Then I came to the third stone

Not long afterwards, I had a very mystifying, almost dis-concerting, dream. I know well that dreams do not necessarily mean that you have received a message from the Lord, but this was one of those dreams where you simply can't shake the feeling. It presses in on you until you have to deal with it. In my dream, I was walking along a path through a great forest, somewhat like the one described in John Bunyan's famous book *Pilgrims' Progress* [6]. Ahead, I could see that the forest was thin-ning out and then ending. I expected to see that now the path would be clear to take the next big step in my life and ministry. But when arriving at the edge of the forest, I discovered that the path ended abruptly and what stretched in front of me in all directions was a vast, hostile, trackless desert, as far as I could see in every direction. I thought to myself, "How can that be? I've been faithfully following the path that I was told I should follow." In a few moments, the Lord said to me, "You have many more wonderous things to discover in My garden before you leave. Turn around and explore all you have missed." If I had not done that, I would probably not be writing this book. Many of those wondrous things are what this book is about.

As is often the case, reaching the third stone allowed me to see the fourth, then the fifth, then the sixth, … until I reached the other shore. This shore seemed rather familiar, and yet very new in many ways. Although it was clear that others had walked there before, it was also clear that few had walked it for a long time. The footprints were old, very deep, yet now almost obscured by the usual evidence of neglect. It was a new place, and yet an old place as well. I had become a new traveler on an old pathway. The old and the new joined together in a wondrous way!

You may not find everything you read here to be new, at least intellectually. One of the things I experienced while reading, studying, pondering, and praying was that God would lead me into these truths in a way that was undeniably new to me—and on a whole new level. It was as if I was discovering things that no one else had ever discovered since the first century—like discovering ancient artifacts deep inside a mysterious cave and covered with centuries of dust and webs. Feeling rather uncomfortable about this, I would then scour the books and available resources even further and find nothing until I settled on the clear, undeniable meaning of my discoveries without the influence of others. Only then would God lead me to other reliable sources that said some of the same things. This happened repeatedly and confirmed to me that I was on firm ground. What I was discovering as new and wonderful truths did in fact come from the Lord and others had also believed and written them, but not heard very often—especially not in the modern church. Each time, it was clear that these matters were clearly spoken of in the Scriptures.

This is how it goes when God is speaking to His people. He speaks through many sources on the same issue, and they all harmonize. The Church must hear and heed these truths! If I can make some substantive contribution to the recovery of discipleship, I will consider my life well spent indeed.

What If the Universe Is Curved?

Now, just as I had to do, ask yourself, "What if the lack of satisfaction with both old and new has been the result of an unintentional and unrecognized side-effect of what we were deliberately doing all those years, always thinking that it was all exactly right. What do you do when you discover that a huge problem that looks nearly impossible to solve, something you never thought would ever happen, was caused by what you intentionally did? It's like the famous Chinese finger-trap. The harder you try to pull out of it, the greater its grip on you. Doing more of what you think is right simply tightens the lock. What then? Should we do what is wrong like some misguided reverse psychology of faith? No, by no means! But, as Albert Einstein once said, "We cannot solve our problems with the same kind of thinking that we used when we created them."[7]

What if most segments of the path after the apostolic age had the same fatal flaws built into them? And what if the problems go far deeper than only the meeting hour, the style of music, which Bible translation is used, the content and order of the church service and what technology is used? What if we finally admit that all those centuries-old flaws left the followers of Jesus unsatisfied and still longing for what He had clearly promised? What if I could show you that nearly all the versions and choices over the span of the last nineteen-hundred years are a bit like gas station fast food compared to the real thing? And what a tragedy if we reached, "…the end of all things…" (I Peter 4:7) only to learn that what most Christians seldom knew in the last nineteen-hundred years, could have been theirs all along. It had been left in plain view in every church, but no one knew how to read the ancient writing. What if the very best wine had been handed down all along but nobody bothered to serve it? Once you've tasted the real thing, I promise that you will never want to go back. You never get tired of it, and you are never satisfied with something else. I fully realize what a radical statement that seems to be and what a tall order it is to fill; but if you keep reading, I can tell you about it and you can decide for yourself.

Must we surrender the church to the forces that would turn it into a social-recreation club, political movement and religious finance mechanism? If you feel the Church has already arrived there, I don't blame you for wanting to climb in the escape pod and push the green button. But, before you do that, I urge you to instead come with me back to the past in order to establish a new future which will prompt you to stay forever.

CHAPTER 2

A BRIEF HISTORY OF DISCIPLESHIP

The results of the studies and surveys comparing the attitudes, viewpoints and behaviors of American Christians to those of non-Christians are far too clear and consistent to be ignored. Failure to grasp the importance of these would be a great mistake and further endanger the future existence of the true church which carries the true gospel to the lost world. What value could the church possibly have in this world if it is not producing Christians that are more like Christ?

Our Lord's Great Commission seems abundantly clear, that we are to, "...go and make disciples ..." (Matt 28:19-20). However, for centuries discipleship has been tragically non-existent, ignored, misunderstood, misplaced, mis-guided and neglected. It has always been something of a mystery to me how and why the Lord's Great Commission could be so ignored and mis-guided over the long years. It is abundantly clear in the Scriptures. Dallas Willard's excellent book, *The Great Omission* [8] asks the same question and provides some valuable thoughts regarding some solutions. There are, in fact, several reasons that such neglect of discipleship occurred; and to escape these great errors and finally get on track, we need to understand how we got where we are, as well as why and how we must escape them.

Discipleship In the Early Church

As I will show you more completely in subsequent chapters, the apostles and early church clearly recognized and understood the Great Commission given by our Lord. The apostles did not limit their work to evangelism, even in those critically important first days and years. They also went about making disciples through quality teaching and leading the new believers into the first essentials of being disciples of Jesus: water baptism, (the) fellowship, (the) prayers, (the) breaking of (the) bread, and devotion to taking in quality teaching from the apostles. (Acts 2: 41-44, (parentheses mine) This is just as they had been taught by the Lord Himself. This formed this first group of believers into the first church. Then daily, they continued proclaiming the gospel and discipling those who believed, bringing them into these first essentials of being a disciple of Jesus. Even though this is one of my favorite Scriptures, we must realize that it reflects only the initial steps of discipleship and church formation. We must also realize that the teaching and discipling they provided was not preaching in church and teaching was not only intellectual content. Preaching was proclaiming the gospel in public arenas, and teaching was teaching *to do*, as Jesus Himself had instructed and demonstrated.

We have a hard time appreciating how long it took to take the gospel into the known world of the apostles. True discipleship also takes time, and it is not surprising that every believer and every church could not be fully discipled in the time of the apostolic mission. This is quite clear from the ministry of Paul, as recorded in Acts. However, no church start/plant is successful until you have a robust group of mutually committed believers, all properly trained in both evangelism and discipleship, and ready to train others. (Most Western churches fail this test, even after many years.) Much more was to come to fulfill the Lord's Commission for all disciples. Soon these first Christians would face administrative problems with resource sharing and then some major leaps in understanding all the ramifications of the teachings of the Christ to whom they had now pledged their faith and allegiance. As promised by Christ, "All the truth..." (John 14: 26) continued to be revealed to the church through the apostles, prophets and teachers until the close of the apostolic era (Eph. 3:4-5) Only then did the apostles and recognized church leaders deem it as, "...the faith once for all delivered to the saints." (Jude 3) Following that, those who claimed or attempted to add were deemed as those who, "...go too far, not abiding in the teaching of Christ..." (II John 1:9)

The apostles accomplished both preaching of the gospel and teaching believers, without confusing the two or neglecting either one. Their evangelistic preaching consistently declared that the predictions of the Old Testament Scriptures were being fulfilled. The Messiah had come. He had been rejected, crucified, raised from the dead and ascended to the right hand of God. He would return to carry out the long-predicted judgment of God and establish His kingdom. They declared that all who would repent, believe and be baptized in His name, would have eternal forgiveness of their sins, eternal life and admittance into this kingdom. This is what Jesus had, in fact, taught them, even as late as the Emmaus road and the Upper Room.

As you continue to examine the record in Acts, you will see that, when they moved out beyond Jerusalem, the apostles continued the same pattern in other areas of Judea, and then beyond to the Gentiles, starting with the Samaritans, the emissary of Queen Candace of Ethiopia, and then the household of Cornelius in Caesarea. Soon, Saul of Tarsus (Paul) is converted, and after a time in Damascus, Caesarea, Jerusalem and Tarsus, Barnabas conducted him to Antioch to join with the believers in that city where, "...they taught many for an entire year". (Acts 11:26). Rather quickly, the focus shifts almost entirely to Paul's ministry until he is transported to Rome to stand trial.

As you follow the ministry of Paul into Asia, Greece and back through Asia, you see that he also followed the same pattern, never failing to both evangelize and disciple, to the extent that he could in each circumstance. However, his opportunities to disciple in some places was inconsistent, sometimes lengthy but other times very brief indeed. Paul stayed in Ephesus and Corinth for extended times, but it is only recorded that he stayed and taught them. There is no record of what he taught. (Acts 11: 25-27, 18:11) In keeping with the words of the Great Commission, I am comfortable believing that it was, "... all that Jesus had commanded them", but it was also limited to the time and opportunities provided. Even in the closing sentences of Acts, we see Paul "preaching the gospel as well as teaching about the Lord Jesus Christ" while still in custody and awaiting trial before Caesar.

What is especially interesting and noted is that, throughout the book, what was taught in these circumstances is not clearly stated or barely hinted. Once again, with the Lord's Great Commission being so clear, and with the greater expansion of Christ's teachings that was subsequently given through the apostles and prophets, it is almost certain that he taught these things. Subsequently he wrote of them again to some of these same churches. It is in these letters that we receive much of the fuller truth promised by Christ, "when the Holy Spirit comes". (John 16:12-15, cf. I. Cor 2: 6-13)

Discipleship During the Post-apostolic Years

How about from the apostolic era until now? Keeping the proper focus on discipleship, as Christ had commanded and the apostles had continued, required each subsequent spiritual generation to faithfully carry it forward without serious error or omission. They had to be certain that the faithful men trained by the apostles such as Timothy, Titus, John Mark, and others also trained other faithful men who would continue it forward to others. (II. Tim 2:2) And as they carried it forward, they had to properly understand and reflect on all the revelation that Christ was giving to His church throughout the apostolic era. Did they? And what would happen if they failed to do so?

If every generation had done so, we would find today's local churches to be abundant gardens of discipleship with every believer being fully discipled throughout their life as well as joyously playing their own part in making other disciples. The normal culture of every local church would be "disciples making disciples". We would also find our local churches radically different in multiple positive ways. The fact that we are now so discipleship deprived is undeniable proof that, somewhere along the way, that transmission did not happen. When? Why? What is tragic, and not expected at all, is that this loss happened far earlier than we might have been aware; and, upon closer examinations, I believe the reasons become obvious.

What Happened to Discipleship?

In his book *Divine Commodity*, Skye Jethani quotes the words of Richard C. Halverson, former chaplain of the U.S. Senate, as follows:

"In the beginning the church was a fellowship of men and women centered on the living Christ. Then the church moved to Greece, where it became a philosophy. Then it moved to Rome, where it became an institution. Next it moved to Europe, where it became a culture. And, finally, it moved to America, where it became an enterprise." [9]

Chuck Swindoll also quotes these same words in his recent book, *The Church Awakening-An Urgent Call for Renewal*,[10] as he expresses his great concern about the state of the current Church.

I certainly have a more positive view of Christianity in America, but the issue at hand is the clear progression away from disciple-making as the primary mission of the church throughout the centuries. It provides a valuable key to understanding the lack of discipleship that we have inherited. How can we understand how our Lord's Great Commission could become "the Great Omission", and what can we do about it?

Once we leave the New Testament period and documents, what was happening in the earlier eras of the church can be found almost solely in the other ancient records of the Church, especially the records of the primary church leaders. These are the "Church Fathers", and the primary sources for their beliefs and practices are their surviving writings which we know as the "Apostolic Fathers", the "Ante-Nicene Fathers" (before the First Council of Nicaea) and "Post-Nicene Fathers" (after the First Council of Nicaea.) Pasted in amongst these writings would be some of the "Confessions of the Church", such as the Athanasian Creed, and Nicene Creed. Following those are all the varied confessions of the many churches and denominations. The average Christian today has probably never read or studied these writings, nor are they likely to. In fact, most Bible college and seminary graduates as well as many evangelical pastors have also not studied them.

What you find as you peruse these historic documents is the great lack of any descriptions, implications or references to discipleship. It would be easy to say this is understandable. It was not the purpose of these surviving documents to instruct in discipleship. They were primarily defenses of the Christian faith, the person and work of Christ, and the person and work of the Holy Spirit. Additionally, until the time of Constantine, the church was in a fight for its life, and many believers and leaders were suffering persecution, imprisonment, torture and death. Doesn't sound like very fertile ground for discipleship. Besides that, if we believe that the Scriptures are the only basis for faith and practice, why should we read or care about the opinions of a bunch of guys that lived hundreds of years ago?

Now there can be little doubt that these were devoted, godly men and women, many of whom were persecuted and martyred for the faith. Almost certainly, we will find them in the extended hall of faith in heaven. It is certainly possible that much of what they did, what they taught, and how they lived, is not fully recorded in surviving documents. Silence can mean more than one thing. But it certainly seems evident that, even at this early point in the church, discipleship was either not in focus, or no one thought it important enough to preserve for future generations. In their writings, they speak of being disciples. They speak of other Christians as being disciples. They quote the Scriptures fluently, copiously, and confidently as they instruct and exhort. In fact, scholars tell us that nearly the entire New Testament, as we have it today, can be recreated simply based on their quotations of the New Testament Scriptures. They instruct their recipients to obey these Scriptures as the word of the Lord, but you would never know how to be a disciple by reading their surviving writings. Of course, as you move forward from Nicaea, the doctrine and practice of the Church deteriorates even more until it reaches the very corrupt medieval church of Europe.

There were a few exceptions, and we know some of these as the "Desert Fathers and Mothers" because they pursued a life akin to John the Baptist, isolating themselves in lonely places like deserts, caves and small deserted islands. They sought to escape the contamination of the world and the organized Church, with its corrupt practices, and to be alone with God. They sought to pursue holiness and total devotion to God. Small portions of their beliefs and practices have apparently survived, usually second and third hand, and they are brief sayings and wisdom for specific matters of holiness. However, this should not be confused with discipleship. Holiness is one goal of true discipleship, but this is not achieved in physical isolation from the world. Other than the 40 days of temptation in the wilderness, our Lord did not practice long-term isolation as the means to achieve/confirm holiness, nor did He teach His disciples to seek it. His instruction was to "go into the whole word". The Monastic system that later developed was slightly less isolationist, but still revolved around the much the same principle. With rare exception, Monastic training was not how to live among and teach others how to be faithful disciples of Christ.

Discipleship Since the Reformation

Many evangelical Christians might think that this was all corrected as part of the Reformation. After all, the Reformers certainly made all the necessary corrections, didn't they? This has been an unrecognized, but common, mistake. The Reformation has had several stages. The Reformers soundly corrected several very important doctrines of the Bible, including personal faith as the sole basis of salvation, the Scriptures as the sole authority of all faith and practice, the priesthood of every believer, and others. However, you would quickly see that people like Martin Luther and John Calvin did not revive any significant aspects of real discipleship.

My research brought me into contact with the writings of other bright stars in this dark time that did not escape to the Reformation but remained as strong witnesses to Biblical faith and holiness from within the Catholic Church. Some of these were such individuals as Fenelon and Madame Jeanne Guyon. These spiritual teachers came closer to instructing discipleship than many modern books, and I found them very helpful in some ways. But they still leave a lot of blanks in the matter of being a complete disciple. One of the more famous books familiar and dear to many modern Christians is *Practicing the Presence of God* by Brother Lawrence [11], but it too includes nothing to instruct others how to consistently enter the spiritual experience described by Brother Lawrence.

Subsequent stages of the Reformation were brought about by later individuals and groups such as the Anabaptists, the Huguenots, the Puritans, the Quakers, the early Methodists, the Baptists the Holiness Movement, the Deeper Life Movement and even the evangelical church and independent church movement. Many of these later reformers "fleshed out" portions of what the original reformers had established only in theology, but the changes were every bit as earth shaking to the community of faith. These later reformers were often persecuted in the same way as the original reformers. They made further positive and necessary reform to the Church, but they also made their own mistakes which would come to light under the larger scrutiny of Scripture. Some of these leaders and preachers left substantial written works about salvation, holiness and sanctification, eschatology, etc. However, as indicated above, that is not the same thing as discipleship. As I researched, I re-read several of my favorite holiness authors and was quite disappointed to find this lack of information in their writings. They are usually written as theologies, sermons or devotional guides, but no instruction for discipleship.

The Problem of the Western Mind

Other things were also happening over these same time spans which, I believe, were far more devastating to the ideal of discipleship intended by our Lord Jesus. As Christianity moved out of Palestine and into the Gentile areas of the Roman empire, it came under pressure to fit into the western mind-set and understanding of Hellenized peoples—Romans, Greeks and dispersed Jews. Jesus did not teach, preach and act from the mind-set of Greeks, Romans, Europeans or Americans. The faith that was given once for all by Christ and the apostles was not western—it was Middle Eastern, and it is truly far more "eastern" than "western."

From the Greeks, there was constant pressure to bend it toward a philosophy. Greeks did not have a truly comparative concept of discipleship as believed and practiced by traditional Jews of Jesus' time. Learning was primarily a matter of intellectual reasoning, based on the thoughts of the famous Greek philosophers. The great philosophers certainly had their "disciples" but not in the same sense as the disciples of Jesus. Therefore, learning Christianity became more and more a matter of intellectual reasoning and logical argument, copying the style of the philosophers and orators. The great apologetic works of some of the early Church Fathers undeniably show this. Perhaps what they taught in the more private sessions of Christian instruction was different, but if so, we don't have any record of it. Paul had written his warnings about morphing Christianity into a philosophy. (Col. 2:8). However, because this style of thinking and learning is what largely shaped the Hellenized mind of the Roman empire, it was almost inevitable.

Side-by-side was a different pressure from dispersed Jews throughout the empire. Therefore, in some areas, there was also pressure to bend Christianity back toward traditional Judaism, starting with, "...they must first be circumcised and obey the laws of Moses" (Acts 15:5). Paul, knowing full well the fallacies of this approach, also warned about this false doctrine in several letters.

Finally, there were the advocates and practitioners of the "mystery religions". Both Paul and John had to repeatedly warn and teach Christians not to fall for what was offered by these, (Col. 2: 20-23) demonstrating and arguing that Christ provides far more than any or all such mystery religions. They clearly and intentionally taught that Christ was "all-sufficient" in all that He offers. No one can offer anything as good, much less, better. These mystery religions do not even come close to competing with what Jesus provides—that is if it is genuine Christianity.

As Christianity moved into Rome itself, it did not escape Hellenized thinking, but picked up another level of contamination. Gradually, barely noticeable at first, but continuing in a relentless pattern, it adopted what it meant to be a Roman. The Roman mind is about hierarchy, power structures, authority and dominance, coupled with ceremonies, rituals and social structures to express these. Even the gods of Rome were based on a hierarchy amongst the gods. On the surface, the doctrinal purity of the Church was continued on the intellectual basis, but under the constant pressure of the Greek and Roman mind and culture, it succumbed, like a person who is gradually poisoned over long-term low doses of a lethal substance. It morphed further, and even more destructively, into expressions of power and authority.

Christians have typically assumed that, under the stern warnings and leadership of the apostles, these false teachings and practices were abandoned, and the Church came back on track and continued faithfully. But if you examine the evidence, we see that this did not happen! Instead, the church continued to be controlled more and more by subtle, but powerful, versions of many of these false teachings and practices. (See II Tim. 1: 15 and III John 9) Some of these teachings and practices crept into Christianity, especially the Greek and Roman influences. By the fifth century, various teachers and bishops were in deadly conflict, using the power of Rome to enforce their particular views and preferences of doctrine and practice. Official condemnation and even excommunication became a powerful and feared tool in the hands of certain factions.

Once Christianity was accepted by the Roman Empire, Church and crown were yoked together with the tragic and destructive consequences that extended for centuries into the medieval church. From that point, a very painful Reformation was necessary, resulting in much spilling of blood across Europe for the Church to get at least two wheels back on the track. Even though it is painful to recognize, all too often the American church is still dominated by this same kind of thinking even now. It is almost impossible for the American Christian to imagine any successful church operating based on a more egalitarian form of leadership and decision-making. It is nearly impossible for us to grasp what Scripture means when it tells us to, "…be of the same mind with one another" (I. Peter 3:8) about anything. It is almost impossible to grasp the fundamental concept of the church functioning as the Body of Christ as taught in the New Testament. Alas, we are still Romans in many ways! How many church splits have been nothing but power struggles between two factions or individuals and their backers?

The Translation Factor

At the same time, something else occurred that is out of sight for most Christians and even for many Christian leaders. The Bible was being translated, and when you translate the Scriptures into another language in another culture, you automatically risk loss of important intended meanings. Modern Bible translators are usually far more aware and on guard against this mistake, but the level of scholarship and careful transmission of original meaning was not so great in the past, especially under the authority structure of Rome. Rome was committed to the dogma that the Latin manuscripts and translations were the officially recognized Scriptures.

We can be blind to the full grasp of Scriptural truths because we are still controlled by "western ears, western minds, and western hearts". The mismatch of mind-set from Middle-Eastern to western also affected the translation process. Good exposition always seeks to help us move across this barrier, but often it is a difference that is so encompassing, it takes real work. Until we are ready to have ears, minds and hearts of the Middle-Eastern people, we will continue to struggle mightily with a true concept of discipleship. One specific failure of proper translation played a large role in wiping out true discipleship and seriously obstructing its restoration.

As you will see in more detail in the Chapter 8, the Great Commission of Christ in Matthew 28:19-20 reads as follows, "Go therefore and make disciples of all the nations, baptizing them in the name of the Father, and the Son and the Holy Spirit, teaching them to observe all I commanded you." A more accurate translation would be as follows: "As you are going, *disciple* all the Gentiles, ..." (transliteration mine). The word for "disciple" is the Greek word *mathetes* and it is the commonly understood term for making disciples in the manner that Christ had done. Making disciples was common practice for rabbis in Israel and the word carries a strong intended meaning of not just students, but apprentices. The second word for teach in this same verse is a different word in the Greek, "...*teaching* them to observe." Making disciples does include teaching, but primarily teaching to make "apprentices".

When the Scriptures were translated from the original Koine Greek into Latin, the word used in the Latin Vulgate Bible for "make disciples" is *doceo* which does not carry the same intended meaning of "apprentice", and especially not the first century concept of a disciple who follows a rabbi. The word *doceo* communicates the western idea of instruction in a school for intellectual understanding, following the western mentality inherited from the Greek and Roman empires from which we came. Since the Latin Bible was used in the Church for centuries, from that point onward, the concept of discipling was by instruction as in a school, displacing the concept of "making apprentices". The Church truly believed it was being faithful to the Commission of its Lord by teaching.

Eventually, the early English translations were achieved (often through great effort and suffering). The Tyndale Bible, the Douay-Rheims Bible, the Coverdale Bible, the Geneva Bible, the Bishop's Bible, and the King James Bible all translate the word "make disciples" as "teach" in place of "disciple". It reads, "Go therefore and teach all nations, baptizing them… and teaching them…." Thus, for many centuries, the Church was prompted to take up a posture and purpose of teaching, along with traditional preaching. Each of these are forms of classroom type instruction, rather than true discipling. Over time, the whole matter of training up children to "take up their part in the Church" was added. This prompted development of the standard forms of catechism and confirmation as the primary means of bringing subsequent generations into the Kingdom of God and the Church. This further reinforced the Western style of instruction rather than true discipling. In all of these, the Church genuinely believed it was being faithful to the Commission of its Lord.

With the rise of the evangelical church came the powerful stream of expository Biblical preaching and teaching (or at least what purports to be) from the pulpits of evangelical churches. Bible-centered preaching and teaching had been valued by some churches previously, but now it gradually transformed into a much stronger stream of exposition of the Scriptures in the pulpits and classrooms. Committed to the task and vison of getting Christians to be well trained in the Scriptures, pastors, preachers, and teachers labored faithfully to bring the word of God to His people. Growing out of the impetus of popular books such as, *Know What You Believe,* and *Know Why You Believe,* [12] and many others, Christians began to realize and embrace that it was, indeed, important to better understand the Scriptures for themselves in order to possess a meaningful level of personal spiritual growth. All sorts and types of Bible translations, study books and study tools were developed. Numerous well-known pastors and preachers came to the fore, eventually resulting in numerous radio and television programs, large churches, more books, more study tools, etc.

The spiritual term and gift of "pastor-teacher" really came into its own during this time, and largely continues to this day in many churches. Millions of Christians, including myself, have been very blessed indeed by the word of God in this approach to church culture, and certainly spiritual growth has been achieved. These fine pastors, teachers and authors also deserve our fullest recognition, thanks and respect. They moved the church a long way along the path of a greater understanding of what the Scriptures say and mean. Through this better exposition and teaching, we came to mentally grasp a more accurate understanding that "disciple" meant something to Jesus and the original disciples that we are very unfamiliar with. But the meaning still lay dormant, a mystery that we barely noticed and certainly did not really grasp. We still labor under the misperception that discipling primarily means teaching, as in a classroom (lesson, sermon, lecture etc.). More recently, it has taken on the connotation of studying between a single student and mentor or small group of students with a mentor to guide, but it is still heavily oriented toward content, not doing. And, still,

31

the Church generally believes that, by evangelism, missions and Bible preaching and teaching, it is being faithful to the Commission of its Lord.

A great many churches who have teaching elements in their ministries would insist that this is discipleship. They are preaching and teaching the Bible—but this is not discipleship. Without fully realizing it, they are teaching and preaching Bible doctrine and theology, not discipleship. It is like teaching someone to play the guitar by having them learn all the notes and fingering, all the scales and all the chords, but never teaching them to play a song, much less many songs. Real life is more like a song that must be made up in each moment of time that unfolds before you.

I can assure you that you will never find me under-valuing or de-emphasizing the great value and importance of the Bible. It is God's word. It is God's mind and heart "breathed" onto the page (II Tim. 3:16). It is "living and powerful" (Heb. 4: 12). "It is your very life" (Deut. 32:47). When I was introduced to exegetical study of the Scriptures, it was a huge and wonderful eye-opener to me! You mean I can understand the Bible for myself, by reading and studying it in much the same way as any other document? I can understand it for myself and be highly certain of its meaning? WOW! I was hooked, and I immediately went about excitedly telling others and showing them how to do the same. It changed my life wonderfully! But it was not discipleship.

Unfortunately, we are still catching up to the true implementation of what we know only in theology/theory. Despite these great blessings, the understanding and practice of discipleship has advanced very little. In fact, the exposition of Scripture as the primary focus of the church, has unintentionally and tragically produced simply more well-informed non-performers of the teachings of Jesus. It produced the intellectual Evangelical Church. Specific ministries have been raised up to explain in greater and greater detail the intellectual basis of the Christian faith and defend it against all intellectual foes. In spite of routine preaching and teaching about the dangers and disobedience of being, "…a hearer only and not a doer of the word…" (James 1:22), our pattern of ministry has left most believers in a weak and anemic condition as far as consistently living out all the commandments of our Lord. We can't quite grasp that obedience as a disciple is not a form of legalism. One major stream of theology in the evangelical church consistently teaches that the commands of Christ are not for Christians today, and we don't have to worry about doing them, because they are based around the Law. Thus, we get to the point when one of the biggest criticisms of the day is that Christians don't act much like Christ.

Meanwhile, our children, and now grandchildren, have observed a Church that preaches and teaches a good story, but it doesn't seem to be real enough to make a significant difference in how we live. Despite many sermons, lessons and daily devotions about, "being doers of God's word" (James 1:22), we are, in fact, only devoted believers, but sadly inattentive to obedience. Over the centuries, the Church has always focused on the more socially heinous sins that are more open and obvious to view; but when we hear Jesus say things like, "You shall be perfect, like your Heavenly Father is perfect," (Matt. 6:48) we start to squirm and even invent theologies to get us around it. So, we live mostly like everyone else because "we are under grace". American lifestyle plus church will do just fine, thank you!

We pursue the America dream far more than pursuing faithful discipleship. We pursue sports, politics and recreation far more than pursuing faithful discipleship. Even at church during "fellowship times", we are far more likely to talk about the weather, economy, sports, recreation and politics than about how the Lord is working in our lives. When someone shares thoughts or questions about obedience, holiness or an experience with the Lord, the response is often a notable discomfort, as if we are guilty of a Christian version of "too much information". When we share prayer requests, it is nearly always about matters that affect our physical needs or our pursuit of the American dream, not about our pursuit of the kingdom of heaven. So why should our children and grandchildren follow us? This is simply a different version of what we baby-boomers observed in our parents and grandparents that prompted our deep questioning of the value of church in our time. By the grace of God, our doubting prompted the further reformation of the Evangelical church, including new churches, new music, new Bible translations, and a new approach to the entire focus of the church. But we still have such a small grasp of the discipleship. We are still in the deadly grip of western mentality and its mental version of Christianity.

What Else Is There?

When we purview the entire landscape of the evangelical church today, we hear the silent admissions saying, "What else is there? We've tried everything we can think of, and it still doesn't work! We are losing the struggle, and many of us are getting really tired!" You hear Christians saying, "Life is really hard! The Christian life is really hard! Why is it so hard? This doesn't seem like it is worth the investment!" Now we hear the same sort of sentiment from the pulpit!

Such responses are the guaranteed result of following a version of Christianity that is not from Christ and His word. I refer to it in this book as "churchianity", and it has dominated the Christian culture for many centuries and continues to do so. But its underpinnings are failing, bringing about the collapse of the entire house of cards. It is in the early process of suffering the fate described by Christ as a house built on sand (Matt 7:26-27), because it was not built on *doing* the teachings of Christ, only hearing them, understanding them, and "believing" them. No matter how grand it seemed, when it falls it will be a great and tragic collapse.

True discipleship is about *doing* the teachings of Jesus. (Matt 28:20) The reason it is so hard is that we have not been pursuing the true Biblical way of Christ, as clearly set forth in the Scriptures. In fact, past generations and other cultures have understood it better than we do now. It is exactly the way that indigenous cultures pass on the knowledge of their way of life generation after generation. When done correctly, it is a wonderful stream of living in the realities of the living water, the living bread, and the living breath of the Lord. Jesus called on us to take up His yoke because His yoke would be "easy and light" compared to other ways (Matt. 11:30). There is nothing about an easy yoke that "is so hard", and the obvious contradiction should warn us that we have a mismatch!

The delay, confusion, and discouragement we are still witnessing shows we still don't quite get it. We all received a very sparse folder about discipleship from our spiritual ancestors and we are still living in that famine. I have been part of the misguided and misinformed herd as well, and I have no desire or intention to unfairly criticize others for our failures in understanding and implementing discipleship. We aren't discipling because we just don't get Biblical discipleship. It doesn't compute! Those who were supposed to disciple us couldn't do so because they themselves had not been discipled. Those who were supposed to disciple them were also not discipled, and those before them, and those who before them, and it goes all the way back through Church history to the first century when true discipleship was allowed to "drift away", like an old rowboat insecurely tied to an old dock. (Heb 2:1) Eventually, the tie rope falls loose, and the boat just drifts away, carried downstream by the strong currents, and eventually disappears into the vast ocean, never to be seen again.

When I reached this point in my search, my reaction was much like John when he saw that the great scroll of the future could not be opened. I wept! (Rev 5:4) I was only comforted when the Lord quickly assured me that He could again open His truth to us. He can and will use His word that is without error or omission to instruct us. It's been there all the time waiting for us to see it, hear it, embrace it and live in it. It can be ours again! Finally!!

Dietrich Bonhoeffer once said, "Christianity without discipleship is always Christianity without Christ."[13] Now that is an extremely radical statement to make! Perhaps suffering persecution and martyrdom under the Nazi regime has a way of forging the truth in a way that is otherwise not seen. He was right! Christianity without discipleship is only "churchianity". It's a version of gas station fast food that comes wrapped in plastic, ready to heat in the microwave, gulp down, and then be on your way to the "more important things" of the day. But it is much too bland and nutrient deprived to build, "a holy people" who are "kings and priests unto God" (I Peter 2:5,9) who powerfully hold out the light of Christ (Matt. 5:16, Eph. 5:8), who love God with all their being (Matt. 22: 37), who are "zealous for good works", (Titus 2:14) and are faithfully dedicated to the one-another ministries of the church in the power and wisdom of Christ. This whole problem has a single solution, and that solution is *true Biblical discipleship* as taught by Jesus and His Apostles. It was lost to us over time, but it can be recovered and re-learned.

We must figure this out together and it must be done quickly. Think of it this way: If you were stuck on the space station and you were running out of fuel, air, water and food, but you couldn't escape until you solved this problem, would you make it off safe, or give up and die a miserable death floating forever in cold space? That is the sense of urgency we must have with this matter, and unless we see it that way, we will not succeed. Not only is the night coming in which no one can work, (John 9:4), but sunset is quickly approaching. We are nearly at the twilight. The very good news is that the instruction manual is still in our possession, and it can still be understood properly and completely because we have a living Teacher who stands ready to disciple us again. So, let us begin our discovery of true Biblical discipleship under our Lord Jesus Christ.

CHAPTER 3

THE BLINDFOLD TASTE TEST

So, what kind of Christian experience do you have? Is it clearly like the very best version of your favorite food, or is it like the fast-food substitute? Is it like the very best wine that only Jesus can provide, or is it like the cheap stuff that is offered after you are well on your way to not knowing the difference? If I blindfolded you and gave you a sample of the two versions of food or wine, would you be able to tell which one was the best just by one taste?

Here is a small description, in Jesus own words, of what His version of Christianity is:

Matt. 11: 29-30 – "Take My yoke upon you and learn from Me, for I am gentile and humble of heart, and you will find rest for you souls. For My yoke is easy and My burden is light."

John 4: 14 – "Whoever drinks of the water that I will give him, shall never thirst; but the water I give him will become a well of water springing up to eternal life."

John 6: 35 – "I am the bread of life; he who comes to Me will not hunger, and he who believes in Me will not never thirst."

John 7: 37-39 – If anyone is thirsty let him come to Me and drink. He who believes in Me, as the Scripture says, 'From his innermost being will flow rivers of living water.'"

John 8:12 – "I am the Light of the world; he who follows Me will not walk in the darkness but will have the Light of life."

John 10: 10: "I have come that they may have (eternal) life and have it more abundantly."

John 14: 27 – "Peace I leave with you. My peace I give unto you."

John 15: 11 – "These things I have spoken to you so that My joy may be in you, and that your joy may be made full."

This was not a slick sales promotion or shell game from Jesus. Jesus doesn't sell Florida swamp land as the greatest vacation spot on earth. When He promises to give us the real thing, He gives us the real thing. Jesus does not give a spiritual version of gas station fast-food.

Now, I recognize we can all have our ups and downs, but even if we temper Jesus' promises with "a dose of reality", what would you honestly say is typical for your life? Is your normal life characterized as being mostly like His description? Would others say that they clearly and consistently see that you have a regular diet of the water of life, the bread of life, the light of life, and a wellspring of living water flowing up out of you? When others get to know you, do they see these characteristics in you? Do they typically say, "This is obviously someone who hangs around with Jesus"?

I can tell you with absolute certainty that Jesus does not give these life qualities through any church ceremonies or rituals; or from walking the aisle (repeatedly) and praying some pre-packaged prayer; or from any Pentecostal or charismatic experience; nor do they come from just faithfully attending church each week, singing songs, listening to the sermons and on the way out saying to the pastor, "Nice sermon pastor. Very interesting".

These promises are not given only to ministers, preachers, pastors or missionaries. These are not restricted to those who have a Bible college or seminary education and spend their entire life in God's service. You don't have to sell your house, quite your job and move to some far away developing country to have it. You don't get them by making certain that you attend church every time the door is open, and you don't get them by faithfully listening to every sermon on Christian radio. It is the promise for all who come to Christ, believe in Him and follow Him through discipleship—His form of discipleship.

Some might respond, "Maybe these are only the ideals of Christianity, and we should not expect these to be true all of the time or even most of the time. I'm reasonably happy with my Christian experience and my church. Why should I expect anything better?" This would be the honest response of many Christians in today's churches, but you must recognize the difference between average and normal. Normal means that something is the way it is supposed to be, a faithful copy of the prototype. The normal for a Christian is to walk in the reality of these promises, at least most of the time. Normal is becoming more and more like Christ. The experience of the average Christian is far below what Jesus said would be true. Please hear me when I tell you that if gas station fast food is all you have ever known, it is hard to believe that there is something that is much, much better. But there is.

Others may immediately ask, "I believe in and follow Christ. Why don't I have these characteristics?" There are very simple, specific and easily solved reasons. But first, you must ask yourself with absolute honesty before God, "Do I really want these to be your normal life experience?" Please be open to what God wants to show you, then keep reading. There are reasons, and they can be corrected.

CHAPTER 4

FINDING OUR WAY BACK

I magine that you are part of a large group of people on a
journey through a trackless wilderness. It leads through a
broad valley between mountain ranges on both sides. Rather
than a great inspired prophet as a leader, you have a map of the
route you are supposed to take. It is a basic map, somewhat like
an old treasure map, and it is rolled up like an ancient scroll. The
primary features on the map, by which you will know you are
on the right route, are prominent landmarks of various sorts.
Interpretation is not always easy. To keep everyone together
and on the same route, a small leadership sub-group has been
selected to have charge of the map and its interpretation. Your
group has been on this journey for many years which requires
that leadership be passed down from time to time. Now this
leadership cycle has included you.

Wanting to be diligent, you want to get some history of the
map and the journey, so you unroll the map backwards to get
some context and perspective. The more you unroll, the more
concerned you become. You see that in the past, there were
several forks in the road. You have always trusted the leadership groups before you to assure that everyone is travelling the

right path, but it has been a long time since any of the predicted landmarks have been sighted. After several days of pondering, you become convinced that a wrong turn was made in the past and you are not on the right path at all. No wonder none of the landmarks have been sighted, and no wonder so much trouble has developed! As you share this with the leadership group, they also come to see your point and reach the same conclusion. You are on the wrong path, and you will never reach the destination like this! The correct path is on the other side of the mountain range to the west. What to do now??

Taking the entire group back to the original starting point to find and pursue the right path seems an insurmountable prospect. You can't even be certain that it is still available, or that it is in friendly territory. That was a long time ago and a long way back. There are indications on the map that some narrow passes through the mountains would take you back to the original path, but these passes are likely to be difficult. They may also be guarded by enemy forces. The last thing the enemy wants to see is your return to the original path. They are planning to ambush the entire group soon, and they don't want their plans to be thwarted. Do you continue along the same route, even though you have definite doubts that you will end at the correct destination? Or do you dare the mountain passes to get back to the original path? That will require courage, determination, and possibly some battles, but at least that would put you on the right path where you were supposed to be. This is not a story-book fantasy or great tale. It is absolutely the decision the church faces at this point.

In order to get back to the right path for discipleship, we must escape from all false, misleading or partial versions. Time is a one-way arrow, so we cannot go backwards in time to take the true path at its beginning. We must journey over the mountain pass to get to where we were meant to be by God. This will require us to clearly identify and face some of the fundamental errors that brought us to where we are. These corrections will not take us away from the clear truth of Scripture, but much closer to it, and this is where we very much need to be. That is the only thing that will keep us from walking in a circle right back to the wrong path. This is a common mistake of people who are lost and trying to find their way out. They walk in a circle. That would be most foolish and dangerous.

Some of these essential corrections are about right understanding of the inspired Scriptures. Others are about correcting common practices, sometimes starting many centuries ago, that are accepted as correct. Other errors needing corrections started more recently, especially in the last 200 years. The past errors may seem small, but if you talk with sailors or surveyors, you know that a small error in direction can eventually take you off course by a long way. Ask the Pilgrims who were supposed to land in Virginia instead of Cape Cod.

To completely explore and correct each of these matters would need an entire volume, or multiple volumes. Therefore, we will focus only on the corrections or clarifications needed for true discipleship. You will see for yourself that most, if not all, of the corrections and clarifications needed are caused by our failure to grasp and implement what the Scriptures clearly say and mean. This is what assures us that the true way is the true way, not simply some different take on certain minor issues that don't deserve much attention.

During Bible college I became aware of the book, *The New Testament Order for Church and Missionary*, by Alex Rattray Hay.[14] It is a fine book and well worth your reading. It proposes a simple viewpoint and describes how to carry it out in both church and missionary endeavors. The overall theme and message of the book is the same as what the Protestant church has claimed to believe: *Read the Scriptures, make sure you understand it correctly, then just accept what it says as true and go do it.* What a novel idea, huh? The New Testament Missionary Union was an active and successful missionary endeavor and organization that had established gospel preaching missions and formed primitive churches in third-world countries, so it was not written on a theoretical basis. You will see throughout this book that the same viewpoint is the basis for all

Read the Scriptures, make sure you understand it correctly, then just accept what it says as true and go do it.

true discipleship. Faithfully following these steps has been the big hang-up of the western church for centuries, and recently it is getting much worse. Unfortunately, we spend most of our time bogged down in the portion, "...*make sure you understand it correctly....*" We believe this is discipleship, but it is not! As you will see in this book, discipleship is training Christians to actually and consistently do what the Scriptures say—go do it!

If the Church had remained on the right path set for them by the Lord of the Church, we would have arrived in our own time with a fully vital and robust life of discipleship for every believer; and every believer would fully and openly embrace it as what it means to be a Christian. Alas, that is not where we have arrived. Making the necessary corrections will be challenging. Some might even seem a bit scary at first. Some parts of the path over the mountains are steep and narrow. But if we do not make the corrections decisively and permanently, we will not be able to find or walk the true path. That will result in a great temptation to turn back again like ancient Israel wanting to go back to Egypt.

In making this climb you might think some areas are much too hard. You may think that only the great scholars can figure this out. But the truth is that children are usually better at it than adults. Many of the things we will be learning and doing come more naturally for a child. Success in those matters will center on whether you are willing to humble yourself as a child and learn from your Master in order to become like Him. (Matt 18:3) This can be very difficult for adults.

There are resting points on the climb, but they are for more than only rest. They are also small meadows for reflection and meditation to gain greater understanding. As you rest, the Lord will instruct you in these times as well. Through it all, you must rest assured that the Lord is with you all the way, in every step and in every moment.

Let us start the journey back to where we were supposed to be to learn the true way of Christ!

CHAPTER 5

CHRISTIAN ATHEISM

I encountered the term Christian atheist in the book, *The Christian Atheist* by Craig Groeschel. [15] Groeschel describes himself as a recovering Christian atheist and explains what he means by that term. In his book, the author explores an array of typical symptoms that might seem contradictory to a claim of being a Christian. Such contradictions, along with others, could certainly prompt the criticism that Christians don't act much like Christ. If such Christians display or have the symptoms Groeschel describes in his book, it immediately suggests that they may not be true Christians. After all, it takes more than a belief in God to make a Christian. However, it is far more likely that they are true Christians, but they have not been discipled properly at all. Proper discipleship could have made a huge difference in the lives of all such individuals.

As you will see in subsequent chapters, the only legitimate Biblical definition of a Christian is "a disciple of Jesus Christ". (Acts 11:26) No one who has carefully examined the New Testament could conclude anything else. But the reason most Christians have not sought out discipleship is because the Church has told them, by both messaging and programming, that discipleship is not necessary unless they want to achieve some advanced level of being a Christian. Otherwise, you are fine as you are, just believing, forgiven, attending church and contributing money and effort to its official functions and programs. A great many churches have no idea how to develop disciples and have little interest in doing so. Welcome to Christian atheism!

You may think the idea of a Christian atheist is a non-sensical contradiction, and I may agree, except we aren't really talking here about only labels and terms. We are talking about actual observed and reported attitudes, viewpoints and behaviors of many American Christians, as reported by themselves and by their non-Christian associates and acquaintances. The viewpoints, attitudes and behaviors described in Groeschel's book are certainly those that you might expect among atheists, or at least non-Christians, but not among genuine Christians. The fact that it is happening is both tragic and discouraging, because, as you read Groeschel's book, it is clear that each of these issues has a simple solution. However, the solution is available from the source that may have caused the problem. It is a bit like asking someone to see a doctor about a contagious health problem when the patient believes the doctor caused the health problem in the first place.

These current behaviors and attitudes are exactly what concerned many of us as we watched some parts of the evangelical church move off to become "seeker-friendly" and "emergent". Once some broke rank, more and more then followed suit (if not in name, certainly in practice). It was the next shiny new remedy to increase attendance and giving—the next ministry fad.

It would be tempting to think this is a new problem brought on by this current movement or pattern in the church.

Unfortunately, I can tell you this problem is not something new, and it is not limited to those churches who pursued these different paths in the last twenty years. In fact, much to my surprise, if you read the writings of church leaders throughout the entire church era and across denominational lines of all types, you will find that it was a common complaint through the entire period. I have repeatedly observed it myself in many church and Christian contexts. In fact, if you are honest in your scrutiny of the New Testament, you will see that many of these same problems were already of major concern to the Apostles in their day. In various forms and combinations, they have continued over many centuries up to, and including, now. It appeared to improve slightly with the birth and growth of the modern evangelical church. However, the move toward seeker-friendly and emerging churches is a reaction against the evangelical church era as we have known it. So, the current situation may be the outgrowth of the evangelical church era. Now, that really complicates the issues, but it doesn't change the answer.

Is There a Legitimate Case?

When non-Christians complain about Christians not being very Christ-like, it is an honest appraisal. The criticism may be unfounded, based on taking the exception as the rule, or a false notion of what Christ was truly like. It could be based on a false notion of what a Christian is, or should be, or who is a true Christian. It is a common mistake to think that a Christian is simply someone who has some vague belief in God and occasionally attends some type of church. Christians have been maligned in all sorts of false ways over the centuries. It may be only another example of blaming Christians for the burning of

Rome. It could also be based on the current politically correct posturing, since Christians continue to insist that the God of the Bible is the only true God, and that Christ is the only way to Him. *However, when combined with the trends within the Church itself, it becomes deeply troubling.* It would suggest that something very systemic is wrong with the forms of Christianity that we have known and practiced over many centuries and within many western cultures.

We can no longer excuse ourselves under the banner, "Christians aren't perfect, just forgiven", and as you will learn, it is also unnecessary. It wasn't meant to be that way and it can be different. Learning to walk in the way of Christ will not make you perfect in this life. However, if there is anything we ought to consistently earn it is that we are genuinely seeking to be like Christ and that we are succeeding enough for that to be recognized.

What I found to be the most thought-provoking part of Groeschel's book was the title and sub-title, "*The Christian Atheist–Believing in God But Living as if He Doesn't Exist*". This is a powerful and accurate way to describe the observable problem. Just to be clear, Christian atheists are not individuals who have a sham claim to belief in God and Christ but are really atheists. It is individuals who are genuine Christians but still act like non-Christians in many ways. The terminology is not as important as honestly recognizing that the symptoms have been around for a long time, much longer than you might think, and there seems to be no working solution put forth. You might call it "being a Christian but living as if God doesn't see, doesn't hear, doesn't care, there's nothing else anyway, I'm under grace and I'm okay with it and you should be too!" This was a common viewpoint within faithless ancient Israel as well, and repeatedly earned the scathing criticisms of the prophets. Eventually, it earned the destruction and captivity of that nation, and they have never yet been fully restored. You might also call it, "Believing in God but believing He never leaves the church building anyway, so who cares?" Sound familiar? That was also a common viewpoint of many of my friends during the nostalgic sixties, to which I have no interest in returning, but suddenly we seem to have arrived there again. What is this, some kind of time warp? Or maybe we never left! Or maybe we are walking in circles! Of course, that would force us to recognize that we are lost.

Welcome to the First Church of Christian Atheists

The symptoms described by Groeschel are manifested, to one degree or another, by four well recognized groups within the Church. Whether they admit it or not, every pastor has analyzed his/her church on the basis of these groups and tried to make improvements or adjustments to meet their perceived needs.

Those in the first group genuinely believe in God and Christ and believe they will go to heaven when they die; but they have little grasp of what it means to be a Christian other than believe in Jesus and try to do what is right when possible. They have never found church very interesting or helpful, so they rarely attend and routinely have many of the symptoms.

Those in the second group genuinely believe in God and Christ and believe they will go to heaven if they die; but they attend church only when it is convenient or when they feel the need to do so. They too have a very limited grasp of what it means to be a Christian beyond that, and they also have many of the same symptoms.

Those in the third group genuinely believe in God and Christ and believe they will go to heaven if they die. They attend church regularly, read and sometimes study their Bible, pray, and sometimes join a small group or participate in some service projects within the church. They would be reluctant to admit it, but they also have one or more of the same symptoms; and at times they ponder why they cannot seem to do better since they are already doing all the church tells them to do. At times, they also ponder if their commitment is worth the effort and flirt with the temptation of leaving it all behind.

Those in the fourth group (and generally constituting no more than 10% of any church) are those who believe in God and Christ and have genuine confidence that they will go to heaven if they die. They attend church regularly, read and study their Bible, pray, and are often part of a small group or participate in some service projects within the church. They also participate in either the lay leadership of the church or the non-vocational ministry group of the church—the volunteers. They are usually the backbone of the church, especially when there is not a plethora of assistant pastors and staff. They are the faithful servants who make their best effort to keep the church functions and activities up and running. They would be reluctant to admit it, but they also have some of the same symptoms at times; however, they generally persevere "by faith" or get help from the vocational pastors to address their struggles and see them through.

Please note that the first three groups are recognized and evaluated based on their mental grasp and professed belief of certain core doctrines of the Bible, and the degree to which they are "churched", in other words, attending and involved in the functions and activities of the church. The fourth group is known by their support and assistance in keeping these functions and activities up and running. None are recognized and evaluated on the basis of consistent Christlikeness.

Most church programs, ministries and budgets are designed to meet the felt needs of the first three groups. They are the "consumers" of the church's resources, and they feel entitled to them. If any of the resources are reduced, changed, or eliminated, they gladly express their dismay and may leave the church to find another church that will "meet their needs". They genuinely believe this is why the church exists—to meet their needs. Leadership also believes this, including the pastoral staff. It seems that everyone has forgotten that there are two levels of needs—felt needs and true needs. When you try to meet the felt need without meeting the true need, another felt need just pops up to replace it. It's another version of whack-a-mole. When you meet the true needs, the felt needs go away, and so do the moles.

The common difficulties and struggles experienced by all four groups are caused by the failure to provide genuine Biblical discipleship as taught by Christ and the Apostles. Any pastor or church leadership group that has set Biblical discipleship as the core goal for their church would be measuring and evaluating entirely different paraments and indicators, as well as implementing entirely different ministries and activities. The results of those ministries would make it far more likely that these Christians would overcome all of the frustrations and shortcomings described in Groeshel's book and many other places as well. For centuries we have been asking how we get Christians to act more like Christ, but the various answers that have been put forward at any given time don't seem to be getting us very far, as evidenced by the symptoms presented in Groeschel's book and a long church history prior thereto.

Revival Anyone?

The long-term traditional solution to the symptoms of Christian atheism has been to hold a revival, with powerful preaching to call sinners to repentance and salvation, and to call worldly Christians to abandon their worldliness and return to a well-churched life. The second-most frequent traditional solution has been to propose a building program. More current solutions include things like implementing the latest church program fad, usually promoted by some large "successful church" and/or celebrity pastor. Some churches have chosen to restructure the church ministry program or organization, or to call a different pastor or additional staff pastors. All these have yielded some fruit in some ways, but once "the new car smell is gone", the same problems usually return. The moles have simply dug new tunnels and new openings. If these things do not lead us *to consistently do* the commandments of Jesus, they will not produce more Christlikeness amongst Christians. We remain stuck in Christian atheism.

We must be willing to fully embrace the truth that the powerful hold of tradition and western thinking blinds us to the true solution. It is only another version of the well-worn, but pertinent, tale of "The Emperor's New Clothes"[16]. Courageously looking through honest eyes, like the unabashed child in this traditional story, we can identify some of those things we are blind to or afraid to admit. Here are some of them. They must be recognized as some of the citadels that obstruct robust discipleship.

The American Dream

"Blessed are you who are poor..." (Luke 6: 20) "But the brother of humble circumstances is to glory in his high position; and the rich man is to glory in his humiliation." (James 1:9) I guess this is what happens to those raised in an impoverished single-parent home in first century Palestine. We can hardly choke down the words as we teach, preach or even read these words. Only an idiot would truly believe them. Very few Christians can take them seriously. In America it is nearly heresy to be serious in meaning them. Preaching on money is the least favorite topic of nearly all pastors, and there are good reasons why. It is nearly impossible for us to imagine desiring to be in a state of poverty. Before we go too far down the road, let us recognize that being of "humble circumstances" is not the same as poverty, unless you are using the U.S. economy and middleclass lifestyle as the basis.

The purpose and right use of money and possessions for the Christian is a subject all to itself, requiring an entire book to deal with it adequately. A number of books and studies are available from various sources. However, any book about the Christian view of the American Dream would have to state at the outset that the American Dream is not only about money. For purposes of this chapter, we need only recognize that pursuit of the American Dream is a major and common interference to pursuing true discipleship, and it is not easy to overcome without real resolve. Resolve seems to be in short supply amongst Christians these days.

Most Americans, including American Christians, believe in some version of the American Dream. They believe they have the right to pursue it as vigorously as possible for them. It says so in our Constitution and right on the Statute of Liberty does it not? Any sacrifice made for God or the church is seen as a true sacrifice because they believe they have a full right to the American Dream. If they devote time, energy and resources to church instead, they believe they are sacrificing some portion of achieving the American Dream to which they are entitled. Many find that a tough trade-off to swallow.

Regardless of what we claim, we are secretly convinced that, however you define the Dream, it will almost certainly require money to achieve it, and it usually does. Since nearly everything in the American Dream wears out, needing repair or replacement from time to time, and with inflation's constant eroding force, we feel we must acquire more income every year. All the specific components in the dream like housing, food, clothing, means of transportation, medical care, hobbies, entertainment, vacations, etc. will require sufficient money to acquire them, even if it comes from someone else. Even if we do not need more money to meet basic needs, we still feel the societal and cultural pressure to gain more money to acquire some of the "good things in life" that also cost money. Rising income and increasing accumulation of possessions are two of the most defining values for American culture. If you lived in a culture where people must be highly mobile to succeed, accumulation of unnecessary possessions would define the fool, since they cannot be carried around without great trouble and effort. If all of your possessions bog you down so that you miss the annual migration of the herds, you well might starve to death this winter, and that would certainly be considered as being a very great fool.

Jesus told us that, "You cannot serve God and mammon." (Matt. 6:24) It is true that the term "mammon" primarily meant wealth or riches. The term itself communicates the concept of having far more than you need. Confusing wealth with "having enough" is a major source of confusion in the minds of most Christians. It's often difficult for us to even sort out the difference or why it is important. It is another example of true needs versus felt needs. The teaching of our Lord was not a criticism of working to acquire the basic needs of life. His teaching was not about how much money you need, or about keeping up with inflation and the Jones. It is about whom you serve, why, and how much you worry about earthly needs. Scripture tells us that we are to work for a living (including support of your surviving elderly parents), and anyone who fails to do so has denied the faith. (I Tim 5:8) Proverbs tells us that only a foolish slacker does not work when it is time to work. (Prov 20:4)

Careful thinking will reveal that you never serve an inanimate object or concept, such as "riches". Meeting the basic needs of life is one thing, but serving mammon means you are seeking what is well beyond basic needs. Serving riches is serving yourself because you have decided that wealth and possessions will provide something additional that basic needs do not satisfy. Riches are usually about what you feel you need to earn acceptance, esteem, security, power and privilege, based on cultural values. However, the disciple learns to live in the wonderful truth that the acceptance, esteem, security, power and privilege that come from following Christ are far greater than any version that can be purchased with money. By following Christ in discipleship, you truly experience those greater values in your life.

Pursuit of the American Dream automatically works against this principle and robs us of the opportunity for true contentment under God's good care and provision. Jesus directs us to seek first the kingdom of God, and all these things (necessities) will be provided. Anything beyond having what you genuinely need is a form of riches, and Jesus said, "The Gentiles eagerly seek all these things…." (Matt. 6:32) The parallel for us would be to say that atheists pursue this lifestyle of constantly seeking material goods that are beyond what they need, and likewise, most Christian atheists do this as well. Both individuals are constantly chasing the acceptance, esteem, security, power and privilege that material wealth tries to provide, but it is like the proverbial carrot dangled in front of the donkey. As most people eventually discover, you do a lot of chasing and not much catching or munching.

Jesus did not advocate or teach that we pursue being impoverished or totally deprived. He simply taught that we should not pursue riches, i.e. *far more than we need*. He taught that "riches are deceitful" (Matt 13:22), and that, "…not even when one has an abundance does his life consist of his possessions" (Luke 12:15). Do you really believe this, or do you just like to say you believe it? What if you had a different Dream?

As a disciple, you will genuinely learn, and adopt with a whole heart, a new view of material goods, possessions and what they can provide for you…or not. This frees you from the chains of materialism by teaching you to grow the eternal wealth above, which is saved in your account for eternity. It also frees you from treading the gerbil wheel of materialism all your life. More importantly, the disciple learns to enjoy God as the primary source of happiness, meaning and well-being. The Westminster Catechism tells us that the primary purpose of the human race is, "…to glorify God and enjoy Him forever". How many churches offer classes entitled something like, "How to enjoy God so that you need fewer material goods", or "How to lower your income needs by learning to enjoy God"? Have you ever had someone arrive a little late for a meeting because they were off enjoying God so much that they lost track of time? Discipleship is the only means to reach this of kind of life, and it should be common amongst Christians rather than a rarity.

Church Activities

Keep in mind that Christian atheism is genuinely believing in God and Christ but acting and living like you don't. There is another aspect of Christian atheism that has crept into thousands of evangelical churches. It is a powerful and subtle deception that rarely registers on the radar of anyone's spiritual awareness. I will refer to this as *church-activity atheism.* Recognizing it and determining to do something positive about it takes a huge amount of honesty before God and courageous, sustained effort.

Without going too far afield, Americans seem to find entertainment, amusements and recreation nearly irresistible, and once mandatory work is done, relaxation and fun are supposed to start. One of the results of the sin of Adam and Eve was God's curse on the ground and on the functions of nature in general. (Gen 3: 16-19, Rom. 8:20-21) This changed their effort to acquire the basics of life from meaningful, satisfying, part-time work into sweaty, back-breaking work that seems to never end. Anyone who has tried to farm or grow most of their own food and clothing by primitive methods can attest to this. It used to be the life of nearly everyone before the industrial age. The primary thing the industrial age did for us is to move "the sweaty, back-breaking work that seems to never end" indoors (that is if you could even find work), and more recently into a cubicle with a computer and a phone.

Since we were not originally designed for this kind of grueling existence, once work is over for the day or the week, we feel a great need to find some balance and solace in activities that provide some enjoyment and distraction from the toil and drudgery. The greater the toil and drudgery, the more intense and sensational the distractions must be to bring relief to our souls. Under the debilitating influence of our sinfulness, these pleasures and distractions can easily become expressions of that sinfulness. This dysfunction has enslaved much of the human race in one form or another. It is quite common for workaholics to try to balance their inner needs with brief, but intense, forms of sensual pleasures that are powerful enough to temporarily numb the senses. It is an addiction that can be hard to break. Meanwhile, your soul is screaming for true fulfillment, which is never reached, further driving the addictive cycle.

When Christianity is introduced into a culture or a life, overcoming the desire and perceived need for sinful amusements and pleasures can be one of the hardest parts of the initial task. In the past, the focus of criticisms from church leaders often fell on the ongoing pursuit of these "worldly pleasures" by Christians. Early in the church age these included the gluttony, drunkenness, pagan temples and gladiatorial games of Rome. Not so long ago, it included the common things such as dancing, theaters/movies, card playing, use of alcohol and tobacco, and gambling. This approach has typically been discarded by most churches because it was finally recognized as legalism of the first order. However, in discarding legalism, we did not really resolve the issues.

The real problem is that most Christians, simply and honestly, have never been able find their Christianity sufficiently satisfying to motivate them to abandon the competing pleasures of the world. Along with that, they also do not know how to incorporate "all other things" into a wholistic and joyful Christian life. The demanding yoke of work and the subsequent need for some balancing pleasures, has resulted in Christians spending far more attention to all the other tasks and distractions of life than to their faith and their church. Such pursuits can be "worldly" and sinful to some degree or other, but rather than criticizing and condemning, the full Biblical solution is to teach Christians how to deeply enjoy God and the life that God leads you into. Only discipleship can teach this. No system of legalism or churchianity will get the job done and teaching them to be "churchy" doesn't work for very long either.

The rise of strong Bible teaching ministries resulted in a new awareness that the traditional forms of legalism were not a legitimate understanding of the Bible, and the New Testament in particular. Gradually, a different view formed about various forms of recreation and amusements for Christians, prompting churches to allow things that had been previously forbidden. Soon, evangelical churches began to inject forms of entertainment, amusement and recreation into the church program, calling it "church activities". I can well remember that proposing to play volleyball in the church parking lot as part of youth group was a rather controversial idea at the time. Not so long afterwards, church softball and basketball appeared. The first move toward accepting movies was to allow "Christian movies" to be viewed in church with a little less guilt. At first, those who attended experienced some inner fear of being struck down dead by God before the film was over. They quietly suspected the pastor of going liberal.

All sorts of sports, recreation, amusements, special interests and special focus activities have now arisen in the church program. A great many of such activities are simply a Christianized version of the same type of activities, clubs and hobbies that keep non-churched people in constant busyness when they are not working. It's called "getting involved". Recently, I have even seen churches advertising for "Recreation Pastors" to be part of their large umbrella of ministry. These activities keep Christians doing the same things they enjoy, but away from the "tainting atmosphere of the world". I believe the ability to offer such church activities was a significant factor in building mega-churches.

At first, some of these activities were intended to communicate to unbelievers that Christians were not just a bunch of strict, straightlaced people who never have any fun. Some of these were begun under the sincere belief that it would bring more un-churched or under-churched people into the church, thereby providing a greater opportunity to present them with the gospel and God's truth about spiritual growth. Many times, they are offered and promoted as "Christian fellowship." All these activities were well-intended, but they are sadly misguided for a specific reason that is very difficult for the Church to admit and truly grasp.

What seems to elude our grasp is that these activities just keep Christians "busy" with things that are fun but cannot provide the deep fulfillment and satisfaction that is found only in Christ. All too often it creates the same kinds of distraction from the more important things of spiritual growth and vitality; but now it is all sponsored by the church, so it is seen as an acceptable way of making Christians "well-churched." This builds a church culture that is based on doing fun things with church friends. The reason for coming to church is to see your friends, catch up and plan some fun together. When there is a call for something that is truly spiritual, related to spiritual growth, ministry or commitment, most Christians are "too busy" with all such activities to fit anything else in the schedule. Everyone is too busy to seriously pursue becoming like Christ. All too often, any call to discipleship brings the response, "I'm sorry pastor, we are just too busy right now with other activities (including church activities)." This usually means madly driving all over the city, county, state, or region to get to such activities, especially for your children. "I mean, Bobby and Susie have soccer, Christy has Irish dancing and science club, and Johnny has baseball, football and computer club. I'm sorry, but there is just no time right now to become a transformed person with Jesus. I have to keep my priorities in line. After all, if Christ were here, He would be offering to serve us by sharing the driving responsibilities to our activities. Right?" Every pastor knows this kind of response all too well. It is a long-standing problem that Christians are reluctant to join a small group unless they already have friends in that group or friends that will join with them. Many Christians seem to be inept at quickly forming new and meaningful friendships, as well as growing and maintaining those relationships.

Thus, we continue making Christians who do not act much like Jesus, but they are enjoying "church" because they enjoy the activities. That's one of the main reasons why they keep attending. Attendance and giving appear stable or on the rise, which makes church leadership think they are doing fine, and everything just continues, but without making Christians who are more Christ-like (unless Jesus has taken up playing second base). If we are not following the way of Him who is the Head of the Church, we are not doing fine, regardless of attendance and budget. Church Activity Syndrome powerfully militates against proper discipleship, and then few become more Christ-like, but they do get better at volleyball. Meanwhile, our new technique of providing and having more fun does not bring more acceptance and appreciation for Christianity. It brings more criticism, and deservedly so.

You can always gauge this problem by simply observing how quickly the church worship area empties after the Sunday church service. There is no tarrying before the Lord to deal with issues of the heart and spirit that may have gripped them during the message. There are no spontaneous mini-gatherings of prayer to seek God in response to the worship time, or to exuberantly praise Him for a blessing bestowed. There are no mini-gatherings to ask a brother or sister to hear confession and seek forgiveness and restoration. (These really did happen not so long ago.) Instead, it's much like a theater when the movie has ended, a crowd after a sports game is over, or the school play when it has concluded. The "program" is over, so it's time to leave and get home to get busy or have some fun. The only way to slow down the evacuation is to offer more coffee and donuts or a cook-out. A cook-out and the afternoon game of their favorite professional sports team on the big screen is even better! The latest fad is a pulpit style that must start each message with several minutes of what resembles a stand-up comedy routine by the host of their favorite late-night show. What then follows is a rather simplified version of a sermon, always avoiding any politically sensitive issues. After all, if we expect them to come, stay, and listen, we must certainly make it fun and entertaining! Right?

Another way to discern this problem is to carefully observe to what extent people ignore God, avoid God and marginalize God in their daily lives while at the same time saying they believe in God. This is the primary symptom of Christian atheism. God never leaves the building! It is my consistent observation over many years that most Christians will do almost anything to avoid hearing and confronting what God has to say to them through His word. It is a commonly observed problem that, if you give Christians any chance to do something that will help them avoid God's truth, they will gladly do it. Nearly everyone who has led a small group or Bible study has experienced this. Christians will talk (about almost anything except God and His word), they will eat, they will discuss, they will plan, they will joke, they will share recipes or cooking experiences, they will play, they will talk about the weather, they will talk about politics, they will talk about their vacation or their fishing trip—anything to avoid hearing God's word to their hearts. This is often painted over as if it were "Christian fellowship". If it is both eating and talking together, it is definitely considered "Christian fellowship". The fact of the matter is that this is another symptom of avoiding and marginalizing God. Church Activity Syndrome has become the proverbial "riding the tiger". Once you get on, you don't dare get off because, once dismounted, the tiger will eat you, and the tiger's appetite keeps increasing.

If Christians found their faith and church deeply satisfying, would we need distractions to keep people attending and staying involved? I promise you, we would not! If Christians could experience for themselves that the value they find in entertainment, amusement, and recreation, can be found in far greater supply in their relationship with their Heavenly Father, would we keep having this problem? I promise you, we would not! Only true discipleship can tap into the deeply satisfying relationship with Christ that you never tire of and nothing else can even come close to matching. I promise you that if you disciple people fully and properly, they will find faith and church so satisfying they won't need distractions to attend or participate, and it will be so joyous that they will think "fun" is kind of stale. They will be the ones to urge that the group get started because they are looking forward to the deep blessings that they will receive, and they don't want to be cheated.

This does not mean that churches must rush out and eliminate these activities. I have been an athlete, outdoorsman and nature lover. Such activities can be enjoyable and enriching experiences in a wholistic Christian life. As I will show later, discipleship is not a form of legalism or drudgery. True discipleship is completely wholistic. Many sorts of activities, recreation and amusements can be part of a disciple's life. Relationships, friendships, and fellowship can also be part of the life of a healthy disciple. In fact, they are vital, and they are part of the blessings Christ has for you, even if you are an introvert. Jesus was a very relational man. He will teach you how to have truly satisfying relationships with many people, and not only your friends or fellow Christians. However, a disciple learns to enter into these things in a way that is directly and intentionally linked to their relationship with Christ and helps them move toward Christlikeness. It does mean that all such church activities must be well-vetted and adjusted to assure that they carry out the discipleship goals. They must only be vehicles to teach and implement a robust, wholistic life in discipleship. This means far more than the obligatory prayer before the first batter comes up or before the first ball goes on the tee.

We are not improving Christianity by adding multiple "updated things" to show how modern we can be. Our substitutes do not result in Christlikeness, and they do not provide the deeply satisfying, transformed life that Jesus promised to those who follow Him. Go back and read Chapter 3, then decide for yourself. Does a cook-out and the big game on the big-screen satisfy like the water of life, the bread of life, and the light of life? We need to respond to the same invitation from God given in Jeremiah 6:16. Reach back to the ancient paths taught by our Lord and bring them forward into our lives. Learn His ways. I can assure you that our current ways are not His ways. Unfortunately, it is also not the ways that have been pursued for many centuries. The ancient paths were lost in the first century and have remained largely lost for nearly all Christians, right up to and including now. The ancient paths of our Lord are the only version of Christianity that will satisfy the deep longing of our hearts, souls and spirits, and we must not accept substitutes no matter how well intended!

What About Christian Freedom?

A very large part of the American and western mind-set is our belief in freedom. A large part of the history of Europe, especially Great Britain and on to America has been about the gradual achievement of religious, political, social, and economic freedom, and the repeated crises and threats that had to be faced and defeated to achieve this. Freedom is a treasured possession in the American Dream. A major part of striving to achieve the American Dream is about the freedom that we believe it will provide for us. Secure home, secure job, secure food resources, secure marriage, secure health, secure nation, secure eternity are all matters which we greatly desire. We genuinely believe that the American Dream will supply these to us.

Unfortunately, when we read passages that say Christ has set us free, we take this in a way that is not meant by the

Scriptures. Without even realizing it, we re-interpret it based on our American/western mind set. It is hard for us to confront the fact that God did not write the U.S. Constitution or the Bill of Rights. He did not sign them, and He is not bound by them. God is the Sovereign Ruler of the universe, the earth and all it contains, including every person and including you. He even owns your soul! (Ezek. 18:4) He has the infinite right to require obedience, and He has the infinite right to condemn any who refuse His rule. It is our terrible sinfulness that makes this so intolerable to us, because, after all, we think we are equal to God and He has no right to order around those who are equal with Him. He needs My permission to order me around! This thinking normally rattles around deep in your mind and soul, not even in your awareness most of the time.

When Americans read or hear that they are commanded to obey, and that God holds them responsible for obedience, it goes down quite hard. If we are free people, how can we be expected to just obey whatever God demands of us. Don't we have a say? Don't we get to vote on this? I thought the church was supposed to be a democracy! Doesn't this require the surrender of our freedom, our free will, our right to choose for ourselves? Yet, it is clearly stated in Scripture that God's commandments, both Old Testament and New Testament, are plainly that—commandments, not suggestions. Disciples are called by the risen Savior Himself to faithfully do all His commandments. (Matt 28:19-20) We can't seem to grasp how commandments can be coupled with grace. We read the writings from great Christian leaders like Peter and Paul, saying they consider themselves slaves to Christ, (Rom. 1:1, II Pet. 1:1) and inviting and urging us to do the same. (Rom. 7:6, Gal. 5:13, Col. 3:24) How are we supposed to go along with that? Great social, political and military wars have been fought to end slavery. Many early Christians were slaves. Some early Christians were masters and owners of such slaves. (See the book of Philemon.) We give thanks to God for being free, and we certainly don't want to go back, but we must understand that this freedom is limited to the human realm, not the spiritual realm.

Now, well down the centuries-old path of western-style freedom, western Christianity has become increasingly accustomed to presenting the commands of God in Scripture more as requests. Obedience is presented as something voluntary, but with sufficient reward to make it worth the sacrifice. If you want the special reward of obedience, then we invite you to obey. We talk about issuing an "invitation" to be saved, or to make a commitment to God. The current strong tendency and pattern is to convert all commands of Scripture into recommendations or guidelines, rather than commands of the Lord God. It's like recommending that you eat less sugar or red meat. It's a good idea, but you don't have to if you don't want to. You are still going to heaven.

How Are We Free?

The Scriptures are explicitly clear about the descriptions of our freedom. The Scriptures tell us that the true Christian <u>has been freed</u> from:

- Eternal judgement and punishment;
- Physical death (No, that is not a misprint. Jesus' promise in John 11:25-26 assures us that those who believe in Him will not pass through the normal death experience as others.)

- The Mosaic Law as a rule of life and source of righteousness;
- The power of Satan to destroy you, your life, and your eternity.

These are part of all the things Christ has done for you entirely by His own power and initiative. They are automatically yours because you have trusted Christ.

The Scriptures also tell us clearly that the true Christian <u>can be free</u> from the following:

- The power of indwelling, original sin
- The falsehood and blindness of sin
- The damage done to who you are because of all the past sources and experiences of sin
- The damage that could be done to you by continuing to take part in sin from all current and future sources and experiences of sin
- Any man-made list of rules/laws that proposes to govern us in a way that is not in full accord with Gods' commands and teaching, or that proposes to replace God with a list of rules
- The power of Satan to make you really miserable, sad, unhappy, afraid, unfulfilled, insecure, and spiritually weak

These are available to you, because of all the things that Christ has done for you, but they are not automatic because they depend on whether you choose and pursue them. Choosing them also requires that you deliberately leave behind what sin really includes, and embrace living a new life centered on God.

You must intentionally embrace and learn how to live out of your resources of all that Christ is as your new source of life. If you fail to do this, it is doubtful that you will enter into the freedom that Christ wants for you. What a tragedy that is!

Notice that the Scriptures do not say or imply that you are free from all authority, restraint, moral laws and commandments, or free from God Himself. You do not own yourself. Believing that you are free to do whatever you please out of your own imagination of what you want to do and be is part of Christian atheism. You are in fact, owned by God (I Cor. 6:20), but God did not purchase you to set you free unto yourself or to do what you want. (I Pet 2:16) He bought you out of the slave market (slave to Satan, sin, and the ruinous effect of sin) to belong to Him; and now you can enjoy the many privileges and enjoyments of being His child. This places you in the wonderful position of becoming all you were supposed to be as the unique creation of God, made in His image and having full, open fellowship with Him. Entering this freedom does not eliminate serving and obeying. A new life centered on God, resulting in serving and obeying, is the pathway toward your freedom!

How's the Weather in Stockholm?

A helpful way to think of all these is someone who has been abducted and controlled by the desires and whims of their captors. They go along because they are forced to. Then they go along to survive. Then they go along to get along. Then they go along with the hope that, somehow, blending in will allow them to escape one day. Eventually they may become a convert, adopting the beliefs and actions of the captors. This has sometimes been called the Stockholm Syndrome.

This is how almost all sin is. First you become a victim, then a perpetrator. We all have a serious version of spiritual Stockholm Syndrome. We are born with it, and our entire human society and mind-set is run by it. Christian atheists will continue to be controlled by their old master/captor unless they choose to escape his control through the power of Christ.

When Christ frees us, He frees us from the condition of being the captive of Satan. He has paid the ransom for our freedom. (Mk. 10:45, I Tim. 2:6) Finally we are indeed free, but as part of being free, God knows that we must also learn a whole new disposition of choosing good versus evil. It was sinful choice that got us into this mess, and now we must learn to consistently choose rightly so we can return to having what is very good. So, He invites, encourages, urges, commands us to join ourselves to Him in full reconciliation. This returns us to being who we were supposed to be—wide-open, unhindered, whole-hearted, loving alliance, fellowship, and service to God, as a child who willingly and glad-heartedly serves the Father. This also requires that we break free of all the false beliefs, attitudes, habits, and patterns of behavior that developed in us while in captivity to Satan. The spiritual version of Stockholm Syndrome is real and very powerful. It takes a powerful force, time and long-term tough love to break it and return us to what is truly normal. Discipleship empowers you to do this.

Hothouse Christians

I used to think I was a pretty good gardener—until we moved to Colorado. Here the combination of weather, wind, soil, water, and insects makes it a whole new contest. The most challenging of all was raising tomatoes.

Garden tomatoes generally start with purchase of very young plants that have been raised in plant nurseries. There they have been raised from seeds and kept in carefully controlled growing environments to make them viable and healthy. These nurseries used to be called "hothouses". Once you believe that weather and soil conditions are safe for young tomatoes, they are purchased and transplanted into your own garden. All too often my experience was that these hothouse tomato starters often did not survive very well, especially if there were a few cold snaps in the late spring. They were started in the nursery under ideal conditions, protected from chilly, cloudy days or turns in the weather. (Of course, in Colorado, that can mean eight inches of snow in May!) When these plants had to live in the real world of outdoor Colorado, they did not fare very well, often dying before they could even blossom. Not very helpful for a struggling gardener like me.

Records, testimonies and writings across the various church eras all demonstrate that most Christians have been somewhat like hothouse tomatoes. They seem to do fine when they are in church, or a church related event, but get them out into the real world, and they don't do very well at all. This isn't quite the same as "Sunday-only Christians", but it is a major fruit of the lack of discipleship. Just as with the current stream of church activities, the well-intentioned response of the evangelical church has been to produce a plethora of para-church ministries and sources to support and care for weak and struggling Christians as they go through daily life outside and away from church. It is a way of taking church and churchy environment with you. It's like carry-out Christianity. This ranges from many thousands of Christian books, Christian radio programs, Christian music and the Christian music industry it has produced, radio stations, television programs, magazines, books, and bookstores to sell them. With the rise of web technology and systems, a whole new layer has been added to provide these ministries and resources online and in web-friendly format. Now you can get them on your smart phone.

As with church activities, these are not necessarily evils that must be abandoned. I have certainly benefitted from such resources over my Christian life. As the Lord is willing, I hope this book will be published and made available through this same network. However, there is an important issue to be faced for correction and healing. Having numerous and readily available resources to assist and encourage Christians is not the real problem. The problem is that a great many Christians can barely survive, much less thrive, outside of a churchy environment all around them. Very subtly, they substitute these resources for God, Himself. Many Christians are barely able to function away from church, church resources, or churchy environment, etc. They don't know how to live a robust, joyful life of being like Christ in a non-Christian environment and they can seldom share the gospel effectively with those around them. This is a direct result of being without any meaningful discipleship. A properly trained disciple can be strong and stable most of the time, even when not in a constant supportive environment; and they can live a faithful, obedient life unto the Lord in spite of adversity. A properly trained disciple has learned that everyday life is a normal, expected part of being a follower of Christ, and has learned to take all of life in stride without losing deep and meaningful touch with the living Lord.

Proper intake of God's word is essential to a functioning Christian. It is both instructional and nurturing for our spiritual life. It is the primary source that tells us the commands, promises and truth that Christ has given to us. God has a very special way of speaking to us in His word and drawing us to Himself through His word. It is the eternal word of God. It is a very great privilege for us to have our own Bibles to read and study. However, we must never believe or allow that the Scriptures become a substitute for God Himself. No disciple who lived prior to the printing press depended on the constant intake of the Scriptures that current Christians seem to believe is normal and essential. Paul did not carry around a complete copy of all the scrolls of all the books of the first century Bible, and no Christian who lived prior to the printing press did this either.

First century disciples were often slaves, servants, or day-workers, etc. and might not read at all. Their daily lives did not require it, so why should they? Their access to what we know as the New Testament was quite limited for centuries. Even once the printing press was invented, a large percentage of the general populations of any country, including Christians, could not read, or could read only at a low level of proficiency; and yet to all of these Christians, Paul urged, "Let the word of Christ richly dwell within you" (Col. 3: 16), and, "...be transformed by the renewing of your mind" (Rom 12:2). If fulfillment of these commands depended on everyone having their own Bible and constantly reading/studying it, with the help of many study aids and resources, then the majority of Christians over time could not possibly fulfill them. Today, most have easy access to the Scriptures and multiple outlets for all of the resources, yet most Christians still do not fulfill these commandments in their lives! This prompts the complaint that too few Christians demonstrate Christlikeness.

The main issue that needs to be faced is that the level of Scripture intake that we think is important and essential in the evangelical church is like a spiritual form of chronic overeating. We seem to believe that reading and studying God's word is more important than living it out. We have promoted the intake of God's word to the point that many Christians can't sense any presence of God without having their Bible open in front of them, or better yet, Christian music playing in the background and their Bible open in front of them. It is like a kind of anxiety that has led many to believe that spiritual security comes from having your Bible close at hand. We used to believe that God lived in the church building. Now we seem to believe that God only lives in a churchy environment that we can create and take with us. Some seem to feel that their spiritual security depends on knowing the correct answers to every question or issue related to the Bible or Christianity. If we don't know the perfect answer, we fall into a kind of panic attack, and perhaps allow a shadow of doubt to enter our hearts.

The Mount Everest of Discipleship

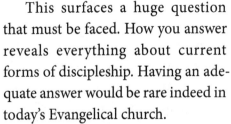

How would you fully disciple someone who cannot read?

This surfaces a huge question that must be faced. How you answer reveals everything about current forms of discipleship. Having an adequate answer would be rare indeed in today's Evangelical church.

How would you fully disciple someone who cannot read? Would you start by years of literacy classes coupled with instructing them in complicated theological questions? Until recently, that would have been my own very flawed viewpoint. However, once you grasp true discipleship, you will see that a high rate and level of literacy is no more required for discipleship than teaching someone to mow the yard or wash the car. Does that shock you? This is the truth of Biblical discipleship.

"Then they recognized them as having been with Jesus..." (Acts 4:13)

Imagine a typical scenario of a visitor coming to your church and as part of introductions at the visitor center, they ask some specific questions about what your church believes. Typically, the answer that will be given is something like, "I don't really know how to explain that, but I can introduce you to the pastor (or elder, or Sunday School teacher). I'm sure s/he will be able to answer your questions." What does that tell this visitor about the reality of the faith of these church members? If it is a church where a strong value of Bible knowledge still exists, a few might be able to provide the answer; but it would normally be in the fashion of a rather theoretical-theological answer while consistently flipping to various passages of Scripture. You may be aware that most unchurched people today do not care much for theology. They are looking for something that can be very real for them, and they judge that by whether your answer is obviously personal and genuine. "They are looking for a genuine, powerful encounter with God..."[17], and they are looking to see if your response shows that you have that kind of deep connection to God. The saddest news of all is that you know this deeply within yourself. You know you are not truly fulfilled! You know that you are not deeply satisfied! That's why you don't know how to answer! You are only putting on a good show in order to fit into the Christian scene. This is absolutely not what Christ wants and it can be different!

Imagine you go to your workplace tomorrow and one of your co-workers asks you why you attend a small group at your church. Would you be able to honestly answer them in a way that makes your church seem like a place that really is worth trying? Providing the best response would communicate that your daily life is so much improved by following Christ, and your small group helps you really understand such things better. It might also communicate that attending small group has helped you overcome some difficult issues in your life that had plagued you for many years. Such answers would communicate that your faith was truly a meaningful part of your whole life—that following Christ has made your life so much better than it was before. Will your answer be spoken with the same kind of cheery delight that you might have in sharing your favorite recipe, or the same kind of enthusiasm as when you tell the tale of your latest big fishing trip?

Such answers cannot be canned or memorized out of a "play book". That's dancing with your head, and its typical of both hothouse Christians and Christian atheists. The inquirer will automatically know that it is fake and superficial, and they will automatically suspect that your faith is also fake and superficial, even though it may be real. Your response must be genuine! The solution is not to practice faking more enthusiasm or having a better sales technique. True discipleship will not teach you a better canned answer. The solution is to make your life and walk with Christ a deeply meaningful, even exciting, part of your daily life. Almost anyone can talk about that! Discipleship will teach you how to have that deeper and exciting life with your Lord, because you are walking with Him and learning from

Him every day. Discipleship is not based on the total volume of the Scriptures you know. It is based on how you grasp it to be consistently lived out in all of life, even if all you do all day long is repair sandals or bake bread.

What Would It Be Like to Escape Christian Atheism?

What has been described above is the current reality of Christianity without discipleship. This is what Pastor Dietrich Bonhoeffer meant by, "Christianity without discipleship is always Christianity without Christ. "[18] That is why it seldom produces Christians who are remarkably Christ-like. In stark contrast to becoming "well-churched", discipleship has the specific and clearly defined goal of making us Christ-like. (Matt 10: 24) No other goal is acceptable. No other goal can substitute. This goes far beyond only avoiding the more obvious sins like lying, stealing, drunkenness, swearing and sexual sins; far beyond obeying the Ten Commandments plus going to church a lot. It goes far beyond being "churchy". Yet it does not require, or even suggest, that you spend most of your time either attending church functions or sitting around reading the Bible and praying all the time. It goes far beyond becoming a well-informed non-doer of the teachings of Christ. It goes far beyond knowing what you believe, or why you believe it, or just believing it very firmly. It goes all the way to faithfully doing it. It does not lead to feeling, "Being a Christian is so hard." Instead, it leads to, "What a blessed life I have! This is incredible! I have to tell others about this!"

How and why we continue to try the same things expecting different results is the true mystery. It is a form of walking in a circle. As advertised, it is a form of insanity. If following what you think is the right path keeps leading you into a box canyon surrounded by your enemies, perhaps we should finally find a different path—the right path this time. Remember—human behavior that is rewarded gets repeated, often to the point of being highly loyal and committed. If Christ promises that He wants us to have a richly rewarding life and this abundant living is only available by following Him in true discipleship, why would we hesitate or propose other ideas in place of His? If we wish to walk in Biblical discipleship, we must dump all the characteristics of Christian atheism and climb back to the true path—the true way that Christ came to give and offered to anyone who is willing.

If you prefer to check the box labeled "No thanks, I don't want an abundant, fulfilling life", feel free. Otherwise, please keep reading.

CHAPTER 6

CHRISTIANS/DISCIPLES/ APOSTLES /LEADERS A.K.A. THE BOOK OF WHO'S WHO AND WHAT'S WHAT

Who Are Christians?

There is much confusion amongst average Christians about the Biblical basis for discipleship. Christians are often quite surprised, and sometimes a bit shocked, to learn that the term "Christian" is used in the Bible only three times, and only in the New Testament. To the surprise of many, the Great Commission does not direct the Apostles to, "go and make Christians…". It directed them to *make disciples*. To understand the historical link of the term Christian to the term disciple, we only need to carefully study the New Testament.

By carefully reading the Book of Acts, you will see that, throughout the time period covered by this book, the followers of Jesus Christ were called by a number of terms. They are "believers", "disciples", "the brethren", "the Way", "the saints", and "the Church". (See Appendix 2 for examples) If you examine any of these passages, or any combination of them, you will see that these terms were used interchangeably for the same people = the followers of Jesus Christ. These are Christians.

Where Did the Term Christian Come From?

The term "Christian" appears only in Acts 11: 26, Acts 26:28, and I Peter 4:16. The information in Acts 11:26 tells us about Barnabas bringing Paul from Tarsus to Antioch to minister to the church there. Then it tells us that, "…the disciples were first called Christians in Antioch". This new term "Christian" was given to those in the church at Antioch who were known to everyone as "disciples". Of course, in the context, it is speaking of the disciples of Jesus Christ. Note carefully that none of the Eleven Apostles from Jerusalem were in Antioch at that time so there is no confusion that the term disciples in this scene was describing those who were known as Apostles. The wording here also tells us this term was invented and applied to the disciples of Jesus by others, not by the disciples themselves. It basically means "Christ-ones", because that is what these disciples were constantly talking, teaching and preaching about—this Jesus that they said was "the Christ". In Jewish terminology of that day, it meant "the Messiah—the Anointed One". Evidently the followers of Jesus did not dislike or resist this new term, so it was eventually adopted and became a common term throughout the Roman empire and throughout history.

Unfortunately, over time, the true meaning of these labels, disciple and Christian, came to be misunderstood. In later years and centuries, few would recognize the term "Christian" as strictly meaning those who are "disciples of Jesus Christ". For the focus of this book, it tells us very clearly that, based on the Word of God, the term "Christian" is intended as an equivalent term with "disciple" and vice-versa. In the true Biblical meaning, Christian and disciple are to be considered as identical. Jesus directed His Apostles to make disciples, and there is no such thing as a Christian who is not a disciple. *You must understand and embrace that, based on the full authority of the inspired Scriptures, Christian=Disciple. There are growing disciples, there are stunted disciples, there are faithful disciples, and there are unfaithful disciples, but there is no such thing as a Christian who is not a disciple.* The inspired Scriptures give no place for any other meaning.

> You must understand and embrace that, based on the full authority of the inspired Scriptures, Christian=Disciple. There are growing disciples, there are stunted disciples, there are faithful disciples, and there are unfaithful disciples, but there is no such thing as a Christian who is not a disciple.

Additionally, for those readers who are in any level of church leadership, it is also very important to grasp that, over time, it has been the Church that has created this misperception about discipleship. It didn't happen by itself. Inadvertently? Perhaps. Unintentionally? Perhaps. But nonetheless it is a fact! Only the churches and their leadership can change this!

What Is a Disciple?

If we are going to walk the path of genuine discipleship under Christ, we need to clearly understand what that means.

Multiple errors and misperceptions have been made about discipleship. A common misperception is that there are "ordinary/everyday Christians", then those who want to be "really dedicated Christians". You know, those who want to spend a lot of time at church, like deacons and teachers—churchy people. However, there is no Biblical basis for being "just an ordinary, everyday Christian". The call of Christ to come to Him for salvation is simultaneously His call to you to become His disciple. There is no alternative, and it is not put off until sometime in the future when you decide to "accept Christ as your Lord". As soon as you cross the line between "seeker" and "believer", it is the desire and intention of Christ Himself that you have also crossed the line to become a disciple. You don't have to wait for some special call from God, or your church, or anyone else. Its automatic. It's by grace, and you don't need anyone's permission to obey what God says in His word.

Some believe discipleship is joining a small group or small group Bible study. Some believe discipleship is joining an accountability group, possibly combined with small group Bible study. Discipleship is not some type of "advanced level of Christianity", like someone who takes an honors course, or a talented and gifted class, or like someone who graduates from high school, then goes on to college, or someone who gets a bachelor's degree then goes on to get a master's degree. It is often misunderstood as only for those who wish to advance to a higher level of responsibility within the church, such as elder, deacon, lay minister, adult Sunday school teacher, or the evangelism team. All of these are inadequate and incorrect, based on the Scriptures.

Discipleship is not a class, or a course, or a 30-day study. It is far more than learning some better Bible study methods, having a daily quiet time and learning some techniques for sharing the gospel. All of these are incorrect or incomplete concepts when put to the test of Scripture. If you wish to enter all the blessings promised and intended for you by our Savior and Lord of the Church, all these must be recognized and abandoned as incorrect and inadequate definitions of discipleship. Discipleship is far greater, far more wonderful, and for everyone who is a sincere Christian. It is the way into the blessed life that Jesus died to give you, both now and forever.

The most heartbreaking thing of all is that secretly, deep down inside, many Christians do not believe they can or should enter a blessed life. They don't think they deserve it. They don't think they can earn it. They don't think they can endure it. Secretly, some believe this is only found in heaven, or they believe this is only for those in full-time vocational ministry. Being rid of these obstacles is an important first step toward entering the blessed life of the followers of Jesus Christ. Please believe the Scriptures that it is not only for some. It is for all Christians. It is for you, and you don't earn it or deserve it. It is by grace!

Christ Making Disciples

During His earthly ministry, Christ went about preaching, teaching, healing and making disciples. We are most familiar with those disciples we know as "the Twelve". The occasion and circumstance of Jesus' call of some of these disciples is described to us in the Gospels.

Having disciples was a common practice for Jewish rabbis in the first century. The Pharisees considered themselves disciples of Moses (John 9:28), and they in turn had disciples. (Mark 2:18) John the Baptist had disciples. (Luke 7:18) The word disciple means a "learner" or "student", but not in the western sense of those terms. More fundamentally, it meant a devoted learner/trainee/apprentice. The word "disciple" can be either a noun or verb. As a noun it refers to a person who is a disciple. As a verb, it refers to the process of training someone as a disciple. Although awkward to our ears, it may be better understood as "disciple-ize".

The process is really quite common and works even in our own world today. We simply don't call it that. You hear of a teacher or speaker who is acquiring some recognition as being especially good or interesting. You happen by or intentionally drop by to listen. You find that what he/she has to say is interesting or helpful to you. It may be challenging. It awakens something in you that calls to you in some way. The more you keep coming back, the more you like what you hear. You feel that you can believe in this teacher and what he/she says. You can believe in his/her message or the cause he/she represents. Eventually you believe in the teacher and his/her message so strongly you want to help. You may start travelling with the teacher as one of his/her supporters. You become something of a "groupie" or "roadie". You might help by finding accommodations, finding food, distributing flyers, helping with the crowds, etc. But when it comes to "teaching time", you are ensconced in your seat, usually up close to the teacher, giving your whole attention to him/her. It's obvious to all that you that you have a strong allegiance to this teacher.

These were all the same marks of a first century disciple in the Jewish culture of Jesus' day. A disciple wanted to spend as much time as possible with a teacher, even travelling around with him, to learn what he said, what he did and how he lived out what he said. By spending as much time with the teacher as possible, you learned as much as you could. You even learned to copy him in as many ways as possible, so you could become like him. Eventually, you might even mimic his words, his speech patterns, his gestures, and his mannerisms. If you discover that he does not live out what he teaches, it is proof that it is a false teaching and a false way, not worthy of believing, copying, or following. Equally important, if the teacher passes off the scene, one or more disciples would often "take up his mantle" and resume teaching and representing his views and practices, similar to when Elisha took up the mantle of Elijah. (II Kings 2: 13-14). This is why the Pharisees saw themselves as "disciples of Moses", (John 9:28) Moses was long gone, but the Pharisees believed they were carrying on his work and mission.

One of my favorite books on discipleship is still an old book that I picked up years ago at a used book sale at my Bible college. It was written by William Fraser McDowell and published in 1935. The name of the book is, *In the School of Christ*. It only cost me thirty-five cents in 1972, but it was truly priceless in its content and how it helped me in my initial understanding of discipleship. It gives the primary structure of what it means to be a disciple and how this prepared the Twelve to do what they were called to do and be what they were called to become. McDowell's summarizes the training of these disciples as: "They heard what He said, they watched what He did, and they came to know for themselves what kind of man He was (paraphrase mine)."[19] The kind of man He was authenticated that what He said and what He did was the truth and completely worthy of following and reproducing. This prepared them to go forth with an authentic message, with matching authentic methods, having become changed men by their Savior. Now, they also lived completely surrendered lives dedicated to proclaiming His message to all.

Who Are Apostles?

Many Christians also do not realize the important distinction between disciple and apostle. When they think of the disciples of Jesus, they think only of the Twelve disciples that are prominently identified in the gospel accounts. However, there were far more than twelve individuals who became disciples of Jesus during His earthly ministry. (Mark 3: 7, 14; Luke 6:13) The Twelve that we know the best are emphasized in the gospels because they were the group first chosen by the Lord to go ahead of Him to preach and heal in His name. They were also the most dedicated "roadies" of the group. By the time of the Transfiguration, they thought they were so dedicated to Him and His cause that they thought they should receive special positions in His kingdom, and would gladly go to death for Him, or even with Him. (Mark 13:41, John 11:16) The special emphasis on these Twelve disciples in the Gospel accounts is retrospective, because when the gospel accounts were written, they reflect what came later in regard to these men as the Apostles (except for the traitor Judas).

An apostle means "a sent one", in other words, someone who is sent out as the authorized messenger and representative of the sender, carrying with him the authority of that sender. If you consistently translate it that way, you will find it helps with all sorts of interpretation issues. The Twelve disciples that we know from the gospels were eventually sent out by Christ on a special mission to prepare other towns and villages for His imminent tour as He began His route back to Jerusalem. Thus, they became apostles, or "sent ones", carrying His message and authority. It included the power to preach, teach, heal, raise the dead and to cast out demons. (Matt 10:1; Mark 6: 7, 12, 30; Luke

9:1-2, 10) This was clearly not an authority they had in themselves, but Jesus gave it to them. In subsequent months, a larger group of seventy was sent out for the same sort of mission. (Luke 10: 10:1,17) Later, they were again sent out by the risen Christ after the resurrection, this time to the whole world, as the initial leaders and vanguard of taking the gospel into all the world. The same criteria of the message and authority of the sender is given again in what we know as the Great Commission. That apostleship never ended. Eventually, Scripture refers to these men as the foundation of the church (Eph. 2:20) as well as the foundation stones of the New Jerusalem (Rev. 21:14). But the New Testament clearly indicates there were many more disciples than those Twelve. (Matt. 4:25, John 4:1-3) In the Upper Room after the resurrection and before Pentecost there were 120 there in Jerusalem alone. (Acts 1: 15)

How Did Jesus Define What It Means to Be His Disciple?

With the current confusion about what it means to be a disciple, or to disciple others, we need to ask the legitimate question: "What does it mean to be a disciple of Jesus?" How are we to go about it, both for ourselves and for others? What should be included, both for ourselves and for others? This question need not be left up to us for arbitrary and varying answers. Christ Himself defined what He meant by this term.

Becoming Like the Master

The first part of His definition was given in Matthew 10: 24-25. Jesus tells the disciples, "A disciple is not above his teacher, nor a slave above his master. It is enough for the disciple that he become like his teacher, and the slave like his master." (Also see Luke 6:40) As described above, the goal of a disciple is far more than just head knowledge. It is to become like his/her teacher and master. Now when you think about it, this is an astounding statement from Christ, and yet it is clearly what He says. One of the complaints about Christianity is that Christians don't seem to be very much like Jesus. *But since Christian=disciple, this should be the exact and overwhelming goal of every Christian and every church. A very large proportion of resources in any church ministry or program should be focused on this purpose.* Every annual business meeting of every church should include a complete and honest evaluation of whether they are reaching or making progress in that goal. This will require a major shift in the focus of all churches. However, if this is clearly the Great Commission of our Lord, how could we determine otherwise? This criteria from Christ for those who are disciples has not changed. If you are a Christian, you are also called to be a disciple, and a disciple seeks and welcomes becoming like the Master.

> But since Christian=disciple, this should be the exact and overwhelming goal of every Christian and every church. A very large proportion of resources in any church ministry or program should be focused on this purpose.

Here are several of Paul's exhortations to Christians urging us to become like Christ and assuring us that this is the goal and purpose of God Himself.

Rom. 8:29—"For those whom He foreknew, He also predestined to become conformed to the image of His Son..."

II Cor 3:18—"But we all, with unveiled face, beholding as in a mirror the glory of the Lord, are being transformed into the same image from glory to glory, just as from the Lord the Spirit."

Gal 4:19— "My children, with whom I am again in labor until Christ be formed in you, ..."

Eph. 4:20—"But you did not learn Christ in this way, ..."

I Cor. 11:1—"Be imitators of me, just as I also am of Christ."

Eph. 5:1—"Therefore, be imitators of God, as beloved children...".

These passages and many others are well preached and well taught in many evangelical churches, and any other churches that still recognize any important role for God's word. *It is God's good pleasure that you become like His Son!* And yet, how many churches enthusiastically and practically include this goal in their annual ministry planning? How many Christians who faithfully attend Bible-believing churches have this as one of their primary life goals that they are actively working towards? How often have you seen a class or small group offer a study of, "Becoming Like Christ"?

Who, Me—Like Christ?

Many Christians would respond to honest questions like this with something like, "Oh my, I don't think I can be like

Christ. I mean, I'm not perfect and don't expect to be anytime soon. After all, I can't become the Son of God." Let me ask you, would you be satisfied with reaching 95% like Christ? How about 90%? How about 75%, or 40%? Most Christians are not expecting to achieve any meaningful part of this until it is done for them suddenly and miraculously by God when they reach heaven. In fact, many Christians are taught that they shouldn't even worry about it or make any attempt toward it, because they are "under grace." Thus, is born the Christian atheist.

To be conformed to the image of Christ does not mean or imply that you can become God or deity. It is not saying that you will become part of the Trinity, or that you will become the only begotten Son of God. It is not saying that you can or should acquire or develop those attributes that are true of God alone, like omnipotence or omniscience. It also doesn't mean that you will walk around performing all sorts of miracles, signs and wonders. It is not saying that you will instantly become perfect. It is also not superficial, as if we should dress or eat like Jesus while He was on earth in first century Palestine. It's also not an alternative persona that you pop in and out of from time to time, like an avatar, when it's time to look or sound religious.

Then what are these verses telling us? As indicated in the verses in Galatians, Ephesians and Colossians, it means you should "imitate Him". Any real thought on this idea quickly reveals that this is not in a superficial or artificial way. The term "imitate" does not describe the process but primarily the result. You will genuinely have and show the characteristics of Christ. Even a small amount of reflection reveals that you cannot possibly do this on your own. You must become transformed by a power much greater than anything within yourself. You will be transformed from who you used to be to a new you that is like

Him. It will become natural to you, not forced, awkward or strange. It is not like David trying to wear the armor of King Saul in order to fight Goliath. (I Sam 17:38-39) When others watch and listen to you, they might whisper to themselves, "That reminds me of Jesus", or "That must be how Jesus was." The longer you walk with Christ, the more you will have and show the mind of Christ, the heart of Christ, the words of Christ, the viewpoint of Christ, the priorities of Christ, the intentions, and purposes of Christ. These are the goals for which you will deliberately and energetically strive. These are some of the same characteristics described as the fruit of the Spirit in Galatians 5, the attributes of love described in I. Cor 13, the mind habits of Phil. 4:4-6, and the life characteristics of Matt. 5-7. Having these consistently in your life, both private and public, inner and outer, is part of what it means to be in the image of Christ. "It is enough for the disciple to become like His teacher and for the slave to become like his master." (Matt. 10: 25) If you are a Christian=disciple, this should and must be your overall goal for life.

I challenge you to stop reading right now, read each of the Scriptures referenced above, then get in front of a mirror and ask yourself, *"Would it be enough for you to become like Christ if it meant becoming a person who consistently has the characteristics of Jesus?* Then ask this question, *"Would it still be enough for you to become like Christ even if it meant*

"Would it be enough for you to become like Christ if it meant becoming a person who consistently has the characteristics of Jesus? Would it still be enough for you to become like Christ even if it meant you did not achieve any part of your own life plan or dream?"

you did not achieve any part of your own life plan or dream?" Paul tells us, "For this is the will of God, your sanctification." (I Thess. 4:3a) All other steps in the path, all other experiences, achievements, events, occurrences and things that mold who you become are subservient to this life goal from God. Do you want to fight God in becoming who He intends you to be, or do you wish to cooperate with God and join with God as your Heavenly Father, in becoming the best and most blessed person you can possibly be? Welcome to the life of a true disciple!

Learning to Obey His Commandments

The second part of Christ's definition is found in what we know as the Great Commission itself in Matt. 28:19-20. In His Commission, Christ describes the overall process of making disciples as "…baptizing them… and teaching them to observe all that I (Jesus) have commanded you" (parenthesis mine). For purposes of this book, we will not deal with the matter of the form, or mode, of baptism that should be practiced, but it must at least be declared that baptism is not optional.

As you continue through the book you will see that obedience to the Lord's commands does not constitute some sort of legalism or something added to the gospel. It is not a work that earns something from God. To receive His forgiveness and eternal life you must declare "Jesus is Lord". (Rom 10:9) This is written by the Apostle Paul, well known as the Apostle of grace and Apostle to the Gentiles. It is quite ridiculous to say that Paul was adding something to the gospel when writing to the Roman church, especially in light of Rome's demand for absolute obedience to, and worship of, the emperor. His command for you to be baptized is His command, not the Church, not some council, and not some preacher. First obedience seals the bond between you and your Savior.

The specific word used by our Lord in His Commission was that disciples were to be taught "to observe" all His commandments. This is a common term used throughout the Old Testament, especially in Exodus and Deuteronomy, to describe Israel's responsibility to obey God's Law for them as a nation. This word does not mean to stand on a hill, watching the commandments go by; nor to put them on display, like a museum exhibit, so that everyone could solemnly walk by to show great respect for them. This Hebrew word means a number of things, joined altogether into one concept. 1.) It meant to protect and guard the commandments as highly valued and sacred to Israel. 2.) It also meant to give focused attention to the commandments to make sure you do not forget or neglect them. 3.) It also meant to give devoted obedience to the commandment. It was to define who and what they were as the people of God, fulfilling God's promise to Abraham. It meant to live in them as their culture and identity. The same multi-faceted meaning transfers over into the New Testament in this Great Commission of Christ.

Becoming a Christian automatically places you on the path of discipleship under Christ. You are entering a whole new way of life—The Way of Christ. 1.) We are to protect and guard His commandments as highly valued and sacred to all who believe in and follow Him (the Church). 2.) We are to give focused attention to His commandments to make sure you do not forget or neglect them. 3.) We are to give devoted obedience to His commandments—a life devoted to learning to obey the teaching of your Lord. We are to live in them as our culture and identity. Afterall, it is *His teaching*, not merely "Church tradition".

However, a disciple under Jesus is not learning to acquire head knowledge, or only to pass a test on paper, or recite a catechism, or mentally assent with a doctrinal statement (even though you don't' understand most of it) so you can be accepted into membership in the local church, or to take copious notes in a notebook then stuff them into a notebook or drawer. Classroom knowledge and book learning are not the primary and ultimate focus of a disciple. This is not school, as in the western mind-set. True discipleship is life training by which you become a changed person by the presence and power of the indwelling Christ. The disciple is learning to do. He/she is learning to do all of Christ's teaching with all his/her heart.

There is a huge disconnect in the evangelical church about the Great Commission. It does not read, "...making sure they *hear* everything I have commanded you". It does not read, "...teaching them to *understand* everything I have commanded you." It does not read, "...teaching them to *believe* all that I have commanded you...". His instruction is that we "teach them *to do* all He commanded". By learning to walk in His way, you come to live in a wonderful new way of life, and you experience an ever-increasing fulfillment of all His promises. It begins to make a completely new version of you. (II Cor. 5:17)

I promise you that becoming like Christ does not come to you by any church ceremony or ritual, or by walking the aisle and praying a pre-packaged prayer, or from any Pentecostal or charismatic experiences. Nor does it come from just faithfully attending church each week, singing songs, listening to the sermon and on the way out saying to the pastor, "Nice sermon, pastor. Very interesting". You do not receive His joy and peace by becoming "churchy". You do not receive His strength and courage by becoming "churchy". You do not receive His wisdom and understanding by becoming "churchy". It comes by learning to become like Him by faithfully walking the path of obedience to His commandments. *This is discipleship. This is to be the primary mission and goal of every Christian and every church.*

> This is discipleship. This is to be the primary mission and goal of every Christian and every church.

I challenge you to see that this is the only Biblical mission and goal of every church. All other legitimate missions and goals that might be chosen for a church are simply portions or sub-categories of this one

Great Commission which the Lord of the church has passed on to us. There is nothing else, and we dare not try to make it something else! There is no need of multiple committees spending months and even years in conventions and symposiums, long meetings, discussions, debates, negotiations and wrangling to determine what it means to be a disciple of Jesus Christ. We need only recognize, embrace and bow to the command of our Lord and King. Only He has the right to define what it means to be His disciple or to make disciples in His name. There is no need of multiple committees spending months in long meetings, discussions, debates, negotiations and wrangling to determine what the mission, vision and goals of the church should be. The mission, vision and goals have all been determined by the Lord in His Commission. It is to take the good news of salvation to the world and to fully disciple all who repent and believe in Him.

True discipleship has not been tried and failed. It has almost never been tried since the first century! Rejecting Christianity based on the many terribly flawed versions that have been practiced over the years and centuries is non-sensical. If you would say of Christianity, "Yeh, been there, done that. Didn't do much for me," it is because you never tried true, Biblical Christianity. True, Biblical Christianity, as taught by Jesus and His Apostles, always works and it never disappoints. (I Peter 2:6) It's just pretty hard to find anywhere. "I'm sorry, we don't have that anymore."

CHAPTER 7

DO YOU REALLY BELIEVE?

W e have seen that to be a Christian automatically indicates a call from Christ to be His disciple. In order to find meaning in this, we must be certain that we know what true faith is before we will be ready to enter fully into all that this means.

We must come to grips with the true meaning of the terms "believe" and "faith". These terms come from the same word in the original languages of the Scriptures. The original meaning of this word cannot be properly translated by a single English word, concept or term. In order to make it easy to "accept Christ as Savior", the essential meaning of these words has been severely blurred and diluted. Because of this, we have quite a difficult time coping with the assertions in various places in our Bibles, including the teaching of our Lord Himself. That is part of the problem, especially if you are trying to turn salvation into an easy formula and prepackaged prayer that can be muttered by someone who is responding to a gospel invitation.

The terms believe/ faith in Scripture mean three things all wrapped together in one word. In various passages of Scripture, different aspects of this term are emphasized. It does not mean making something exist because I choose to believe it exists. It means to believe a fact, as in, "I believe that the earth is round." It also means to trust or entrust, as in, "I believe that the earth is round, therefore I am confident I won't fall off the edge." It also means to commit to, or hold allegiance to, as in, "I believe that the earth is round, therefore I won't fall off the edge, and I have joined the crew of Christopher Columbus tomorrow to prove it." Then throughout the voyage, you follow each command of Christopher Columbus because you have no doubt or lack of trust in what he knows. You don't' always understand or agree with his decisions but you fully expect to arrive at the destination that he has anticipated. In light of this, we see the overall Scriptures telling us that to believe in Christ (or have faith in Christ) means you believe what He says is true (fact), you are willing to show your belief by completely trusting Him to do what He has promised (trust/entrust), and you are committed to doing what He teaches is true (allegiance) even if you don't always understand it at first. To leave any of these out means you do not really believe in the way that the Scriptures call us to do.

True faith is not a version of, "I guess I favor believing more than disbelieving. I can go along with believing so far." Then, you go through life silently gathering evidence that either favors or disfavors continuing to believe. Each encounter with such evidence weighs in one direction or another, with the goal that before you die you still fall on the believing side of the line. This is not the faith that saves. This is what "salvation by sacraments/ church membership" has done to us. It was once unknown in the true church, but now, under the "big tent" philosophy of the evangelical church, it has infected a much bigger sector of the entire church. The current church mantra seems to be, "Come and belong, and along the way we hope you will believe." This is basically the old traditional view of parish ministry. Meanwhile, it assures a larger attendance to become well-churched and join in the church activities. This does not mean that those who are "seekers" (those who are still watching, listening and considering) cannot or should not be welcome to attend and participate to the extent they wish. We should certainly welcome and love them. But the clear distinction between true Christian by genuine faith and those who have not arrived there yet should not be blurred or erased. This is not the model of the church presented to us in the Scriptures at all.

The faith that saves says, "I believe, and I am all in, no matter what. Are you kidding? Why would I go back? No going back for me, no matter what!" This is why the Scriptures always present to us two dependable tests for genuine faith—perseverance (I'm not going back) and works (I sincerely seek to do what He says.) Faith/belief that is only mental assent/mental acquiescence cannot bring any transformation and no Christlikeness because it is not true faith. It is, "…dead, being by itself". (James 2:17)

Though true faith starts out small, it is still genuine and sincere. It starts like a sprouted seed and steadily grows into a fully mature plant bearing fruit. Discipleship is what helps you receive all you need for growth and benefit from all that God has provided for your growth. It also keeps you deeply in touch with the One who tends the garden. Without discipleship your growth will be stunted and slow.

How Real is God to You?

After all these years, I find myself forced to the same conclusion expressed by a number of other influential Christian leaders, such as A.W. Tozer and Dallas Willard. *Many people who believe they are Christians do not really believe in God, at least not the real God who actually exists and is presented in the* Scriptures. (Ex. 3:14, Isa 44:6) Such Christians, from the lowest seat to the highest office, only believe in God as a mental abstraction, a concept, a working theory from which to operate—in other words as a theology. God is not as "real" to them as other things in their world that they consider real. Now this may be only that no one has explained it to them properly. Once you hear it correctly, you may know that you really do

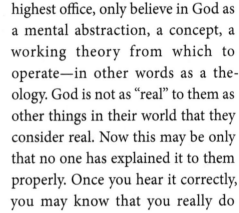

Many people who believe they are Christians do not really believe in God, at least not the real God who actually exists and is presented in the Scriptures.

believe. In order to enter true discipleship, you must also face this penetrating question and issue for yourself and within yourself. Your faith in God may be truly genuine, but you owe it to yourself to make certain. Do not side-step or avoid this issue. It is much too critical.

To even the casual observer, it is obvious that pagans believe in the reality of their gods more than many Christians believe in the reality of the One True God. When pagans do what they believe is displeasing to their gods, they have genuine fear, and they want to do whatever is necessary to appease their gods as fast as possible, and at any cost—even sacrificing their own children. The "reality" that they have in their belief is what we sometimes call "superstition". The one true God of the Bible is the ultimate reality that exists, and it is imperative that we see and relate to Him this way. Nothing is more real than He. Compared to the real God, everything else is nothing but a mist that evaporates away. (Ps. 102: 25-27) If we do not relate to God in that way, we can never become who we were meant to be by God.

Some would argue, "Isn't the uncertainty about God the reason we believe in God by faith?" Did you know that the Scriptures never say, or even imply, that we are to believe anything by faith? As indicated above, the words faith and believe are the same word in the Bible. It is only the difference between the noun form or the verb form. (Remember your grammar classes?) To say that you believe by faith is the same as saying "you believe by belief", or "you have faith by faithing". It's nonsense. Hebrews 11:1 tells us that, "...we understand by faith", but this is not the same thing as saying you believe by faith. Jesus told us that, "Blessed are they who did not see and yet believed." (John 20:29), but this is not believing by faith. Jesus was speaking to Thomas who had refused to believe Christ's own promise to return from the dead after three days. He had also refused to believe the testimony given to him by his fellow apostles and several others who had already seen Christ resurrected and appearing to them in living color. They had handled Him. They had watched Him eat before them. Yet Thomas refused to believe their testimony.

Luke clearly tells us that after the resurrection, Jesus, "...presented Himself alive by many convincing proofs, appearing to them over a period of forty days...". (Acts 1:3) Scripture provides us with more than enough convincing proofs to completely believe it, but it leaves enough room for doubt that if someone is looking for an excuse (very subtly) to dis-believe, then dis-believing can still seem reasonable, because you didn't see it right in front of your own personal eyes. Faith is not a fantasy, fable, fairy-tale or wishful thinking. Faith in God does not mean we hope God exists. God is not created by believing in Him and He doesn't disappear from existence by our dis-belief. The very name of God is "I AM". (Ex. 3: 13-14) The book of Hebrews tells us, "...he who comes to God must believe that He is (He truly exists) and that He is a rewarder of those who seek Him." (Heb. 11:6, parenthesis mine)

Uncertainty in our faith can be driven by our strong sub-conscious view that nothing that is intangible is real. This is the result of our long-standing secular culture. However, most people believe in gravity without seeing it. You only feel the effects. Most people believe in oxygen but have never seen it, and you certainly know the effects. You have probably never seen electricity, but you still believe in it. You believe in x-rays, but you have never seen them, heard them, or felt them unless you have accidentally suffered radiation burns by a high dose. Natural gas cannot be detected by any of our normal senses, but if not carefully controlled and contained, it is deadly. It certainly exists. People believe in love, but they have never seen anything except the results expressed in tangible ways. Many things that are not "tangible" are very real. We see only a very small range of visible light. We hear only a very small range of sound waves. There is far more light energy than we see, and far more sound energy than we hear. That doesn't mean it doesn't exist or is not real.

Scripture tells us that God is spirit. He is completely intangible, but you can still believe in Him as who and what He is—the absolute Real Being. You can believe this with absolute certainty because, throughout human history, He has revealed Himself to various individuals and groups in very tangible ways that gave no room for doubt. He proved Himself to them in ways they could not deny or escape, and they made a record of it in some way. The very power of their encounter with God drove them to proclaim or publish it so others could benefit. Those encounters have been recorded for us in the ancient records we call the Bible by those who witnessed them. It is exactly as the writer of Hebrews said, "God, has revealed Himself at many times and in many ways..." (Heb 1:1, my paraphrase). They are not simply ancient superstitions carried over to us in the Bible. They are ancient encounters with the One True God of the Bible. Peter declared to his fellow Jews, "We are witnesses of these things", (Acts 2:32) and, "We did not follow cleverly devised tales...but we were eyewitnesses of His majesty." (II Peter 1:16)

If you don't believe in God's reality just as much, or more, than the chair you may be sitting in, you don't really believe in the God who really exists. Scripture tells us that God hides Himself both in light and in thick darkness. (Ps. 18:11, 104: 2) This is simply to express that God is invisible to our eyes, like many parts of the light spectrum such as ultra-violet and infra-red. He is "cloaked". Not only is He intangible, He is "wholly other". He is Spirit. The reason science cannot investigate, analyze, and prove or disprove Him by scientific means is because science is entirely and strictly limited to two aspects of our knowable reality—matter and energy. God does not consist of matter or energy or any combination of both. He created both, but He does not consist of these. Therefore, He is completely invisible to all science as we know it so far. It is like being nose-blind or color-blind. We cannot discover or locate God by a radar beam or a tachyon sweep. At times He has taken deliberate steps to express His presence in ways that are tangible to humans, like fire, smoke, thunder, wind, a soft voice, a thundering voice, etc. Even though God is "intangible" to us, due to our very limited range of awareness and perception, He is always completely and perfectly aware of all the expressions of yourself. He sees every move, hears every word, knows your thoughts even before you do, knows your emotions even before you do, (and even when you cannot express them in words), knows the intentions of your heart, even before you do. More importantly, He wants to interact and relate to you in all these things.

You, on the other hand, are tangible, and therefore you do many things to express yourself in completely tangible ways. If you do believe in the true God that exists, you can respond to Him, react to Him and relate to Him in the normal, tangible ways. You can know with absolute certainty that He sees, hears, smells, tastes and knows every one of those expressions. He is, after all, omnipresent (present everywhere all at once), and omniscient (knows everything all at once- even things that we do not know). He wishes for every one of His born-again children to relate to Him in ways that are completely normal for them, because all ways are "normal" to Him. It's part of His being omniscient.

This is how Jesus lived, and as a disciple it is how you can, and should, live also. You are called to it. Jesus died to give this incredible gift to you. The gift of truly knowing the One True God who really exists. (John 17: 3) This will be very important for living in true discipleship, and you don't need anyone's permission to do so. You only need to grow in conscious awareness of His presence and activity as being the absolute reality that surrounds you and engulfs you constantly. This is not eastern mysticism. It is what the Bible tells us. Discipleship will teach you to actively and intentionally live this way.

So, why do we have such a common problem of avoiding God, marginalizing God and keeping Him on the periphery of your life, as if that is normal and acceptable? It is not primarily because He is intangible. *If you wish to enter into true discipleship, you must face the truth that it is your sinfulness that prompts you to think of God and respond to Him in any way that is not based on absolute reality and fully worthy of Him. It prompts you to deny God, avoid God, marginalize God and keep Him on the periphery of your life instead of at the center of your life.* This is part of the sinful nature that you inherited from your family tree, extending all the way back to Adam and Eve when they believed Satan's lie. They believed that they would become like God (therefore equal with God) if they would disbelieve God's warning and disobey God's commandment. If you are equal with God, you don't need Him for anything important, unless you feel terribly guilty about some great sin you have committed or need some kind of miracle to solve a serious problem that you can't solve (which would prove you are not equal with Him). Otherwise, He is "out of

If you wish to enter into true discipleship, you must face the truth that it is your sinfulness that prompts you to think of God and respond to Him in any way that is not based on absolute reality and fully worthy of Him. It prompts you to deny God, avoid God, marginalize God and keep Him on the periphery of your life instead of at the center of your life.

sight, out of mind". When it's "time for God", you may give some attention to Him, otherwise, you've got lots to do and a short time to get it done. It's head down, leaning into the wind, nose to the grindstone. No time for God and no transformation to become like Christ. This is caused by one huge problem—you don't really believe in the Real God who truly exists.

The Critical Importance of True Faith for the Disciple

Disciples must have true faith, not only "mental assent or mental acquiescence". A disciple is seeking to sincerely follow Christ and consistently live in His commands and teachings. This will not happen if your faith is only mental assent or mental acquiescence. It will not happen if you don't believe that God is real. Such a claim is based on a deeply flawed concept of faith. True life always expresses itself, and spiritual life is no different. This is absolutely essential in order to walk the pathway of discipleship to which your Lord has called you. As indicated above, one of the essential elements of discipleship is obedience. You will have little interest or commitment to obedience if you do not truly believe in the reality of God. You cannot say that you have faith in Christ for salvation if this faith does not also prompt allegiance to Him as your Lord, or if you have no desire or intention to obey Him as part of following Him.

All the famous individuals described in the great Faith Hall of Fame in Hebrews 11 are described on the basis of what they *did* because they had true faith. Able offered a better sacrifice. Noah prepared an ark. Abraham left his homeland, travelled to Canaan, and wandered all around Palestine living in tents his whole life. Abraham offered his son on the altar of sacrifice. Moses parted the sea. Joshua brought down the walls of Jericho. Rahab hid the Israeli spies. David killed Goliath in combat, etc. Their genuine faith prompted them to act in concert with God.

When God directed Moses to part the Red Sea, Moses did not go back into his tent to have an iced tea, saying to God, "I know you can do that God. Go ahead, while I get some shade." God's command to Moses was to stretch out his hand and staff over the water. (Ex. 14:15-22) Only when he did so was the sea parted. This was not by Moses' power, but by God's direct and deliberate power, but God waited to act with His power until Moses showed the clear sign of faith—he picked up his staff, walked to the water's edge and held it out over the water. There is an action partnership between God and those who follow Him. It is not a partnership where you do anything that requires any great or supernatural power. But it requires you to have the kind of faith that moves you to take the actions that God commands. As you take the actions God commands you to do, you are looking to God to provide what is great or supernatural power. Faith that is real obeys. It obeys because it is based on spiritual sight, not physical sight. (John 20:29)

The essential role of "doing" as the expression of truly believing is not limited to miracles. In fact, the more you examine this issue, the more you will see that doing is the strongest test for believing. The following example makes that point very clearly.

Let's say that you come from a part of the world that has no knowledge or experience with electric lighting. All the light that you know comes from the sun, the moon, the stars, or some version of fire. As far as you know, that's all there is anywhere in the world. While visiting a friend in a developed part of the world, you enter a dark room at night, expecting your friend to light a match, candle or torch for light. Instead, the friend walks over to a little plastic rectangle and small lever on the wall, flips the lever to an upward position, and suddenly light comes from the ceiling! After several extremely frightful moments, your friend explains electricity, electric lighting, and shows you how to flip the light switch on. Eventually, you believe it—at least you say so. However, the next night when you enter the room by yourself, you continue to light a match or a candle for light.

Do you really believe in electric lighting? No, you don't. When you truly believe something, you automatically and consistently walk over and flip the switch. You barely think of it most of the time. You just do it!

It is an indisputable fact: You always consistently live out what you truly believe. Either you don't really believe it, you don't think it is necessary, you don't know how to do it, you are afraid of doing it, or you don't think you have the power to do it.

Here is the next truth for you to fully embrace for entering Biblical discipleship. *It is an indisputable fact: You always consistently live out what you truly believe.* If you say you believe God's word, but don't consistently seek to live it out, you reveal that something else is going on and it is a direct challenge to anyone who claims to have faith. *Either you don't really believe it, you don't think it is necessary, you don't know how to do it, you are afraid of doing it, or you don't think you have the power to do it.* Any of these can be the explanation, and in the context of discipleship, all pastors, teachers, leaders and disciple-makers are under obligation to find out what it is, then lead that person to embrace full faith obedience. This must start with confronting whether you truly believe what God says, or you just like to say you believe it because it is expected. This is full-spectrum discipleship and cannot be done alone by the pastor, or pastoral staff or the "leadership group". This further requires that, as other writers on discipleship have said, the church must be a culture of discipleship. There is no other legitimate mission for the church than discipleship. Evangelism and missions are only getting people through the gate, not an end in itself. It is only the start of being a Christian=disciple, not the whole purpose.

When we are led to believe that salvation is the call to heaven then going merrily on our way spending life in seeking the American Dream coupled with churchianity, we can never embrace discipleship. The very core of discipleship is obedience. Often, obedience is dismissed as being "works" which are opposed to pure faith, but this is clearly not what the Scriptures tells us. When we are led to believe that discipleship is optional, the call to discipleship will be inaudible to our ears. Our busyness dulls our hearing of the voice of our Lord calling us to obedience. As long as our balance between believing and not believing stays on the right side of the line, we are okay. Right? We are under grace, right? Tragically, this means no transformation, no becoming like Christ.

How would you respond to the following statement: *If you really, really, really believed in the true God, the One who has revealed Himself in creation, in history, in the ancient writings we know as the Scriptures, and finally in His only begotten Son, you would not dare to disobey His commandments or even His suggestions and preferences.* You would not even consider doubting Him, ignoring Him, marginalizing Him, or treating Him as if unimportant or less important than yourself and

If you really, really, really believed in the true God, the One who has revealed Himself in creation, in history, in the ancient writings we know as the Scriptures, and finally in His only begotten Son, you would not dare to disobey His commandments or even His suggestions and preferences.

other things in your life. You would also never think of Him as a kindly old grandfather with a long white beard who is always nice to everyone and looks the other way when you sin. Not only would you obey God's commandments, suggestions and preferences, but you would do so with great love, joy, and wonderful sense of fulfillment and privilege. He is your Heavenly Father, and you love Him with all your heart, soul mind and strength. (Sound familiar?) Every good thing that exists comes from Him to you as a gift.

Do you wish to be free of this debilitating falsehood that keeps you from truly knowing the One True God that actually exists? Only discipleship under Christ can free you of this debilitating sickness and chain of slavery, restoring you to a right relationship with God based on who He really is. This is not merely a theological or intellectual exercise. It is a very real experience of right relationship with the One True Living God through His Son, Jesus Christ. This life change will radically change your life and elevate your worship experiences, both corporate and private, far beyond anything you have ever known. It will hugely enhance your prayer times. It will also hugely increase the joy of your obedience and life in general—so much so that you will be prompted to obey just to get the joy of it. It will be almost addictive!

CHAPTER 8

WHAT IS THE GREAT COMMISSION?

As you study the Bible and listen to messages and lessons in church, or on your preferred technology, you may already know that Matt. 28:19-20 has been considered the Great Commission of our Lord before He left earth and returned to the Father. The term "commission" implies that this was a command of Christ for the disciples to carry out a specific mission. Just as with the Twelve and the Seventy, He again sends them with a specific, established, and authoritative mission, along with His assurance of His continual ongoing presence with them. To properly grasp the full meaning of the term, we must see it as not merely as a "commanded mission", but also as a "Co-mission". Before His ascension, having fully accomplished everything needed as the basis for forgiveness and redemption, He sends His disciples to continue doing what He Himself had been doing; and as the holder of all authority in heaven and earth, He would be with them always in this mission.

As you read Matt 28:19-20, you can see that the focus of the Great Commission is clearly making disciples. However, if you are a real student of Scripture, you also know that through the years, preachers, teachers and scholars have struggled mightily to grasp and embrace why this Great Commission is not more clear in its directive for what we know as evangelism or sharing the gospel. It is routinely used as the mandate for evangelism and missions, but it really does not address that except by implication. How can the Great Commission be so ambiguous toward evangelism? There is a reason!

Those who are most committed to evangelism, such as evangelists and pastors who lead strongly evangelistic churches, automatically assume and portray this as the commission to preach, proclaim and spread the gospel of Jesus Christ. They automatically and vociferously equate "making disciples" solely as making converts. This is their all-consuming purpose of ministry and the churches they lead—win people to Christ and salvation. These types of churches and ministries usually downplay, ignore and even spurn the task of making disciples, as if Jesus had not even addressed this in His Great Commission. Other times, they equate making disciples with nothing more than training others to be soul-winners. Sometimes they have negatively characterized working toward spiritual growth and transformation as "navel gazing", as if Jesus also spurned it and so should we.

Others recognize the primary meaning of this commission from Christ to be the task of making disciples, more in line with the true meaning of the term. They also tend to wonder and struggle with how to include evangelism within the Great Commission when it seems so narrowly focused on making disciples. Surely, such a Great Commission should focus on this great task. To avoid the appearance of excluding or under-emphasizing evangelism, they usually conclude and promote that you can't make a disciple unless s/he is first converted by salvation. Of course, this is correct, but these pastors, teachers and churches are typically more single-purposed in the direction of teaching and spiritual growth with a minimal evangelistic ministry. These have been slow to energetically embrace that walking in the steps of Jesus and learning to be like Him automatically demands that we become witnesses and soul winners.

Jesus was not only a soul- winner. He was a soul hunter! He deliberately and energetically sought out and saved those He had been sent to save. Each one was one of, "...those You have given Me." (John 6:37, 17: 6, 9) Only true disciples will learn to do this also—be a soul hunter who operates by the power of the gospel and the work of the Holy Spirit! As described in Chapter 6, the teaching and spiritual growth emphasis that are commonly associated with discipleship has not been done in a manner that is completely faithful to the true principles of discipleship that Jesus intended when He said this. To properly grasp the total scope of the Great Commission given to us by our Lord, we must understand with clarity what His own mission was, and how He passed it on to His followers before returning to heaven.

The Mission of Christ

Christ had a mission to fulfill on earth, and He stated it in a number of places and settings. Although one overall mission, it can be best understood by looking at each aspect that was included. These two aspects fall under the two primary headings, evangelism and disciple-making.

115

1. Seek and Save the Lost

The first part of Christ's mission is recorded in several places in the gospels, including Luke 19:10, "I have come to seek and save the lost." Even though, in Luke's chronology, this statement of mission is stated in a later time frame of His ministry, we must not misunderstand this structure. Jesus' words in Luke 19 are recorded there because they were pertinent to the situation and scenario in which He spoke them. The gospel records clearly indicate that Jesus pursued this aspect of His mission from the beginning, and it was a primary focus.

Jesus didn't merely set up shop in a strip mall in Jerusalem or Nazareth to allow people to come if they wished. He went out seeking them. He traveled all over Israel and the nearby Gentile areas seeking out those He had come to save. Several of His parables were about seeking out the lost and saving them. Our Lord's direction to Nicodemus about the need to be born again to enter the kingdom of God is in the early days of His ministry. Nicodemus comes seeking an interview with Jesus, but it is quite clear from the record in John that Jesus quickly turned the tables on Nicodemus. It was no longer Nicodemus seeking an amicable theological inquiry and discussion with this new rabbi, but Jesus hunting his soul so he could be saved from his lost condition. Soon thereafter, Jesus sought out the Samaritan woman at the well, who then put Him in touch with a whole town. The reason He had to pass through Samara was specifically to keep His divine appointment with her to save her soul, as well as many of her neighbors. Later, He sought out Zacchaeus. He did not wait until Luke 19 to suddenly change His mission from disciple-making to one of evangelism. It is quite evident in the gospel records that He pursued this part of His mission during His entire earthly ministry. It is especially highlighted in John's gospel. It was there on the bank of Jordon that John proclaimed, "Behold the Lamb of God who takes away the sin of the world." (John 1: 29) However, later that same day, before Christ launched into any of His mission of salvation, He initiated contact with those who would become His first disciples. (John 1: 37-42)

2. To Bring Transformation

The second part of Christ's mission is recorded best in Luke 4: 18, "The Spirit of the Lord is upon Me because He has anointed me to preach the gospel to the poor. He has sent Me to proclaim release to the captives, and recovery of sight to the blind; to set free those who are oppressed; to proclaim the favorable year of the Lord." (Luke 4:18-19). Our Lord did in fact preach the good news to the poor, but it was not limited to how to get to heaven when you die. His good news included His mission to bring freedom and transformation. He did, indeed, physically healed those who could not walk, those who could not see, and those who could not speak, yet He never freed those who were physically captive or physically oppressed. He never emptied any prisons. He never changed any oppressive laws, policies or institutions of Rome, and He never freed any slaves, even though the Roman empire was full of such people, and He never set up feeding stations throughout Palestine. What we also see and hear from the Lord is that He came to give spiritual sight to the spiritually blind; to give spiritual speech to those who have been paralyzed from speaking about the glories of God; to give full spiritual mobility to those who were spiritually lame; to give release and freedom to those who were captive to their sin; and to give freedom to those who were spiritually oppressed by their failure and guilt. This was all part of His "good news".

Sin doesn't only condemn us to hell, it also blinds us, cripples us, twists us, poisons us and makes us very dysfunctional in multiple ways. It has literally ruined the human race from being who and what we were supposed to be. It ruined you from what you were supposed to be! Only Christ can change that, and He did it by the power of His death, burial, resurrection and ascension to the right hand of the Father. Therefore, the mission of our Lord also set His sights on this gigantic problem. It was His plan and purpose to recover the human race by salvation and transformation, based on His death, burial, resurrection and ascension. The crowds would come and go, come and go, but as this occurred, He was carving out a few to be saved and transformed. Sometimes it was one, sometimes it was many. As He preached and taught, He was pulling them out of their "lostness" and bringing them into the process of being redeemed— bought back to God as God's own possession. Once returned to God's possession, He does not want to leave them in the practical misery of their former lostness. He wants them to be fully redeemed, fully returned to being what they were meant to be. He also came to transform. This is discipleship. As a disciple, you will learn how to personally enter into all of the benefits and blessings that are available from Him, both in this life and eternity. This will transform you beyond what you ask or think.

The gospel records clearly show that our Lord's good news was not limited to how to get into heaven when you die. He came to bring forgiveness and eternal life. He urged individuals and crowds to believe in Him for eternal life. For those who chose to believe in and follow Him, He also began to develop that eternal life into the real-life experience of a changed life here and now as well. If you have chosen to trust and follow this Savior, you will certainly receive forgiveness of your sins and the assurance of a future in heaven. However, this does not simply plug you into a position of attending church, listening politely and attentively, becoming a "nice person" and learning how to be another cog in the wheels of church ministry. This isn't fulfilling a destiny of becoming another sprocket in the machinery of the church program and activities until heaven.

In discipleship, you will learn to have real-life release and freedom from the sin and dysfunctions that have kept you captive all your life. You will learn to have freedom from your failure and guilt. You will learn to see with spiritual sight. Jesus said, "…the mouth speaks out of the heart," (Matt. 15:8) so your heart will be freed up and filled with the praises, glories and truth of the Lord. You will learn to develop spiritual mobility and agility, truly becoming a fully functioning member of the Body of Christ. These do not come instantly, but they can begin more quickly than you might imagine. Are those changes that you can embrace and seek?

We must finally and fully embrace that our Lord's ministry always carried these two primary aspects of His mission. He spoke of the need to be saved, and the need to be changed to enter the kingdom. He spoke to crowds, and He spoke to individuals who came to Him. Those who came to Him came not only to be saved, but also to be freed from what sin had done to them, physically, emotionally, spiritually, socially. When He went to the cross, He went to save us from the consequences of our sin as well as from the power and effects of sin upon us and within us. This was the mission of the King who came to bring the kingdom of God to earth, not just a suitcase of doctrines to leave behind for debate, discussion and preaching. Save and restore! Save and transform! Save and make them wholly fit for the glorious kingdom He was going to bring, and do it by the power of grace, not the feeble works of lost sinners!

Clearing Up the Confusion

The confusion about the Great Commission is entirely of our own making, based on erroneous assumptions about the closing passages of the gospels. To clear this up, let us look at post-resurrection passages in the New Testament with careful observation and thinking. There are a number of essential things we need to observe about these important passages.

First, we must recognize that the Great Commission in Matthew 28: 19-20 is not intended to be a different way of saying the same thing as given in Luke 24: 44-49 and John 20: 19-23, as if these authors failed to get their heads together and get the story of the Great Commission straight between themselves "before it goes to print". Very capable conservative scholars, such as Gleason L. Archer, have shown quite clearly how to harmonize all the resurrection and post-resurrection accounts. [20] Both Luke and Paul make it completely clear that Jesus appeared to the apostles several/many times over a period of forty days, speaking about the kingdom of God. These appearances were outside the tomb, on the Emmaus Road, in the Upper Room, in Galilee—the location of the Great Commission. These appearances and directives are described for us in Luke 24: 36-53, John 20: 19-23, Matt. 28:11-20, and Acts 1: 3-8. Many others may not be included in Scripture, and they need not be. Other subsequent appearances were to James (in an unspecified location), to five-hundred brethren (in an unspecified location), and months later to Paul on the Damascus Road. (Acts 9: 1-9, I Cor. 15: 5-8) There are insufficient details to determine the exact order of these appearances, but it is very clear that they are not all the same single event, told from different viewpoints. The direction given by Christ on Easter evening, as described in Luke 24 and John 20, was not the same direction given forty days later, as described in Matthew 28. There was no conflict or contradiction because they were not intended to be the same.

Second, by calling it the "Great Commission", we imply, intentionally or not, that this is the most important commandment of Christ to His church, above all others. We cast it as Christ saying to the disciples, "Guys, if you don't remember anything else I have said or done, at least remember this. This is the last thing I'm going to say to you, so this is the most important of all." Of course, there is no Biblical basis for this. Each and all of Jesus' commandments and teachings are entirely true and of tantamount importance, therefore all being "great". His command to forgive your brother seventy times seven is not any less important than His command to proclaim the gospel throughout the world and make disciples. Perhaps we need more great city-wide crusades to teach the importance and ability to forgive others.

It would appear that the term "Great Commission" was popularized by William Carey, one of the first modern missionaries in the western church. Regardless of its origin, we must grasp the fact that the passage itself does not assign such a label, nor imply it. The Matt. 28 account simply reports one of those several post-resurrection encounters of Christ with His disciples. It is likely that the Matt. 28 passage may not be the final encounter, nor does it state that it is the most essential directive and greater than all others. It cannot be used as being the most definitive, overriding or exclusive directive from our Lord following His resurrection. If you wish to assign ranking of importance to

Jesus' teachings, He specifically said that the first and greatest commandment is to love God with all our heart, mind, soul and strength. He said the second-most important is to love our neighbor as ourselves. The lack of obedience to these are what drives our failure to share the gospel, not the failure to assign first ranking to this "Great Commission". He also gave the "new commandment" that we love our fellow Christians as He loves us. (John 13:34) He made no effort to specifically assign more-or-less importance of that new commandment compared to the others. Our failure to achieve Biblical discipleship drives the lack of obedience to all these commandments. Our ignorance of the entire subject may not be all our own fault, but the weak effort to discover and implement it cannot be mistaken for anything other than lack of love for one another.

The inspired Scriptures do not tell us that there was a single, all-encompassing statement from Christ to define the "Co-mission" of the apostles or His church. It seems quite clear from the Scriptures that there were two components of the overall Commission given by Christ after His resurrection. These were the same components that made up His own ministry, both included in His final directives to the disciples before His final ascension. Luke 24: 46-48 records His directive to proclaim the gospel of repentance and forgiveness in His name, not only to Israel, but to all nations, starting with Jerusalem. "Thus it is written that ...repentance for the forgiveness of sins would be proclaimed to all the nations (Gentiles) in His name...". (Luke 24: 47) John 20: 21 records this mission in a general way that clearly describes it as being the same as His mission. "As the Father has sent Me, I also send you...". Both aspects of the "Co-mission" are clearly demanded. Matt 24:19-20 directs more clearly that they (and we) are to fully disciple those who respond to the gospel call by baptism and then teaching them *to do* all that He commanded. This combination, together, constitute the Great Commission. To neglect or unbalance either one or the other is a failure to be faithful to the commands of Christ.

Embracing this understanding helps us finally grasp the true meaning of Matt 28: 19-20. The traditional KJV translation of verse 19 reads as, "...go and teach all nations...". The NASV reads, "Go therefore and make disciples of all the nations...." This has been awkward to Biblical translation because, as many scholars and interpreters have rightly pointed out, the grammar used in these verses recommends that it would be better translated, "As you are going, make disciples of all the nations..." Our Lord's words sound as if the disciples know the first aspect of their mission—going into all the world. His instruction to them to go and proclaim the gospel and the forgiveness of sins in His name, given in the Upper Room and other appearances, is now forged together with the second aspect of their Co-mission—making disciples. This is exactly what He had been doing for the entire 3-4 years of His earthly ministry, and now He sends them out to continue this same dual aspect Co-mission, but now to the ends of the earth. When you think about the real experience that the disciples had been through with the betrayal, trial and crucifixion, it is perfectly understandable that Christ had to approach the subject of taking the good news to other lands and people in a staged explanation and do so more than once over the period of forty days. Getting it through their heads that it now included going to the Gentile peoples of the world took even longer.

I greatly wonder at why we have been so slow to understand and embrace that these two goals or emphases in our Lord's

Great Commission are not mutually exclusive tasks given to us. They are not in competition or conflict. In fact, the division that has been amongst us in this matter is deplorable! Christ certainly pursued both equally, and we dare not exclude or diminish either one. The equally deplorable fact is that, whether any given church is dedicated primarily to evangelism or to discipleship, the primary approach to accomplishing the task by those in the church has been to invite unsaved and unchurched people to church so the pastor can achieve the goal for them. This is simply a window into the fact that true Biblical discipleship is not being done. Every disciple can become an effective gospel-sharer as well as taking an effective role in disciple-making. This is, in fact, what Christ wants. We have His word on it!

We must cease pursuing all the distractions and substitutes of churchianity and zealously pursue His clear directives. We must decide once and for all—is Christ Lord or not? Those who truly embrace Him as Lord will do as He says—nothing else and nothing less! But it is a learning process, and it must be the learning process of a disciple, seeking *to do* all His commandments and become like Him. When you become like Him, you instinctively and powerfully do what He did. You enter co-mission with Him, knowing the full reality that He is with you always.

Once again, I urge you to stop reading, put down what you are doing, get in front of mirror and ask yourself if this is a Co-mission that you will embrace with your Lord. You will only get to the doing of it effectively by entering and persevering in discipleship. Please, make that decision now!

WHAT ABOUT OBEDIENCE?

T hroughout the Scriptures, God has given commandments. God gave commandments to Adam and Eve, to Abraham, to Moses and Israel, to David, to Paul, and many others. Christ's Great Commission is itself a command. In all cases, it is clear that God expected obedience to His commands. However, in all of these, superficial obedience was not what God was after. It was obedience from the heart. Thus, David is described as, "a man after God's own heart." (I Sam. 13:14) As demonstrated in Chapter 6, Jesus defined a disciple as one who is learning to obey all of His commandments and teachings in order to become more like Him. Jesus clearly stated that it is the wise builder, who hears, believes and *does* His commands, whose house survives the storm—not the one who only hears and believes. (Matt 7:24-27) This seems straight-forward enough.

The problem is that the Church has wrestled with obedience throughout its history, both in theology and practice. In seeking to bring about obedience, and without understanding its true source and purpose, much of the Church has been crippled with various forms of legalism. Since we did not really under-stand what legalism was, trying to correct it led to other equally serious problems. The more recent and popular versions effectively deny the need for obedience because we think it takes us back to legalism... and so we keep travelling in circles... and we do not produce Christians that become like Christ.

The Witness of Scripture

The Scriptures are actually quite clear on the matter. Here is a brief sample of the matter, as stated in the New Testament alone:

John 14: 15 – "If you love Me, you will keep My commandments."

John 14:21 – "He who has My commandments and keeps them is the one who loves Me, and he who loves Me will be loved by My Father, and I will love him and will disclose Myself to him."

Rom. 1:5 – "...through whom we have received grace and apostleship to bring about the obedience of faith among all the Gentiles."

Rom. 6:17 – "But thanks be to God that, though you were slaves, you became obedient from the heart to that form of teaching to which you were committed."

Rom. 8:3-4 – "For what the Law could not do, weak as it was through the flesh, God did: sending His own Son in the likeness of sinful flesh and as an offering for sin, He condemned sin in the flesh, so that the requirement of the Law might be fulfilled in us who do not walk according to the flesh, but according to the Spirit."

Rom. 15: 18 – "For I will not presume to speak of anything except what Christ has accomplished through me, resulting in the obedience of the Gentiles by word and deed."

Rom. 16:19a – "For the report of your obedience has reached all;"

II Cor. 10:5 – "We are destroying speculations and every lofty thing raised up against the knowledge of God, and we are taking every thought captive to the obedience of Christ…"

Phil 2:12-13 – "So then my beloved, just as you have always obeyed, not as in my presence only, but now much more in my absence, work out your salvation in fear and trembling…"

Add to this several verses about pleasing God:

Phil 2:13 – "…for it is God who is at work in you, both to will and work for His good pleasure."

Col. 1:9-10 – "For this reason also, since the day we heard of it, we have not ceased to pray for you, and to ask that you may be filled with the knowledge of His will in all spiritual wisdom and understanding, so that you will walk in a manner worthy of the Lord, to please Him in all respects, bearing fruit in every good work, and increasing in the knowledge of God;"

I Thess. 2:4 – "…but just as we have been approved by God to be entrusted with the gospel, so we speak not as pleasing men, but God who examines our hearts."

I. Thess. 4:1-2 – "...as you received from us instruction as to how you ought to walk and please God...that you excel even more. For you know what commandments we gave you by the authority of the Lord Jesus...".

Heb. 13:16 – "...And do not neglect doing good and sharing, for with such sacrifices God is well pleased."

I John 5:3 – For this is the love of God, that we keep His commandments; and His commandments are not burdensome to us."

Most of these are written by Paul, widely known as the Apostle to the Gentiles and Apostle of grace. Those from the Gospel of John are taken from our Lord's words to His disciples on the night before He would be crucified for the sins of the world to provide the fullness of God's grace. He told the disciples that the Last Supper was the symbol of the New Covenant in His blood. (Luke 22:20) It seems quite clear that neither John nor Paul thought that obedience was in opposition to faith or grace. If we added the many other individual commands in both Old and New Testaments, the list would be much longer indeed. This should make it quite clear for anyone who accepts the authority of Scripture that obedience to God's commandments is necessary and important for the followers of Jesus. This also seems straight-forward enough.

Unrolling the Map of the Past

Following Christ's Great Commission, the Apostles labored and sacrificed to spread true Christianity throughout the Roman empire and the world at large. Their work constantly encountered external forces that sought to morph it into something different than originally intended and proclaimed by its Founder. The Church struggled courageously against these forces, often at great sacrifice, but inexorably it was changed. This is attested by the late writings of the New Testament, and after that it only worsened. Many of the verdicts expressed by Christ in the early parts of the book of Revelation describe doctrines and practices that are appalling! They were way off the path!

A great many of these changes leveraged the Church toward embracing doctrines, rituals and ceremonies that made Christianity more amenable to the indigenous religions and surrounding culture. Over time, it moved the Church away from the "simplicity of Christ" (II Cor. 11:3) (repentance, sincere faith, and a life of learning to live in His truths). Instead, it substituted rituals, ceremonies, forms of legalism and "Christianized" pagan teachings. Many of these changes became the erroneous doctrines, dogma, and practices of the medieval Church. The Church taught that these earned favor and acceptance with God because they were seen as having been given by God as the "means of grace". Instead of a people who lived in the abundant riches of grace by personal faith, the Church "dispensed" the grace of God through the sacraments. Performing and participating in these sacraments were seen as the works necessary to be acceptable to God, fitting one for heaven. At this point, they were not only off the path, but they had lost it altogether! Enter the Reformation!

The Reformation, driven by "sola Scriptura" (by the Scriptures alone) and "sola fide" (by faith alone), brought back the correct doctrine of salvation by personal faith. However, it included nothing about discipleship. It did not properly correct/

realign the Biblical understanding of the inseparable connection between faith and obedience. They stumbled over the fear that seeking obedience somehow implied that faith alone was not sufficient. They feared it implied works. They also routinely fumbled the matter of how law and grace fit together properly. Luther seriously flirted with the idea that both the book of James and the book of Hebrews should not be included in the New Testament due to their content concerning the importance of works.

Subsequently, under the influence of all the "free from the Law" offshoots, it has produced a view that law, commandments, and works are somehow in opposition to faith. Under this faulty belief, if we add anything to the gospel of grace by faith, we have left the true principle of sola fide (only by faith). Far too often, obedience has been painted as being some version of works, which is seen as conflicting with pure faith. Yet, it is typical for obedience to be promoted as being important for Christians. Despite the clear guidance of Scripture that, "For by faith you are saved…not as a result of works…created in Christ Jesus unto good works…" (Eph 2: 8-10), it has resulted in a very mixed message that confuses many Christians. In fact, most Christians do not even connect the concept of such "works" with the word "obedience", nor with "Christlikeness". Much of the evangelical church still does not understand how obedience can be important or how to explain it.

The most recent version of this "free from the Law" viewpoint is to take any and all commandments or directives as automatically non-applicable for the Christian, because they are seen as expressions of law and they can only lead to an inescapable sense of failure and slavery, per Romans 7. This faulty view would say that if there is any value to commandments at all, they should only be taken as recommendations or guide-lines. Therefore, there would be no need for any Christian to accept or value any commandments from Scripture, much less, "...observe them as being the vital center of your life". Trying to obey God's commands is seen as a futile effort which is not important or necessary since "we are under grace." If you achieve some obedience, that's great, but if you don't that's okay too. We're all going to heaven anyway. This seems to be obliv-ious to the call and promises unto a transformed life in Christ by learning obedience. This is the apex of "easy believe-ism" decried by those like Bonhoeffer.

If a disciple is to learn how to live out all the command-ments of Christ, but all commandments are automatically rejected as "law", how is any discipleship possible? In that case, it would empty the Great Commission of all meaning, and Jesus must have been very confused! Jesus always accepted people for where they were, but He was never satisfied to leave them there. He knew very well the cruel torture of people who were captive by their sinfulness, and He came to release them! He wants the same for you!

All of these reflect the confusion we still have about things like Law, works, grace, faith and commandments. These issues have been so difficult to resolve because the issues of salvation and obedience quickly get mushed together in the discussion. Sooner or later, the conversation comes around to, "How much can I sin and still be/stay saved?" This is never the viewpoint of Scripture, and it is just another strawman to challenge us to a futile duel. The Scriptures never mush these together. They are always inseparably connected, but in the right order. We have complete assurance of salvation by grace through faith in the blood of Christ; and we are instructed, encouraged and urged to always obey. There is no line in the Scriptural sand that would encourage us in any way toward disobedience or even neglect, but that is only following a genuine personal decision to trust and follow Christ.

Works (Earning) vs. Grace (Gift)

Part of the solution is to clearly recognize what a "works" system really is. The Apostle Paul defines it as one in which we earn what we receive. (Rom 4:4) The fundamental concept of "earn" is that the value of what you do equals the value of what you receive in return (within that economy). So, in Jesus' parable of the workers in the vineyard, a full day of working in the vineyard earns a denarius in payment. It is "wages", not a gift. It is something you have worked for and now you deserve payment. (Matt. 20:1-16) A works system says God owes you His forgiveness and blessing/reward, based on certain kinds of obedience. But the words "earn" and "grace" do not belong in the same sentence together. The fundamental definition of grace is undeserved favor or free gift! You don't deserve what is unearned and you don't earn a free gift!

Imagine you were living on the street, homeless, jobless, and living entirely on the meager social safety net. One day, another homeless person you know comes by and says, "Hey, they're giving out free meals down the street at the shelter." Very glad to hear this news of free food, you walk down the street and enter the building. A pleasant host welcomes you, directs you to the food line, and you have a feast on comfort food. Did walking down the street to the shelter mean you earned the meal? No! It was free! You just put yourself in the necessary position to receive the free gift.

Imagine that you receive a legal notice in the mail one day, informing you that a rich uncle has died and left you a very sizeable gift of money in his will. You never even knew you had a rich uncle, and you certainly never did anything for him at all. The notice says that to receive the inheritance requires you to attend the reading of the will at the office of the attorney. The office is not so far away, so you feel like it is worth going. At the reading of the will, you discover that his gift to you was $250,000! Did you earn this gift by travelling the short distance to the attorney's office? No! You just put yourself in the position to receive this free gift, per the terms of the will.

Take a simple illustration from nature. Baby birds in the nest, chirping their heads off when mother bird returns with food, does not mean they are earning the food. They are simply putting themselves in the position to receive what the mother bird is providing completely free. Their job is to keep chirping as loud as possible and open their mouth as wide as possible until satisfied. Doing what God requires by His commandments only puts us in the position to receive the free gift and we are not earning our salvation or our sanctification. The value of what you do has no value compared to the value of what you receive. You are just putting yourself in the right position to receive the free gift, no differently than baby birds who chirp madly for food.

If you have made a sincere personal decision to trust and follow Christ, there is no reason to fear or hesitate to energetically pursue obedience. No amount of obedience earns what God has given you in Christ, nor does it earn any blessing God will give you. Obedience has a completely different purpose, and you will never be sorry that you pursue it. Its purpose is to bring you into the wonderful freedom that Christ came to provide (Luke 4: 17-19). We also have no need to fear or avoid good works. Works are simply the overt expressions of obedience of every kind and degree. It is the automatic outcome. It is what can be seen and heard by others when you obey the Lord's commands and teachings. Even when not seen by others, they are seen by God and rewarded, but they are not earned. (Matt. 5: 16, 6:1)

Good works are not done to earn God's favor, blessings, forgiveness, or a place in heaven. They declare that we have become people who are transformed by the *grace* of God (unearned, underserved). We love because we have been loved, and now we relish extending love toward others. We forgive because we have been forgiven, and now we relish extending forgiveness toward others. We are patient because we have received God's great patience toward us, and now we relish being patient toward others. We are kind because we have received God's great kindness toward us, and now we relish being kind toward others. We do these things because we love doing it, just as God loves doing it to us. We live transformed lives given by our Savior, and our good works shine forth as lights in a dark place to the glory of God. (Matt. 5:16, Phil. 2:15)

The True Source and Purpose of Commandments

God made humans in a certain way. He made us to be a certain kind of beings that live in all the ways He intended for us. By living in these ways, we could experience all the happiness that was intended by God. If we went outside those ways, we would lose that happiness. In the creation account of Genesis, everything up to Chapter 3 was described as "good" or "very good". Part of the way God created for us was to have the power of free choice, within the limiting parameters that He set for our choices. One of those parameters was to suffer the consequences of choosing wrongly, and that is what happened. The first human pair chose to seek both good *and evil*, rather than only good. We have been suffering the consequences ever since. Now we must live constantly encountering both good and evil, around us and within us. This forces us to constantly deal with both happiness and unhappiness, rather than only happiness.

Since humans are extremely oriented toward happiness, pursuit of obedience should have been self-sustaining, but now sin also brought pleasure (sinful pleasure), seemingly bringing happiness. This made the internal moral compass confused and undependable. With the mind darkened by sin, the conscience became seared, and the heart would either accuse or defend wrongdoing. (Rom. 2:15) This showed that a remnant of God's moral law was still within us, but also that our sinfulness was too great to abide in that witness. With the sovereign power of God to control all things, it would eventually bring curse—unhappiness. Lesson learned too late, and it seems not very well remembered! We just keep on doing it! Perhaps worst of all is that we continue to believe that we are fully capable of making our own moral decisions. Clearly, we are not!

There is only one solution to a confused and undependable internal moral compass—outside direction that is true and dependable from a source that is all-loving, all-wise, and all-good. This is the God of the Bible, and His commandments communicate the true and dependable source of direction that we need. His commandments are not some stark program for trying to be good enough to get into heaven when you die. They are expressions of His grace, and they are all steps into blessing, happiness and regaining who you were supposed to be.

If you look carefully, you will find that, over time, the detail and complexity of the Biblical commands generally increase. They also increasingly focus on things like innermost thoughts, feelings, and intentions of the heart. Eventually, the commands include things that you might not think are even in your control, such as forsaking anger, being tenderhearted, always forgiving others, (Eph. 4:31-32), and controlling what you think about as you see another person, etc. (Matt. 5:27-28)

Most of the Old Testament centers on the Law of Moses. Other than the Ten Commandments, most of these commandments are about the worship, sacrifices, rituals and ceremonies prescribed for Israel. Only a limited portion is about social laws and how to treat other people. In the New Testament, the commands and teachings stem from Christ and the Apostles, reflecting the giant step beyond the Old Covenant to the New Covenant under Christ as Savior and Lord. They are far more focused on individual behavior, how to have a deeply meaningful relationship with God and how you should treat others.

In the Old Testament, the commandments were paired with the system of positive and negative reinforcement, often described in Scriptures as blessing and cursing. Obedience would bring blessing and disobedience would bring curse. Fundamentally, blessing meant, "things will work out well for you and you will be happy". Curse was, "you will have suffering, misery and things will go very badly, making you very unhappy." (Deut. 27-28, Ps. 128:1-2) (As a matter of fact, this is the Biblical meaning of both curse and blessing.) These were primarily physical blessings, but the emotional and mental aspects of such blessings cannot be discounted. The blessings promised to Israel for their obedience were nearly all physical blessings—protection from enemies, protection from diseases, good weather conditions that result in good harvests, etc. But, by the design of God, each of these would also bring a sense of inward happiness. Such blessings would certainly identify Israel as a "special people unto God", especially in the corrupt ancient world. This special people of God would live in happiness and fulfillment because of righteousness.

In the New Testament, you discover that the nature of the blessing has changed. God is no longer establishing a special people on a special patch of ground in the Middle East. He is spreading His offer of love and grace to all people throughout all the earth. He is demonstrating through His church that those who repent and receive His gifts will be blessed in far superior ways that do not depend on a wonderful land, with wonderful crops, wonderful protection from enemies, and wonderful health and prosperity. Now, His people live in blessings that work even though they don't have special physical protection and provision. Now we have, "…every spiritual blessing in the heavenlies in Christ" (Eph 1:3), and they work in all the normal situations of life, including, "…tribulation, distress, persecution, famine, nakedness, peril, or sword." (Rom. 8: 35). Now, we are indwelled by His Spirit and that works equally when outward things go well or not, or even when you are thrown into prison for witnessing.

God does not make arbitrary laws and requirements for His children. His commands keep guiding us back to what we were supposed to be. The message that God keeps trying to hammer home is that obedience brings a wonderful sense of blessing (happiness) because it is what you were meant to be—in His image, but less than Him. Being like who you were supposed to be makes you feel good! (Do you really believe that you will not be happier when you are gentle and patient instead of harsh and demanding?) What God is truly trying to move you toward is what the Psalmist says in places such as, "Blessed is the man who does not walk in the counsel of the ungodly, or…" (Ps 1:1), "You have put gladness in my heart, more than when their grain and new wine abound." (Ps 4:7) This is what Jesus was speaking of in His teaching, describing the one who will blessed. "Blessed is he who…". (Matt. 5: 1-10 ff)

When you love, worship and serve only the One True God, you will be happy! When you honor your father and mother you will be happy! When you love your neighbor, you will be happy! When you forgive those who wrong you, you will be happy! When your life is full of, "…love, joy, peace, patience, kindness, goodness, faithfulness gentleness and self-control…" you will be happy. When rightly understood, all of God's commandments have one overall purpose—returning you to what you were supposed to be, in His image and "just as if you had never sinned". Do you want to be happy all the time? It's quite simple and available—obey God all the time. Easier said than done, huh?

To finally recognize that obedience is the core and ultimate purpose of Christianity might hardly seem necessary, but our wandering off the path for nineteen centuries has brought us to that point. No matter what portion of the Scriptures you consult, it is abundantly clear that what God was seeking throughout all periods of history was obedience—even in the innocence of the Garden of Eden. All the commands of the Old Testament and New are aimed at avoiding or ending wrong behavior, attitudes, thoughts, feelings and intentions of the heart and/or prompting righteous behavior, attitudes, thoughts, feelings and intentions of the heart! God's revelations were not to form new doctrines to be studied, discussed, debated and preached, but to produce changed people! We very badly need to be changed! Disciples openly declare that they hereby choose the pathway of becoming such people, and by doing so, enter into the joy, peace, and satisfaction of becoming what God intended for them all along. "Blessed are those who…". (Matt. 5: 1-10 ff). If you study the blessing passages in all of Scripture, you will see the kind of people that God intended to create. Now, through His Son, He implements His ultimate power to do this, based on His work of grace through faith, not the feeble abilities and works of fallen humanity, but *grace through faith.*

It seems we have missed the whole point of this pattern on the part of God. Obedience would bring happiness/blessing/good, and disobedience would bring unhappiness/curse/evil. Obedience is not a poison word and does not necessarily bring any sense of failure or slavery. When Paul writes about discouragement, failure, despair and the sense of slavery, he is talking about pursuing obedience based on our human effort or legalism, not the obedience that comes through faith. (Rom. 7) As you will see in subsequent chapters of this book, this requires walking the path of true discipleship.

What kind of Church might we have if this would actually occur? We would have a Church comprised of people who are like Jesus Christ! As you look over some of the many "blessing passages" in Scripture, imagine for yourself what it would be like to be like what is described. Is that a version of you that you could fully embrace and be abundantly glad of it? Only Christ can teach you how if you follow Him in discipleship. This is what produces Christians like Paul and Silas who are found praying and singing hymns of praise after a beating and imprisonment in Philippi. (Acts 16: 25) Notice that they didn't need a "powerful worship band" with a truckload of electronics!

CHAPTER 10

WHAT ABOUT
SELF-DISCIPLINE?

Throughout all eras of the Church, few have properly grasped that obedience to the commands of Christ, and the Scriptures as a whole, is not consistently achieved through some form of legalism. If Law and legalism cannot bring us to consistent, joyful obedience, then how do we get there?

To some, this suggests the current version of "do-nothing grace", otherwise stated as, "If God wants me changed, He will do it Himself. I don't have to worry about it or pay any attention to it at all. It will just happen." But this denies the obvious fact that all commands in Scripture are addressed to the people who are supposed to obey, not to God. God is not commanding Himself to make you obey or to change you to get you to obedience. He has already done everything He must do to get you there. However, for you to learn to live in obedience, you have an essential role that cannot be avoided or discounted.

Sometimes, it seems we would be better off with no will of our own. It is very difficult for us to imagine any way of dealing with, "Thy will be done, not mine," (Luke 22:42) without just extracting our free will like a bad tooth. To us, free will automatically implies that we always struggle to yield to God but fail most of the time. This is based on the subtle belief that our self-will is hopelessly captured to being in opposition to God's will. If your "free-will" has been captured by some other force, you do not have free-will! This would make the entire point moot and we know within ourselves that it is not.

Thomas Henry Huxley once said, "I protest that if some great Power would agree to make me always think what is true and do what is right on condition of being turned into a sort of clock and wound me up every morning before getting out of bed, I should instantly close with the offer. The only freedom I care about is the freedom to do right; the freedom to do wrong, I am ready to part with on the cheapest terms to anyone who will take it from me" [21] In other words, if someone would completely take away my free will and make sure I always make only the right choices, it would be a great deal. This viewpoint may seem attractive (or perhaps desperate) at first. It has been repeated in various forms by some, and you may even agree with it, but believe me, it is not what you really want. Being assigned to such a status would be terrible. The gift of free will (actually the ability to choose between known and available alternatives) really is a wonderful thing, and once you learn to handle it in Christ, you will find it one of God's best blessings. God made you to be like Him, and He does not want you to act or perform like a robot.

Self-discipline In Discipleship

To overcome the weaknesses of legalism, the traditional solution in the Church has been to add self-discipline. Those who joined themselves to monasteries or abbeys did so to work toward holiness—dedication of their whole self and life to God, His service, His kingdom and His Church. Achieving holiness and sanctification under this approach required, and often imposed, great discipline. This included various forms of denial and deprivation, such as fasts, watches (sleeplessness), imposing harsh tasks, arduous journeys/pilgrimages, self-administered whipping, and others. Nearly all approaches to holiness and sanctification, both past and present, have been heavily based on the concept of self-discipline to be the driver of the legalism that was thought necessary. Unfortunately, most forms of modern discipleship do the same.

Most discipleship programs in the current Evangelical church have been centered on learning the Bible more thoroughly, learning to share the gospel with others, participating in some service and ministry, and learning to play a stronger role in the overall structure and ministry of the church. It is often a tool to identify and develop future leaders or future teachers. Many programs link you with an accountability partner and/or support group who seek to mentor you and hold you to your commitments in these endeavors. Much the same as historic monasticism, this depends heavily on personal self-discipline and the peer pressure of your mentor, your accountability group, or others in the program. To be fair, such self-discipline and peer pressure is usually limited to simple things intended to keep you more mindful of what Scripture tells us to do, as well as urging you to become a more well-churched Christian. The knowledge that others are supporting you and praying for you can be helpful. However, as you should immediately perceive, this is simply a new version of monasticism that doesn't require you to live "on-campus".

A great many churches who have teaching elements in their ministries would insist that this is discipleship. They are preaching and teaching the Bible—but this is not discipleship. Without fully realizing it, they are teaching and preaching Bible doctrine and theology, not discipleship. It is like teaching someone to play the guitar by having them learn all the notes and fingering, all the scales and all the chords, but never teaching them to play a song, much less many songs.

Unfortunately, this concept is now a well-entrenched approach to typical Christian discipleship. But it seldom leads to a truly transformed person that is brimming over with the new life in Christ. It is only the vestiges of monasticism trussed up and re-packaged in a protestant evangelical wrapper because we don't know what else to do. Even the current revival of the classic spiritual disciplines can still be based on this approach. In a permissive society, it is not even an interesting offer to most. In a permissive church, confused about faith and works, it is also not very interesting.

The Scriptures are rich in verses that extoll the virtues of self-discipline, self-control and diligence. In these verses, various words and terms are used for the word "self-discipline/self-control", each with a slightly unique meaning. When we read the gospels, we come away with an image of Christ as being a very self-disciplined or self-controlled man, so the effort to become more like Him automatically implies that we too develop self-discipline.

Linking self-discipline with Christian discipleship appears to be reasonable. After all, the words discipleship and discipline come from the same word do they not? This apparent link, based entirely on the English translations, is well meant, but unfortunately, somewhat misguided. It stems largely from Paul's exhortation to Timothy, "...discipline yourself for the purpose of godliness" (I Tim. 4:7b.) Paul seems to be comparing the bodily discipline of the Greek gymnasium with the "discipline that brings godliness", as if they were similar and could use similar methods. However, all too often, self-discipline is the dancing partner with legalism. Its legitimate role in Biblical discipleship is less than usually presented.

False Notions of Self-discipline

The first concept that is normally built into traditional self-discipline is to grit your teeth and make yourself do something you don't really want to because it's the right thing or the good thing to do. The view that self-discipline can achieve the expectations of a disciple implies that you can learn to consistently and joyfully have and demonstrate the traits and characteristics of Christ by simply gritting your teeth and making yourself do them. However, if self-discipline was the answer, all that was needed was a commandment to be self-disciplined. Perhaps this should have been the 11th commandment? As Paul states, "If righteousness comes by the Law, Christ died needlessly." (Gal 2: 21b) If strict self-discipline was the primary element for successful Christian discipleship, the best disciples would be former special forces, top athletes, ninjas, and Samurai warriors. Such is not the case.

The other concept normally included in traditional training is repetition of correct movements—it's the "reps". This develops correct muscle strength as well as agility, precision, hand-eye coordination, and muscle memory. This results in instinctive correct movements. This is done in the "practice sessions" or "training" that are familiar to all athletes, just as in the Greek gymnasium. However, the practice sessions are not the actual competition event or the battle. The role of self-discipline in this is the focused determination to faithfully and assertively do the reps. You can almost do them in your sleep. Training and self-discipline can be used for these purposes. This kind of self-discipline can train the body, but not the heart.

Similarly, many mental abilities can also be developed by self-disciplined practice. This applies to memorizing a poem, speech, multiplication tables, music scales or Bible verses. This kind of self-discipline can train the mind, but not the heart. It is from the heart that one believes. (Rom. 10:9) It is from the heart that one speaks with the mouth. (Luke 6: 45) It is from the heart that one loves fervently, like Christ loves. (I Peter 1:22) It is from the heart that the fervent prayer of a righteous man flows. (James 5:16)

Unfortunately, real life does not have practice sessions, nor does the Christian life. It is full-time, full-tilt game time all the time, and you should never think otherwise. How would you hone your athletic skills if there were no practice sessions, only full-tilt game time all the time? This is what discipleship requires. How do you have "practice sessions" for kindness, gentleness, goodness, longsuffering, etc.? How do you practice building faith or being full of joy? In true discipleship, these are only meaningful as you go about all aspects of ordinary life. It requires a new set of instinctive thoughts, feelings, reactions, etc. and these do not come from "reps" in practice. It must come from the heart—a transformed heart.

The Truth About Self-Discipline

Self-discipline seems to be a commonly understood term, both in Paul's time and ours. However, for many Christians, numerous attempts and failures, whether real or perceived, have led them to conclude that they do not possess this magical power, and therefore they cannot pursue discipleship. In fact, this term is normally misunderstood, and demands more careful thought.

If you travel the pathway of self-discipline, you are quickly confronted with the Romans 7 syndrome. You quickly discover with Paul that, even though you want to do good, you don't seem to have the ability to consistently and powerfully implement the good. It is more than only building better habits, and your best efforts of self-discipline do not possess the power to push very far into it. It is far greater and deeper than that.

This is not the situation where you still are not yet convinced to do the good. What the Scriptures clearly say about this is, "...*the willing (to do good)* is present with me, but *the doing* of the good is not." (Rom 7:18b, parenthesis mine) You do want to do good, and you try to do good, but for reasons that seem inexplicable to you, you can't pull it off. The sinfulness within your old nature is far too automatic, powerful and obstructive to consistently complete the most determined effort to do right. Self-discipline will not overcome this powerful enemy within. Even when supported by mentoring and support groups, it still holds the same weakness which Paul clearly states in Romans 7.

Depending on the power of self-will and self-discipline does not get you out of the control of the sin nature, and Paul's direction to Timothy here in Chapter 4 does not contradict that! Those who attempt this (and there have been many who tried) soon discover that you cannot discipline yourself to love God with all your heart, mind, soul and strength. You cannot discipline yourself to love your neighbor as yourself, or to love your fellow Christian as Christ loves him/her. You can discipline yourself to pretend that you love, but only superficial, mental love (in other words "act like you love"). It cannot bring you into, "Love the Lord your God with all your heart, mind soul and strength." (Deut. 6:5, Matt 22: 37-38) It cannot bring you into, "...love one another fervently from the heart". (I Peter 1:22) Loving someone fervently from the heart requires real love, not pretend or superficial love. It cannot come from the well of self-discipline. Completion of numerous study books and repetitious memorizing of Scripture verses that talk about these things will not bring you into these realities in your life. If self-discipline was the solution, Paul would have said so as he wrote Romans 8 and Galatians 5, but he didn't. The personal righteousness desired and intended by Jesus for His disciples requires something far more. It requires transformation.

How Should We Understand Paul's Directive?

Long before the letter to Timothy, Paul had written that self-control was part of the fruit of the Holy Spirit. (Gal 5: 22-23) He had already stated in his letter to the Colossians that strict rules controlling your behavior do not have the power to control the lusts of the flesh. (Col. 2:20-23) In earlier parts of this same letter to Timothy, he tells us that the "secret of godliness" is not strict discipline, but Christ Himself. (I Tim 3:16-17) Immediately before His direction to Timothy about self-discipline, he indicates that doctrines promoting strict abstinence from what God has given as blessings is a sign of false doctrines

(I Tim. 4: 1-5). Was Paul contradicting himself in the very same letter and in the very same paragraph? What did Paul mean as he wrote to Timothy?

1. Self-Discipline

The word used by Paul for "discipline yourself" is the Greek word "gumnazo", from whence we get our English word "gymnasium". However, it is correctly understood not as a place where you exercise, but what you do there to exercise. It means "to train"[22], but not just any kind of training. This training was intense and strenuous, thus it means "to train strenuously". This is a far more accurate meaning of Paul's directive to Timothy = "intensely train yourself for godliness."

The training in the ancient Greek gymnasium would push you to your maximum effort and skill to excel, thus it truly means "strenuous training". It's like long bouts of wind sprints or "line drill" in football or basketball practice until you feel like you are going to drop. Then the coach's whistle says, "Go again!" The perspiration is pouring off of you and you are breathing so hard you feel you may pass out. An even better picture is extreme circuit training, using the same maximum effort. This was the training in the ancient Greek gymnasium. To achieve your best effort, it was common to strip off nearly all clothing to bare minimum or even nakedness, to remove any hindrance whatsoever. In fact, the related Greek words, "gumnos" and "gumnotes" mean primarily "nakedness or destitution as shown by scant clothing". [23]These terms are used in a number of places in the New Testament.

2. Godliness

We must also properly understand the goal which is to be pursued by this self-discipline. It is "godliness". Routine use of the English word "godliness" in Scripture is a bit mysterious. Like a number of other words used in English translations of the Bible, it stems from the Latin Vulgate and then old English, rather than the meaning in the ancient Greek of the New Testament.

You might expect this word to be a compound word, joining together the word for "God" and the word for "likeness" = godlikeness = godliness. To my great surprise, I discovered that the Greek word used by Paul contains neither. It is the word *eusebius/eusebia,* consisting of the prefix "*eu* = good" and "*sebia* = fear". It literally means "good-fear". Furthermore, the word *sebia* was closely connected to the concept of worship, therefore it could be understood as "good-fear worship" or a "good-fear worshipper". In that day, bowing/kneeling down before someone to show the appropriate expression of honor, fear and surrender was the common practice. It was used this way of slaves to masters and worshipers to the gods. What does this mean for purposes of discipleship?

The term godliness is used numerous times by Paul in his pastoral letters, as does Peter. Vines describes the New Testament use of this word as, "...to be devout, ...piety which characterizes a Godward attitude, doing that which is well-pleasing to God, reverence manifested in actions." [24] Unfortunately, the word pious/piety has also lost its true meaning in American culture. It is also not properly understood by most in our day. To some, devotion and piety seem too passive, almost timid. To others it is commonly linked to the word "self-righteous". To others it could mean constantly disagreeable, along with a full-time scowl, very plain clothes, and no fun in life. Is that the goal and result of discipleship? How could that possibly align with other Scriptures where we read about Jesus, "I delight to do Thy will?" (Heb. 10:9). If that were the case, how could first century Christians be described as those who have such joy that it is beyond their ability to express? (I Peter 1:8)

When we look carefully at these uses, we distill the core meaning. The proper focus of the term godliness is as Vines suggests. It is the practical outworking of what you profess to believe. In other words, do you actually practice what you say you believe? Does your behavior truly and consistently reflect what you say you believe? You say you fear God and you say you worship God. To fear and worship God should be expressed in truly obeying God. To put it in Paul's words elsewhere, "You who preach that one shall not steal, do you steal? You who say that one should not commit adultery, do you commit adultery? You who abhor idols, do you rob temples? You who boast in the Law, through your breaking the Law, do you dishonor God? (Rom. 2: 21-23) Do you practice what you say you believe? Do you practice what is preached in your church? We could appropriately assign the term "spiritual and moral integrity" for this characteristic because they truly do fear God and worship God. It is someone who sincerely bows before God in worship and therefore sincerely seeks to obey and please God in all things, in all situations, and in all moments. It is a sincerely "God-focused person", not because you spend all your time in church or reading the Bible, but because you are truly devoted to attending to God and pleasing Him. It is a person who lives with constant attention and orientation toward God, with all aspects of their life brought into alignment with that fundamental viewpoint and purpose. Anyone who follows you around can quickly know what you believe simply by what they observe in your daily life and situations. This is the correct way to understand the word godliness and the correct goal of the self-discipline of which Paul speaks.

Making the Link

How does self-discipline get us to godliness? If it's not gritting your teeth and/or the reps, what is it? The secret lies in understanding Chapters 6-12 of the book of Romans. Here, Paul explains how the Christian can not only escape the power of sin, but also have the power to live out righteousness. Part of this explanation tells us that the body is involved. Not only must we, "…no longer present the *members of your body* to sin as instruments of unrighteousness…", but also, "…present your *members* as instruments of righteousness to God". (Rom 6: 13) He tells us that, in the battle for obedience, "…there is a different law in my members, waging war against the law of my mind and making me a prisoner of the law of sin." (Rom 7: 23)

From the time of conception, the body and soul are woven together, and they develop interwoven together. The body learns to obey one master—your soul, your inner person/inner self. Over and over, the body is instructed by its master to carry out unrighteousness. It is "programmed" by the sinful inner self to carry out its directives. Since the body and the soul are woven together, this makes the response of the body to the dictates of the soul nearly instantaneous.

When a person is born again by sincere personal faith in Christ, a new inner self is created; but s/he is a "babe" that must grow and develop. (I Cor 3: 1) However, the body remains the same, still controlled by the impulses of the old inner soul. As spiritual growth happens, there must now be a new link between the new person and the body to do the bidding of this new, still developing, master. Now, to live out righteousness, the body must be retrained in many ways. It is quite similar to training a wild, unbroken colt that is used to getting its own way. The body does not have the inner programming to do what is commanded by the new inner person. It must be re-programmed in many ways. This training goes far beyond assenting to a new program or assenting to the right of a new master. The body simply does not know how to perform these new tasks now ordered by the new inner person. Even more than this, it is actually inherently resistant to this new program. We are tempted to call this "habit", but that is not quite accurate because habit is too neutral. As the new inner self grows, the body must be reprogramed and retrained to do the bidding of the new self. It is very difficult for Western Christians to truly grasp this at first.

As a new person in Christ, you must now retrain yourself, to assure that the body carries out the promptings of the new inner-self rather than the old self. This requires attention and deliberate focus. It requires determination. It requires what we would call self-discipline. This is the only true role of "self-discipline", as taught in the Scriptures. This is what Paul spoke of in his words, "I discipline my body and make it my slave..." (I. Cor 9:27). It is always about the body and the retraining necessary to overcome its original programming under the old inner-self. This is why Paul concludes his argument in Romans by, "Therefore, I urge you, brethren, by the mercies of God, to present your *bodies* a living and holy sacrifice, acceptable to God, which is your spiritual service of worship." (Rom 12: 1)

This connection between the soul and the body, and therefore the new self (new soul) and the body, gets almost no attention whatsoever by most of the modern Western church. The modern church is far too superficial, oversimplified and utilitarian for this. It requires mediation, reflection and especially meditative prayer. It doesn't come from answering five questions in a "study book". Only God can explain this to you and teach you how to truly grasp these things. That's why the Evangelical church can make no real sense of these instructions from Paul. It's great preaching material! It sounds wonderful, and enlightening and challenging, but no one understands it or knows what to do with it!

All the discipline pictured by the ancient Greek gymnasium, or any other highly disciplined regimen, is limited to the abilities of the human mind, soul and body. But this can never be thought of as the means to achieve transformation. These are puny when compared to the transformation brought about by the Holy Spirit through the finished work of Christ. Only that kind of transformation turns a Simon into a Peter or a Saul into a Paul. The ability to preach great sermons or work great miracles is not the focus. Transformation takes you from who you are to who you were supposed to be, and that is for every single Christian on the planet! You were not meant to be only a pew-sitting Christian who listens politely, says nice things to the pastor, has some fun with friends and then goes on your way to spend your life pursuing the American Dream.

And Yet I Show You a Better Way...

All forms and levels of self-discipline are, in fact, a modification or narrowing of values and priorities, followed by a modification of how you spend your time and energy to fulfill those values. It is all about deliberate choices, which is within the ability of nearly everyone. These choices are driven by a powerful and deeply instinctive cost-benefit analysis. You choose based on what you genuinely perceive to have the best pay-off, and whether the pay-off is "worth it". Your cost-benefit analysis is normally based on your experience, or on any desired improvement in your experience. Your cost-benefit analysis may be wrong or misguided, but that is what drives your choices. It is unavoidable. You make these choices yourself, so you alone control them, and you can always do so.

What you truly believe drives your cost-benefit analysis to the desired goal. It cannot be faked or lied to. Your perseverance in your choice is an undeniable measure of the strength of your belief. If you quickly surrender and quit, it means you really didn't believe, thus, the huge importance for disciples to really, really, believe what Christ has said. If you truly do not believe that the best blessings come from obedience to His commands and teachings, you will not value it and you will not pursue it with the strength of self-discipline. There will always be sufficient distractions and excuses that can interfere and keep you "too busy" to seek Christlikeness.

Think about it carefully. How much self-discipline does it take to enjoy your favorite food, or your favorite activity, or your favorite view of nature's vista, etc. More likely, it takes some self-discipline not to eat too much or stay too long. If you could feel this way about obeying Christ's commands, would you welcome it? Would you like to say that you genuinely look forward to forgiving and being reconciled? Would you like to say that you genuinely enjoy being kind to those who don't deserve it? Would you like to say that you genuinely enjoy loving others fervently from the heart? This requires one thing—a transformed heart, and only Christ can deal this out! This is true Biblical discipleship!

Spiritual Training—a Unique Discipline

In coming chapters, we will explore, "...the mystery (secret truth) of God which is Christ in you." (Col. 1:26-27) The transformation that God calls us to is only possible by this truth. This, "Christ in you" requires concrete realization of, "It is no longer I who live, but Christ". (Gal. 2:20) This is for every single true Christian, but to realize it requires a "stripping off of the old man and putting on the new man". (Eph. 4:22-24) This requires your active and deliberate participation. It must be learned step by step, and it moves you toward the goal of "godliness". It is indeed a "training" in the "Way of Christ". True discipleship trains you in this. To be clear, the secret truth that leads to godliness is not self-discipline as we think of it, but all that is in Christ. (I Tim. 3:16) He is available to us as our sole resource for "everything pertaining to (eternal) life and godliness." (II Peter 1:3, parenthesis mine) The bottom-line result is that God *gives* you self-discipline from your spiritual resources in Christ! That's why it is described as a fruit of the Holy Spirit!

True Biblical discipleship is not something that feels like training for the Olympics or military special forces. Being a devoted follower of Jesus Christ does not require you to do some spiritual equivalent of getting up at 4:00 am, running twenty miles with a forty-pound pack, then splitting three cords of wood by hand before you swim three miles across the icy lake for breakfast, all while quoting Bible verses and rehearsing your techniques for sharing the gospel. Biblical discipleship will include self-discipline, but it must be the right kind, and in the right way. First you must decide specific matters in your heart, mind, and soul. Until then, it is puny, easily becomes the victim of legalism, and not the pathway to true godliness. You must decide that you are tired of gas-station fast food and believe that there is something far better.

True spiritual discipline is not forcing yourself to do what you don't want to do merely because it's the right thing to do. Spiritual discipline is far more like learning to let go (stripping off all that hinders your focus = "gymnasium yourself"). Proper use of the classic spiritual disciplines can put you in focused connection with God so He can strip from you the thoughts, feelings, words, and intentions of the old nature. Learning to let go frees the Holy Spirit's power to be released into you, instilling transformation. When you come into transformation, you will enjoy loving God, your fellow Christian, your neighbor, even your enemy. You will do it just for the sheer joy of it, and the joy of pleasing your Lord. Of course, when you enjoy it, it becomes powerfully habit forming, even addictive. It becomes automatic, just like flipping on the light switch when you enter the dark room. You hardly even think about it because you really believe it. (Subsequent chapters will deal with this more completely.)

Surrender of your free will is not necessary at all if you simply and deliberately choose, out of your free will, to do the will of the Father. This simply says, "I can choose whatever I want, and I choose obedience because that is the best path for blessing." This is what Jesus did. He wants His disciples to learn to do the same, and they can. But this kind of transformation only comes from Christ, and it only comes to those who enter discipleship under His mentoring. He infuses it into you by His Spirit.

Are you feeling like you are about to cross a yawning crevasse by walking across a simple ladder? It is a thrill you will never forget and never back away from again, but you will never know it unless you take your first step onto the ladder. Don't look down. Look to Jesus! He will have you safe in His hands.

Another helping of Tiramisu anyone?

CHAPTER 11

THE DEADLIEST
DEAD-WEIGHTS

As you will see in this book, several fundamental errors have occurred in church history. Some occurred very early along the path, and others in more recent times. These errors have put us on the wrong path and affected many of the subsequent decisions at other forks in the road along the way until we arrived where we are now—off the path, and unable to live deeply satisfying Christian lives that attract people to Jesus. These are still huge problems that must be cast aside and left as junk along the road if we are going to make it back to the true path. It is like trying to carry a grand piano on the tailgate of your covered wagon, still thinking you can make it over the pass just fine. But it won't happen!

Life is Good in the Middle of the Road

Most people, including most Americans, want to believe they are a basically good person, and they work hard to keep that thought going in their mind and conscience—regardless of their actual behavior. Under the influence of, "I'm okay, you're okay", that belief has strengthened even more. Typically, this is one of the initial hurdles for sharing the gospel in modern western culture. With the current ban on making any judgments at all, it is even worse. Within the Church, the forsaking of belief in true repentance and any real sense of pursuing a godly life has brought this poison into the center of all churches and into Christian living.

We see our spiritual condition like traveling down a road. As long as we stay more-or-less in the middle of the road most of the time, we think we are doing fine. Sure, from time to time, we drift into the ditch on one side or the other. But as long as we get ourselves out as quickly as possible and back in the middle of the road, we are still good, and God expects nothing else. If we don't commit serious sins like murder, adultery, theft, or drug dealing, we think we are basically okay. I know I need a Savior, but actually, I'm not such a bad person, and I don't need to change. No matter if we were unkind to the server at the restaurant last night or demonstrating some road rage toward the driver next to us in traffic or selfish toward our spouse after work. No matter if we are arrogant and rude at church. This is all covered by God's grace. Right? Middle-of-the-road is quite comfortable to churchianity.

According to God's assurance in Scripture, all of these can and will be forgiven and your salvation is not in jeopardy. However, that does not mean that God is okay with these behaviors. Middle of the road is not all that God expects on this side of heaven! Our calling is to be holy like the One who called us is holy. (I Peter 1:15) To be holy is not "middle of the road". Unfortunately, the church has not taught us how to be such holy persons. Most Christians believe that this is reserved only for the pastor and maybe those who want to be special, high-level, high-performing Christians.

This is the classic example of the double-think that seems so prevalent within the evangelical church. It stems from the role that the church has chosen to take up, described so well by Dallas Willard as "sin management". [25] Being a Christian starts with admitting to ourselves and to God that we are sinners needing to be saved. Yet, we continue down the road under this lie that we are okay! We are not okay! That's why the compassionate Savior came to save us. That's why the compassionate Savior came to save you! And saving you includes saving you from all aspects of your ungodliness and sin, carried out every day as you pursue living in the "middle of the road". As Jesus warned, middle of the road is the "broad road that leads to destruction" (Matt. 7: 13).

We don't seem to recognize that the broad road leading to destruction is not only about hell after you die. The entire road is pot-holed with destruction. It is full of land mines that will blow up your life while you go your own way down the middle of the road. (Isa. 53:6) Going your own way down the middle of the road is what brought you to realize you needed a Savior. Your sins are real, and they permeate a big chunk of your life down-the-middle-of-the-road. The call of Christ is to "the narrow road that leads to life" (Matt. 7: 13).

The fantastically good news is that, once you enter the narrow gate and begin to follow the narrow road, you discover that it actually leads to a wonderful, exhilarating freedom. (Ps. 119: 44-45) As we begin to travel the narrow road and pursue true holiness, we discover that the road begins to widen in a miraculous and beautiful way. It is not really as narrow as it appears from the outside, and a beautiful new land opens up to your eyes and heart that you never saw or imagined before. This is part of God's wisdom which hides His truth to the so-called wise and reveals it to babes. (Matt 11:25) Discovery of this new promised land does not require that you take flight on a ship bound across the ocean to an undiscovered country. It only requires that you turn your feet to true Biblical discipleship.

Faith Without Experience

For most Christians, the great lack of Biblical discipleship has resulted in a Christianity that is taken "by faith", with little matching experience with God. Their actual daily experience is focused almost entirely on briefly hearing or reading about what they should believe "by faith" (believe by having faith). This is a widespread symptom of not properly understanding what belief/faith really means, along with the lack of teaching the "how" of discipleship. Christians have been led to believe (by faith) that no experience is even available, or at least not available very often. They are led to believe that you must be some kind of very special person to have any meaningful experiences to accompany your faith. Sometimes they are led to believe that it is somehow sinful, worldly, dangerous, or even heresy to expect any experiences. Expecting any experiences is seen as a lack of faith. Receiving spiritual experiences is reserved only for special people who have special ministries and status with God—the spiritual super-heroes. This view and influence is extremely subtle, which keeps it off our radar, but it is very powerful. We are barely aware of it, as if it were nothing more than annoying, fuzzy background that should not be there and is generally ignored. You know, just some technical flaw in the program.

To be clear, we don't base our understanding of God and the truth of the Bible based on emotions and experience. However, the reverse is also a terrible mistake. If you don't experience your theology, something is very wrong. If you don't experience proper emotions about your faith, something is very wrong. This mistake has been made by far too much teaching and preaching in evangelical churches that inadvertently disparages or suppresses any experience with God. A very influential and long-standing theology in the evangelical church has been that the facts of faith are not something to be experienced. "That's why we call it faith."

When presenting the Biblical truth about our position in Christ, classic dispensational teaching says that none of the things we receive in our position in Christ are to be experienced. We are to take them as truth by faith in the word of God, the Bible. But this can only mean that they are not necessarily experienced at the moment we receive them, in other words, in the moment we are born again. However, much of what we receive by being in Christ certainly may and should be experienced as we go forward in real life as a child of God. More precisely, you should absolutely experience much of what God has done for you, and the longer you walk with Christ the greater the experience gets. To be born again is very real. You experience the difference. You will feel the difference within you. Being made alive in your spirit by the indwelling of the Holy Spirit is real and you will feel the difference. Learning to be "filled with the Holy Spirit" is real, and you will feel it as it happens (and it has nothing to do with speaking in tongues, being slain in the Spirit, or faith healing.)

In Gal. 3: 2-3, Paul asks the Galatians about their experience of receiving the Holy Spirit, and whether it came from hearing with faith (their salvation experience) or when hearing the teaching or preaching of the Law. Of course, Paul is expecting them to answer that they received the Holy Spirit when they heard and accepted the message of faith in Christ. Paul is establishing his theological argument about faith and Law on their *experience* of receiving salvation and the Holy Spirit. This is not some reference back to charismatic experiences at the time of their salvation. But it undeniably means that the Galatian Christians could remember back to the specific time when they received the Holy Spirit. Paul was not expecting them to respond with something like, "I guess I need to talk with my pastor about that"; or, "I'll have to look that up in our doctrinal statement"; or, "I'll have to check my notes from the small group Bible study." Paul expected them to fully remember that there was a moment in time when the Holy Spirit came to indwell them, and it wasn't when they were listening to a sermon on how to be saved by keeping the Law. A great many Christians today would have a very hard time giving the answer Paul was prompting. A great many Christians today would respond by saying, "I guess I need to talk with my pastor about that"; or, "I'll have to look that up in our doctrinal statement"; or, "I'll have to check my notes from our small group Bible study."

The entire emotional aspect of our humanity has been so sadly ignored and neglected in the evangelical church that is as if we are afraid to speak of it, lest it cause speaking in tongues. This is both one of the causes and effects of intellectual Christianity. It is as if we are trying to purge Christianity of all emotion, lest it get out of hand. It is as if we are trying to produce a Christianity that is pure intellect, so it is absolutely free of all contaminating emotions. We have even defined love in a way as to purge all emotion from it, making it an intellectual commitment to the well-being of others. We have computers that can do that! It's as if we have been watching too much science fiction/space fantasy! Meanwhile, it produces a Christianity that can never become so enjoyable that no one ever wants to walk away from it. As seen from the outside, it impresses observers, inquirers and seekers, to say that our faith is not a real experience.

However, it is indisputable that the Scriptures teach that the True God Who Really Exists wants His people to experience Him, not only in the future in heaven but having a full foretaste now. Multiple Scriptures, both Old and New Testament, practically scream that God wants us to know Him. In Hebrew thought, knowing something or someone always included experiencing that which we seek to know. Otherwise, the whole discussion and debate about world religions revolves only around who has the best ancient book and the best scholars of that ancient book to explain it to us. This is not true Biblical Christianity!

The reason we can be so certain that Christianity is unequaled by all other religions is that, in Christianity, we have the great satisfaction and fulfillment of actually experiencing the God Who Really Exists. There is a much greater experience out in the future, but the foretaste is now, and it is real! Imagine what the world might have been like if Christianity was compellingly real, and that such reality always transformed the faithful to be like Jesus. What a different world we might have today!

This is similar to the problem of distinguishing between faith and works. Works do not provide salvation, but living faith always results in works. Works are the fruit of genuine faith. (James 2: 14-26) In exactly the same way, experience does not prove truth, but much of genuine Biblical truth is a reality that Christians can and should experience on a regular basis. The experience confirms and lives out faith, just as genuine faith lives out in works.

In fact, works are part of the experience side of faith. As our Lord promised, obedient living will absolutely increase your perception and awareness of His presence. (John 14:21, 23)

Biblical discipleship will teach and enable you to have a life that experiences God's presence and blessing regularly, including a healthy, balanced, robust and enjoyable emotional life. Your relationship with God will include healthy, balanced, robust and enjoyable emotional aspects. You will fully enjoy expressing and sharing your emotions with your Heavenly Father; and you will fully enjoy receiving His emotional relationship with you. This alone will make true discipleship a radical change for many evangelical and liturgy-based Christians. It may be the first time you really enter into knowing your emotional self and the emotional attributes of your Heavenly Father who made you in His image.

Reason, Faith and Spiritual Understanding

Some of the most critical historic confessions of the Church are based on an attempt to explain the "wholly other" by the human concepts and language of intellect, logic, and reasoning. When faced with concepts that are clearly beyond intellect, logic and reasoning, then theologians invented terminology to describe them, making it faintly grasped by others of intellect, logic and reasoning. But when you grasp it by intellect, logic and reasoning, you still don't function with God very well, because it is only mental knowledge about a subject that cannot be known by mental knowledge alone. It is not spiritual knowledge, and so it is not spiritually functional knowledge. (Welcome to the evangelical church at large.) This is why so many attempts at spiritual discussions are so awkward. Every pastor knows this experience quite well.

The average Christian of any country and any era is not someone of great intellect, logic and reasoning. Most of us are just people, ordinary people going about the normal life of just people. Many of the early Christians, as well as Christians in under-developed countries with primitive churches, could not even read. If the "great minds of the Church" can only faintly grasp the spiritual truth of God and the Bible by using intellect, logic and reasoning, how do you expect the average, ordinary Christian to grasp it by that approach? Can you imagine trying to explain to a twelve-year old passing through confirmation that the Triune God is "one in subsistence, but three in distinct persons"? S/he can memorize and repeat this back to us, but they do not grasp it at all. We embrace with Paul that, "…now we see in a mirror dimly". (I Cor. 13: 12), but we do see! Primary reliance on intellect, logic and reasoning does not make the dim mirror any clearer. However, proper discipleship teaches you that the right combination of faith, reason and experience will let you see more clearly.

When our Lord rose from the dead, He spent part of that day walking incognito with two disciples on the Emmaus road. The conversation revealed that they had still not grasped the meaning of the Scriptures about His resurrection. He referred to them as, "…foolish men, slow of heart to believe". (Luke 24: 25) As a student of Christ, how could they be slow of heart to believe? Didn't Christ use enough logic to get through to them? Yet they had not really believed and were on the road out of Jerusalem as if completely giving up on the great hope that Jesus was the Christ. Later that night Jesus appeared to the other disciples in the upper room. We are told that He explained the

Scriptures about Himself from the Law, Psalms and Prophets. (Luke 24: 44) Surely Christ knew full well how to explain these many passages using all necessary reason and logic, yet we are told that He had to, "…open their minds to understand the Scriptures" in order to get through to them fully. (Luke 24:45) This is a powerful illustration of Biblical spiritual understanding.

Paul wrote to the Corinthian church that, "not many wise, not many mighty, not many noble" were called to salvation in his preaching (I Cor. 1:26). He goes on to remind them that when he came to them, he did not present the gospel, "with superiority of speech or (human) wisdom" (I Cor. 2:1, parenthesis mine) and his message was not in "persuasive words of wisdom" (I Cor: 2:4. A few moments later, he declares that he does speak, "God's wisdom to those who are mature" (I Cor 2:6); but it is not "human wisdom, but a wisdom taught by the Holy Spirit", and therefore it is indeed grasped by those who are "spiritual". (I Cor. 2:13-14) John writes to the churches that true Christians have an "internal teacher" that gives the assurance that they truly know God and are true followers of Christ. (I John 5:10) These passages are well taught and well preached in most evangelical churches. Yet we continue to teach people to try to understand the Scriptures by human intellect, logic, and reason. We try to bring God's revelation to the minds and hearts of His people by using a completely faulty approach. Little wonder that they don't grasp it in a spiritually functional way.

This is why Paul told the Ephesian church that he was praying for them to be given, "…the spirit of wisdom and revelation in the true knowledge of Him (God)." (Eph. 1: 17) Without this spiritual link and function to the spiritual truth in Paul's letter, the readers would not fully grasp the truth of what he was writing. How many Christians are praying the prayer of Eph

1:17 on a regular basis? How many pastors are earnestly praying this prayer for their people on a regular basis? Without Biblical spiritualty, believers do not truly grasp the great spiritual truths that are presented by the Spirit—inspired Scriptures that we seek to explain. But Biblical spirituality has not been taught.

We will always use our minds and words to teach the Scriptures, but it must be done in a way that provides spiritual wisdom, spiritual understanding, spiritual insight, and spiritual nurture. It must be done with "words taught by the Holy Spirit" to accomplish spiritual functioning. We cannot depend on intellect, logic and reasoning to substitute for spirituality and spiritual grasp of God's presence and God's truth. Otherwise, Paul's words to the Corinthians are speaking into the air. If we had our evangelical way about it, we would change Paul's statements to say that he *always* used careful intellect, logic and reasoning to express God's truth. Spiritual truth is not understood by leaning entirely or primarily on intellect, logic and reasoning. It is understood spiritually. (I Cor. 2:14) You have to grow, "… ears that hear". (Matt. 11:15) You have to grow a heart that hears and perceives (John 12:40, cf. Matt 13:15) Once you perceive it correctly in your spirit, your spirit explains it to your mind, and sometimes that takes some time. Discipleship teaches you how to use proper Christian meditation. Without this spiritual meditation, your spirit will have limited opportunity to explain things to your mind. When it happens, a light comes on in your understanding and you smile delightfully because you have just experienced a small piece of the spirit of wisdom and revelation for which Paul prayed. The disciple learns to understand God's truth by developing spiritual learning skills and spiritual understanding skills, not primarily intellectual learning skills.

These are available to every believer. But Biblical spirituality has not been taught.

J. Vernon McGee used to tell of his occasional experiences discussing Scripture with the woman who was responsible for cleaning their church building. He described her as a very simple Christian woman with limited education, but Pastor McGee remarked his surprise, and yet delight, at what a solid grasp she had for some deep spiritual truths—the truths which he regularly preached and taught at his church and on his radio programs. She had learned spiritual learning. She grasped truth that was missed by many others because others tried to grasp it intellectually, but she had learned to understand through her spirit. This is the way of Biblical spirituality, and all born-again children have that right and privilege. You have "the software" to learn it, but you must learn to use it. The internal operator and tutor is the indwelling Holy Spirit in His teaching and guiding ministry to every believer as they take in the God-breathed Scriptures.

Now, intellect, logic and reasoning are not some kind of evil, and they need not be discarded entirely or discounted unfairly. Jesus, Paul and other authors of the Scripture used these to express the Word of God. We cannot make sense of the world or express any thought without use of these. I am using these as part of writing this book, and you are using them to read it. Both Jesus and Paul were master tacticians in the use of logic, reason and debate, but Paul also speaks of the "spirit of your mind" (Eph 4:23) In the end, we must realize intellect, logic and reasoning are inadequate to truly grasp God, His attributes, His presence, His truth, or His actions within and around you, because God is spirit. We must be willing to fully hear and embrace the teachings of Scripture. They teach that truly grasping God's truth is a spiritual function, and we must learn to teach believers to develop spiritual understanding. This comes only from Biblical spirituality.

Biblical Spirituality

Scripture tells us that God is spirit. (John 4:24) He has always been spirit, He is now spirit, and He will always be spirit. Even though He exists as spirit, He possesses the full spectrum of personhood in every way that we can understand. He possesses, mind, will and emotion. In other words, He possesses thoughts, feelings, and the power of free choice. He is also fully capable of carrying out anything He chooses out of those thoughts, feelings and intentions. Because we are created in His image, we also have mind, will and emotion, along with our physical existence, and we also possess a spiritual component. We are physical beings but with a spiritual aspect or component. When God breathed into Adam the "breathe of lives", it made him "a living soul". (Gen. 2:7) Our spirit is not the same thing as our soul, but these two communicate back and forth with each other at a deep level of our being. Our spiritual component was given to allow us to have open, free and natural relationship with our Heavenly Father who is spirit. God wanted us to have spiritual awareness and capacities. He gave us spiritual awareness and capacities. In other words, humans started out being spiritually alive. Being spiritually alive allows us to actually experience the presence of God and what He is doing.

Scripture tells us that when sin entered the human race, it brought about spiritual death, separating us from God. Paul writes things like, "...and you were dead in your trespasses and sins" (Eph. 2:1, 11, cf. Col. 2:13), "...at that time you were separate from Christ, excluded from the commonwealth of Israel, and strangers to the covenants of promise, having no hope and without God in this world". God had warned Adam and Eve that, if they should partake of the tree of the knowledge of good and evil, they would die. (Gen 2:17) Of course, they did not die physically until many years later, but the open, free and natural relationship with their Creator and Heavenly Father was gone because they had died spiritually. Instead, they fled and hid. Spiritual death had struck the human race. The positive relationship with God was gone. The positive awareness of God was gone. Now the blame game starts. The criticism game starts. It prompts us to blame God for everything we don't like. It prompts us to see the splinter in the eye of others but be unaware of the log in our own eye. (Matt 7:3) These were all outward symptoms of becoming spiritually dead to God.

The deep flaw that resulted by that one choice to "taste evil" is passed on to each subsequent generation by natural conception and birth. (Ps. 51:5) Something died within us that interrupted and obstructed our ability and our desire to have fellowship with God. God "disappeared" from our awareness and focus. It's like having a two-way radio with the antenna snapped off by a storm wind. We keep listening, but we can't hear anything. We keep talking, but apparently, no one can hear us. Is anybody listening? Does this thing even work? Hello? Hello? Oh, well. After all, if you believe you are equal with God, you have little use for Him anyway. Of course, the reaction of Adam and Eve automatically reveals that they did not really think they were equal with God; otherwise, why run off and hide at His approach? They had been tricked by the master of lies and deceit.

What passes down to us as part of our deep sinfulness is the inability to be aware of God, and our automatic reaction to run off and hide from God. We instinctively choose to not acknowledge God. (Rom 1:28) If you can't be equal and can't hide, the next best thing is simply put Him out of your mind. This makes Him disappear from your awareness. Just ignore Him, then claim that He doesn't even exist. This allows you to live under the complete pretense and self-delusion that You are god! You will choose what is right for You. You will decide for You what is right and wrong—and by the way, since You are god, everyone else must do what You say. If someone else doesn't want to do what You say, there is a fight brewing. Watch any group of four-year-olds and you will see it clearly. That's what sin has done to us, generation by generation, and we are powerless to break out of it ourselves, even when we recognize how destructive it all is. This perpetuates the deception even though you know it is a deception. It's called denial. It's called thinking You are the center of the universe.

When we sincerely repent of our sinfulness and trust Christ fully for salvation and eternal life, He gives eternal life, as promised. Eternal life is not limited to forgiveness of our sins. Eternal life is not only a promise of heaven when we die. It is a new level and kind of life that comes into existence within us, starting from the moment that you are born again and then enduring throughout all eternity. This new source and form of life comes into your being and merges with your whole self. This allows our spiritual awareness and sensibilities toward God to start functioning. We have been made alive in spirit and alive to God. (John 3:5-8, Rom. 8:10, Gal. 5:25; Rom. 6:11, Gal. 2:19, Eph. 2:5) But as indicated in Scriptures, this new life starts as a "new creature" that has come into existence, as a "babe in Christ". Now it needs all the same things you needed when you were physically a new-born infant. It needs to be nurtured, kept secure, cleansed, cared for, doctored, exercised, trained. S/he needs to grow. If it does not receive these at the right times and in the right forms, this new version of you does not develop properly and normally. It remains dominated by the former version of you (the old man), described in Scripture as "natural" and "carnal".

But remaining carnal is not what God desires for any Christian. God's desire is that each Christian learn to live out your new-found spiritual aliveness. He commands us to, "...walk by the Spirit". (Gal. 5:16), not just for the "religious moments", but for every moment of your life. As you do this, you become more "spiritual". You learn to see all moments, and all that each moment includes, as "spiritual" because the One True Living God, who is spirit, is at the center of each of these moments (except for sin of course). You can sense God's presence in each moment and all that each moment includes. The world becomes a glorious place full of what God is doing in you, in others around you, and in the world around you. Churchianity cannot teach you this. Law/legalism cannot teach you this, no matter what list of rules you use; but the disciple of Jesus learns this.

Once again, the primitive church often knows more about this than the sophisticated, well-informed Western church. Missionaries tell of experiences when they were holding gatherings for preaching or training until native Christians would suddenly come and tell them, "We sense in our spirit that government troops are coming. We must dismiss the meeting now, so everyone can leave safely." Sure enough, hostile government troops would arrive later looking for the Christians, and everyone would be gone, safely in their villages and homes.

Centuries of Church history, right up to and including now, have demonstrated an overwhelming failure in this aspect of true Christianity and discipleship. As soon as the Church turned to the Western mind-set, with its focus on intellect, logic and reasoning, it lost its hold on the spiritual and the unseen realities which are clearly declared and demonstrated throughout the Scriptures. The Bible is absolutely loaded with teaching and descriptions of the unseen reality that is "wholly other", beyond the seen reality, but still truly real. However, it can be experienced by grasping the "beyond reality" in your spirit which is now alive to God. Eventually, you begin to realize that the spiritual reality is somehow woven together with the physical reality that we are familiar with. Somehow, they are inseparably tied together. They are woven together in one great fabric of reality. Both dimensions are taking place together in each moment and each event.

The sophisticated intellectual church has a very hard time with this. It's kind of "lost in the fog" of good doctrine. It can only be learned more completely in discipleship under Jesus. We all have a great, instinctive longing to know the "greater reality" that, somehow, we sense must be out there beyond ourselves and our world. We have a vague, ancient memory of it, but we can't seem to get in touch with it anymore. It is that "something greater", that even primitive people sense. Paul tells the Athenians that it is the unseen Provider of Blessing for which we seek and grope, looking for His identity and meaning. (Acts 17:27) It is, in fact, "the vacuum at our center which can only be satisfied in God.[26] Augustine put it, "...thou hast made us for thyself, and restless is our heart until it comes to rest in thee."[27] The terms "restless" and "finding rest" are about experience and feelings, not intellect or doctrine.

As part of their 2014 book, *Churchless*, George Barna and David Kinnaman write, "The number of churchless adults in the U.S. has grown by nearly one-third in the past decade. Yet the startling truth is that many of these people claim, "...they are looking for a genuine, powerful encounter with God—but they just don't find it in church."[28] Amongst the statistics in this book are that sixty-five per cent of unchurched people consider themselves to be "spiritual" people, and, "...fifty-one per cent say they are actively seeking something better spiritually than they have experienced to date". [29] (Remember this is a 2014 statistic.) Do you suppose that if they found the real presence of Jesus at a church, they would find satisfaction? They aren't looking for another chance to play softball, golf or have a barbeque. They aren't looking for another chance to have a faux-spiritual experience, and yet Biblical spirituality has seldom been taught or displayed for nineteen centuries. We fail to teach it or display it, so after centuries of neglect, most do not know it. There are only few who do. Unfortunately, many of those have been forced out of their churches to make room for more progressive approaches that attract a larger audience.

Meanwhile, younger Christians and those superficially churched have begun to explore and experiment with non-Christian religions and cults because those seem to offer spiritual experiences that reach out to the spiritual reality beyond us. They seem to offer a spirituality that is more tangible, not just theology and church activities. True Christian spirituality eliminates these threats and voids, providing a rich and deeply meaningful spirituality that is directly tied to our everyday experiences. It is tangible and offers real connection with the Real God in everyday experiences. He is real and knowing Him is a real experience. It is woven into the very fabric of our lives.

The ancient Celtic Christians and other small groups of simple people knew this, but it wasn't passed on successfully.

Then the medieval Roman Church killed it. Christian spirituality does not require great world conventions to decide what the forms should be and how to make sure every Christian and every church does it the same way. Uniformity is not the way to this wonderful and deeply personal Christian spirituality. Only a robust and real living out of what the Scriptures clearly tell us will do that. This is learned in discipleship under Jesus.

Some will say that what I am suggesting is a form of Christian mysticism. This can be a clever scare tactic. It suggests that Christian spirituality is one of the heresies that have been rejected and condemned by the Church in the past. Some forms of mysticism have been rejected and condemned because they were not Biblical. Without apology, true, Biblical spirituality is a mysticism, and it is the kind that is absolutely taught and advocated repeatedly in the Scriptures, both Old and New Testament, and this is exactly the point. The Scriptures practically scream the teaching of Biblical spirituality. All you need do is to consult any accurate exhaustive concordance of the Bible to see all the verses that speak of the role of the Holy Spirit in the life of the Christian. But you can't explain the person and role of the Holy Spirit in terms of intellect and reasoning. It is only our many centuries of western mind-set that makes us blind to this. Even when Paul took the gospel and word of God to the west, he emphasized the spiritual basis and content, not the intellectual.

My purpose here is certainly not to cause anyone to doubt their faith, their relationship with God, their salvation in Christ, or their certainty of eternal life by faith in the Son of God beyond that which is always appropriate. The Apostle Paul wrote to those who thought they were Christians in Corinth saying, "Test yourselves to see if you are in the faith; examine yourselves." (II Cor. 13:5) We must be willing to recognize and embrace that, even though there has been much effort to keep the Church on a Biblical track, we have missed a huge portion of what Christ fully intended to give to His Church, according to the Scriptures. It is both no ones' fault and everyone's fault. We don't know what we don't know, but we can know it. It's been right in front of us in God's inspired word and we must stop missing it and neglecting it and substituting other things. We must stop substituting our versions of churchianity for true, Biblical Christianity. It can be done, and it must be done!

We must finally recognize that our hearts are not hungry for more church activities. We are hungry for the Living God! We must finally recognize that our hearts are not hungry for more special effects in the form of special lighting, faux-fog and computer-generated images. We are hungry for the Living God! We must finally recognize that our hearts are not hungry for more intellectual understanding of the Scriptures that does not change our lives. We are hungry for the Living God who speaks these Scriptures to us, and stands before us with open, loving arms inviting us into His truth and transformation. In the depth of our soul, we long for a satisfying connection with God. Only a deep connection with God satisfies our hearts, and Jesus Christ came to give us that. That is what the Church is supposed to be dealing out. Everything else is just another, "…cistern that won't hold water," instead of, "…the fountain of living waters". (Jer. 2:13; John 7:37-38) Nothing else will do. Everything else is just another version of gas station fast food.

Discipleship is the process that teaches you Biblical spirituality. It will be quite new to most, but it is truly essential. You cannot learn it in a fifteen minute "quiet time with God" or "Thirty-day journey with God" (in other words thirty fifteen-minute quiet times), or a week-end retreat. But you also do not need to attend a Bible college or seminary, or sell your house, quite your job and move to an undeveloped country. Firstly, you would probably not learn it at a Bible college or seminary; and secondly, if you go to an undeveloped country where there are primitive churches, they are more likely to teach you than you teach them. You do not need to seek a Pentecostal or charismatic experience. Biblical spirituality does not come that way. It only comes in the true Way of Christ, and no other way. You do not have to wait for heaven to have this. It is for here and now, "that we may know the things given to us by God," and, be "lights shining in the world to the glory of our Father". (I Cor 2: 10-12, Matt 5:16, Phil 2:15) Christianity should consistently produce people who will be open displays of what God intended the human race to be. Only Biblical spirituality will do that, because it produces an amazing transformation by the power of the Spirit of God and the power of His word. We were meant to be spiritual people. But Biblical spirituality has not been taught!

As with the travelers of the Oregon Trail, it is likely to be painful to discard some of what we see as cherished things. But as you leave them behind, finally, and start on the right path, you will see that it was well worth freeing yourself from the junk to gain true freedom and fulfillment as our Lord promised. "Who told you that you needed all that stuff?"

Go back and read Chapter 3. Then ask yourself again if you truly want the things that Jesus promised, as summarized there. These tremendous blessings are only available as you walk in the true Way of Christ. They are not available in any other way. Only Biblical discipleship teaches you to walk that path. What do you really want: faux-Christianity = churchianity, or the real thing? Then you have to unload the wagon of "all this stuff" and start climbing over the pass back to the true path.

CHAPTER 12

THE SOURCE OF OBEDIENCE— THE GLORY OF HIS GRACE

The Scriptures clearly establish that obedience to the commands and teachings of Christ is not optional for the Christian. It is an inseparable part of being a follower of Jesus Christ. As described in Chapter 6, it is the fundamental definition of being a disciple. Obedience does not in any way earn salvation, keep salvation, or "pay God back" for salvation. It is learning to walk in "the Way of Christ", as any disciple would want to do. You will be putting yourself in the position to receive God's undeserved and unearned blessings; and as you do so, you enter all the joy and freedom that He promised to those who believe in and follow Him. Since disciples are learners/apprentices, these are things you learn over time as you walk with Him. The longer you walk with Christ, the better you learn to do them, the more you enjoy doing them, and the more you enjoy the life that God has given you.

To move you along this path, God does not, and cannot, use any form of legalism. That would only fail due to our inability to consistently obey. Instead, He has put in place the most powerful provision possible for getting you to obedience—grace and transformation. This is a process that replaces the old you with a new you that is Christ-like. It will still be you. You will still look in the mirror and see the same image of yourself that has always been there. However, inwardly it will be a new you that gradually sheds what is sinful, selfish, unbalanced, distorted and displeasing to God. You will also escape the damage done by sin and shed all that makes you unhappy or unfulfilled.

The thought of living in obedience based on grace may take some time and adjusted thinking on your part. As described in earlier chapters, far too many Christians think of grace and obedience as have nothing in common, like two extreme ends on the spectrum. However, they are mutually supportive partners to guide you along the same path. Make no mistake, obedience flowing out of grace is what the Scriptures teach, and it works so well you may be taken by great surprise as it unfolds in your mind, heart and life. The truth of Scripture does not leave the Christian in the constant struggle described Romans Chapter 7. It moves on to the triumph of Romans Chapter 8. It opens the doors to a life that is described by Jesus in His statements summarized in Chapter 3 of this book. It opens the door to a life that you would describe as, "I'm having a blast! Why would I ever go back or look for something else?"

God's Righteousness—Imputed and Imparted

As part of the opening of Paul's letter to the Romans, he declares that the righteousness of God is revealed in the gospel. (Rom 1:16-17) Any attentive reading or study of the book of Romans makes it abundantly clear that this letter describes far more than just the gospel we think of as "how to get saved". It certainly is the gospel that tells how to receive eternal forgiveness from God, but it also tells us what He has done to provide the way back toward actual righteousness—"just as if we had never sinned". It is far more than justification. It is also imputed righteousness, which then becomes *imparted* righteousness. Imputed righteousness happens in an instant. Imparted righteousness happens over time, sometimes in small increments, other times in big chunks. We call the developing change "transformation". Imparted righteousness is the definition of transformation. These all flow forth from God's grace (undeserved gift) and both require deliberate, personal faith in what God has given before it can become a personal reality. Through His own dear Son, this eternally righteous God gives away righteousness to those who have none because He is the only One who can give it. We cannot obtain it or develop it any other way. After all, the righteousness once possessed by the human race was originally given to them by God. They did not develop it by following a bunch of rules. The value of such gifts is incalculable! Are you really unwilling to take simple steps to receive such wonderful gifts?

The Scriptures tell us that the will and plan of God for each and every Christian is transformation into the image of His dear Son. (Rom 8:28-31) In the current arena of discipleship, and transformation/spiritual formation, much is discussed and debated, but transformation must always be correctly linked to its true goal—obedience. It is the full circle of what Paul wrote about throughout the book of Romans. It connects his purpose stated in Rom 1: 5, "...to bring about the obedience of faith...", to his ultimate exhortation in Rom 12: 1-2, "...present your bodies as a living and holy sacrifice acceptable to God". This exhortation only has meaning in consistent obedience.

Otherwise, the transformation that he urges has no goal and no purpose, and in fact, does not occur. No matter how sincere, being, "…transformed by the renewing of your mind…" must never be seen as merely gaining a lot of Bible knowledge or an intellectual understanding of a "Biblical world-view".

"I in You and You in Me" (John 14:20)

Of course, this all starts with Christ in His teaching in John Chapter 15. On this night before his death on the cross, He gives a profound description of the union He was going to establish between Himself and all who sincerely follow Him. For this purpose, He uses the metaphor of the vine and branches. It is the same relationship and union that the Apostles would later describe more fully as "in Him". But it is a union that will only become real to us if we deliberately choose and learn to "abide in Him". This should be the image that is desired and pursued by each and every Christian (disciple), and the church must be dedicated to seeing this come into reality in each and every sincere Christian (disciple). Yet, you will rarely find it stated in the vision or goals of many churches.

This image was not given to describe a theology to be discussed and debated, but the actual experience of having this oneness with the Master. The branch is a biological extension of the vine. The branch originates from the vine and lives entirely from the life energy supplied by the vine. As you pursue this kind of connection with Christ, you should find that it is an actual experience, not merely a theological belief that you believe by faith. As you develop more and more goodness, you will also feel the wonderful goodness of your Lord who is transforming you to be like Him. As you develop more and more gentleness, you will also feel the wonderful gentleness of your Lord who is transforming you to be like Him. As you develop more and more spiritual courage, you will also feel the wonderful spiritual courage of your Lord who is transforming you to be like Him. As you develop more and more faithfulness, you will also feel the wonderful faithfulness of your Lord who is transforming you to be like Him. Not only are you becoming like Him, but you are also coming to know Him. This fulfills the promise of Christ in John 14: 21,23.

This is one of the powerful themes in John's writings, especially his letters. The way he writes is a beautiful weaving of deep meaning that made the ancient Celtic Christians truly love and favor John's portions of the New Testament. They express a very Celtic frame of mind. Many of the churches in "Asia" where John ministered were likely European Celts. We find John's gospel and letters difficult only because we are approaching them from a doctrinal perspective rather than a living experience perspective. We see them as some lofty ideals that can never come to actuality. But the ancient Celtic Christians saw them as a beautiful tapestry depicting the deeply satisfying relationship of the soul with the Lord who made us. This is the heart-yearning of Christ for each and every one who sincerely believes in and follows Him. It is transformation for those who follow Him as a disciple. As you edge into it, you will feel like you are edging into the outskirts of the lost Eden and the coming Kingdom.

Your Standing In Grace

In Romans 5:1-2, Paul describes salvation and forgiveness as our, "...*introduction into this grace in which we stand*." Receiving Gods' forgiveness of our sins and His promise of eternal life is an introduction into a new standing or status with God as being a permanent and continual receiver of grace—a "favored one" (cf. Luke 1:28). This is undeserved and unearned. Paul writes further of this subject in remaining chapters of Romans, explaining how this standing of grace is the spring from which flows this working of God to bring His people into righteousness. This is the starting point in the pathway of walking in grace.

This grace standing allows God to apply unlimited grace to every part of your life, as well as your eternal destiny. This standing never changes. It is the permanent gift of God through His beloved Son to all who sincerely believe in Him. It is never withdrawn, diminished, paused, or put on hold. It is never affected by outside forces. This means that in every moment and every situation, God treats you as one who inherits the benefits of all that Christ did for you in His suffering, death, burial, resurrection, and ascension. By choosing to trust and follow Jesus Christ, you have entered the narrow gate and set your foot on the narrow path. As you turn and look at the gate from the inside, you see the words, inscribed in God's own handwriting, "Chosen before the foundation of the world," (Eph. 1: 4, II Thess. 2:13) and you stop to wonder how such a thing could be.

Paul also writes of this grace standing in Ephesians and Colossians. He describes all the magnificent perfections of Christ in His Person and work, and then links these to all the benefits and blessings that pass to us as an inheritance because we are "in Christ". Because of this standing, God has granted us, "...every spiritual blessing in the heavenly places..." (Eph. 1:3) and they are all *in Christ*. Additionally, Paul tells us that this was the secret plan of God from before time and the universe began. (Eph. 1:4) As he describes these matters, he writes that these actions are, "...to the praise of the glory of His grace", (Eph 1:6) and "to the praise of His glory" (Eph 1:14).

As Paul describes our rich position in Christ, he tells us things like:

"...all of us who have been baptized into Christ Jesus have been baptized into His death, ...that we too might walk in the newness of life" (Rom. 6:3-4);

"...our old self was crucified with Him...so that we would no longer be slaves to sin" (Rom. 6:6);

"...God... made us alive together with Christ...and raised us up with Him, and seated us with Him in the heavenly places in Christ Jesus..." (Eph 2: 5-6);

"...in Him you have been made complete..." (Col. 2:10);

"...having been buried with Him in baptism, in which you were also raised up with Him... (Col. 2:12);

"...He made you alive together with Him..." (Col. 2:13)

Paul tells us that all the fulness of the Godhead is in Christ, and because we are "in Him" we are also "complete" in Him. (Col. 1:19, 2:9-10). This assures us that we have a complete source for all the specific traits and characteristics that are in Christ (not including His diety). These can also be ours through the transformation that God provides, reflecting the meaning of, "...walk in the newness of life." (Rom 6: 3-4) It is fully described by all the individual commands and teachings given to Christians by

Christ and His apostles. We can be Christ-like, and this is what even the unbelieving world expects of us. Unfortunately, we do not expect it of ourselves. Somewhat secretly, we believe this idea must be some kind of heresy.

Peter also writes of our grace standing in II Peter 1:3-4, "…. His divine power has granted to us everything pertaining to life and godliness through the true knowledge of Him who called us by His own glory and excellence. For by these He has granted to us His precious and magnificent promises, *so that by them you may be partakers of the divine nature….*" (italics mine) Based on grace, God has provided everything necessary for the followers of Jesus to be like Him. The reason that both Paul and Peter can then write commands and exhortations for obedience is based entirely on the power of this "grace-by-faith" provision from God.

When Paul writes commands to Christians, calling us to such things as humility, gentleness, patience, tolerance, abandoning falsehoods, persevering against personal sin, discarding wrath, anger, clamor and slander, he speaks from the basis of our grace standing that he has described in earlier parts of his letter. All these are found in Christ, and it is God's full intention that they be in us as well. After describing our provision in Christ, Peter says, "…applying all diligence, in your faith, supply moral excellence, …knowledge, …self-control, …perseverance, …godliness, …brotherly kindness, …love." (II Peter 1: 5) All these are found in Christ, and it is God's full intention that they be imparted to us as well, but it also takes deliberate partnership from you as well.

Even though God is applying His sovereign grace in us, we still have a role or responsibility to fulfill as part of this wonderful process. God chose to make you a being with free choice, and He always works in cooperation with that choice. The teaching of our Lord, recorded by John in chapter 15 of his gospel, combines both our position in Christ and our role for "abiding in Him" to fully experience the blessings of this position. Peter's words call us to the responsibility and privilege of a living faith in God's promises and provision, and we are to be diligent about it. We must activate and apply what God has given us. If you do not apply all diligence toward this transformation, you will not receive the fruit of what God has promised.

This is not a contradiction, inconsistency by mere human authors of Scripture, or suggestive of any form of legalism. It is the wisdom and power of God, but you have an active role. You must deliberately choose to embrace and cooperate with His gifts by putting yourself in the position to receive them and act on them (faith). Just as with your salvation, it is *grace by faith*. (Eph 2:8-10) In each issue and each experience, God will be working to fulfill His promise to "work all things for good" (Rom 8:28) and enable us to "...partake of the divine nature". (II Peter 1: 5) But understand fully, the good that He is working toward is not to make you happy, as if He were simply some cosmic genie. He is making you into the image of His Son, and that will make you happier than anything else! Just you wait and see!!

God is not satisfied to make us robots or remove our free will. He wants us to feel the wonderful fulfillment of intentionally and gladly choosing obedience, as His born-again children. The more you do this, the more you experience real change and the more you experience what you were meant to be—in His image. That brings an ever-increasing sense of joy and fulfillment so that obedience becomes light and easy, just as Christ promised (Matt 11: 28-29). Part of that joy comes from the transformed ability to choose what is the true blessing—righteousness. The undeserving redeemed also become the undeserving transformed! This completes the circle of God's eternal plan of grace, and He is glorified by it all. It is truly to the praise of the glory of His grace! This is so far beyond what any form of legalism can bring to you that it is like comparing travel at light speed to the stroll of a turtle.

The Complete Gospel

The Scriptures are abundantly clear that the "good news" of the gospel includes the wonderful provision that we do not need to remain what we had always been before we came to Christ. We can be changed! The undeserving redeemed are intended to become the undeserving transformed! Those who view discipleship and sanctification as unnecessary "navel-gazing" that consumes church resources and diverts from the mission of soul-saving do not know the gospel of the Scriptures! Those who were once given over to, "…a depraved mind, being filled with all unrighteousness, wickedness, greed, evil, envy, murder, strife, deceit, malice, gossips, slanderers, haters of God, insolent, arrogant, boastful, inventors of evil, disobedient to parents, without understanding, untrustworthy, unloving, and unmerciful…" (Rom 1:28-31) can be transformed by the power of God's grace. We can become holy, sanctified, loving, kind, forgiving, good, faithful, wise, patient, joyful, gentle, self-controlled, peace-seeking, peace-making people. It does not depend on your natural personality or temperament. We can be what He always intended us to be—like Him. As described in Chapter 8, this fulfills the second major component of the Great Commission, declared by the Lord in Luke 4:18-21. Without this, we do not have a complete grasp of His Great Commission or His gospel. It is all by grace and all to His great glory!

There are no Christian atheists amongst those who learn to walk in the daily realities of these wonderful gifts of grace. Each and every symptom of Christian atheism, including each one created by the modern Evangelical church, is overcome, abandoned, and replaced by true Christlikeness. You quickly discover that becoming more like your Savior is a lot more fulfilling than improving your volleyball serve!

CHAPTER 13

THE COST OF DISCIPLESHIP

"Christianity without discipleship is always Christianity without Christ." [30] This declaration by Bonhoeffer is huge. It is every bit as challenging as Luther's ninety-five theses. As implied by the title of his book, Bonhoeffer's settled viewpoint is that there is a cost for becoming a disciple of Jesus Christ, and from his viewpoint, that cost can be high. Bonhoeffer certainly paid a high price for his faithfulness to Christ during the Nazi regime of WWII. Throughout the centuries, a great many followers of Jesus Christ have also paid a heavy price for their witness and faithfulness, and this is a common viewpoint and theme in much information about discipleship.

When you read Bonhoeffer's book, you find that he presents a degree of balance between this cost of which he writes and the great value and reward of discipleship, but it is not particularly easy to discern. This balance can often be missing from the majority of other treatments. It's as though we feel that we must invite people to discipleship with, "Come and be a disciple, and boy are you going to be sorry!" Bonhoeffer rightly connects discipleship with obedience and warns against "cheap grace". We wonder how grace can be negatively labeled "cheap" when the fundamental definition of grace, as used in the inspired Scriptures, is "free and undeserved". It is free by the specific will of God because Christ paid the entire cost! If all that Christ did was all-sufficient before God, then what additional cost could there possibly be?

Sometimes you will hear Christians speak of grace as, "… free, but it will cost you everything". This is very confusing to almost everyone who hears it, even in Christian circles. We learn to say it even though we don't really understand it. It is one of the elephants in the room that everyone tries to ignore.

Jesus certainly spoke of the cost of discipleship, but His emphasis was far more on the benefits and blessings. We find the Apostles doing the same, including Paul who said he had, "… suffered the loss all things and consider them as rubbish in light of the surpassing value of knowing Christ…" (Phil. 3:8) To the Ephesian elders, he declares that, "I do not hold my life of any account as dear to myself, so that I may finish my course and ministry…" (Acts 20: 24) Paul fully anticipated that his obedience to the Lord would cost him dearly. Yet he considered this cost, even his life here on earth, as "worthless" in comparison with the benefits.

In the Western Church (both evangelical and not) the real problem is that we often see the wrong elephant in the room! We see it with traditional views of legalism and self-discipline as part of discipleship and we are thinking of all the things we will have to give up to in order to become a disciple. Discipleship is seen like a gigantic version of giving up something for Lent, except it goes on and on, leaving us poor, ragged, hungry, and sad. We must understand that this would only be another version of, "cleaning the outside of the cup but leaving the inside full of corruption." (Luke 11:39) However, when we learn to see the "cost" with the eyes of Jesus, we will see the elephant more like the big, old, worn-out, sofa that takes up way too much floor space in the room. In order to accomplish the redecoration that we desire, this thing just has to go to the dump! It's worn and dingy and quite frankly, kind of stinks. Giving it up doesn't seem to be much of a "cost". It seems more like a great relief and benefit! It is very important that we have an accurate understanding of this issue. What is this cost of discipleship and how costly is it? Let's make sure we correctly understand the cost, so it doesn't catch us unprepared and so we don't shoot the wrong elephant!

The Light, Easy, and Restful Yoke of Obedience

In the first century it was common for the Pharisees to refer to the Law as being "the yoke of the Law", or "the yoke of Moses". The Pharisees referred to the Law in this way because, to them, it seemed like a heavy burden to bear; but as the premier, obedient, Separate/Pure Ones (that is the meaning of Pharisee) of Israel, they would take it up, out of great sacrifice to themselves, to please God and ensure His blessings upon Israel. That is how they saw obedience to God's commandments. It is how we see it as well. Jesus described it as, "…tying up heavy burdens and laying them on men's shoulders then making no effort to help". (Matt 23:4) Peter referred to it as, "…a yoke which neither our fathers nor we have been able to bear". (Acts 15:10) As you probably know, a yoke was a tool or implement for work, and usually hard, sweaty, demeaning work. It meant you were carrying something or pulling something that was very difficult to do, but using the yoke made it a little easier.

In complete contrast, the promise of Christ was that if you took up His yoke, you would find it light, easy and restful to the soul. (Matt. 11: 29-30) This was part of His invitation to those who are, "...weary and heavy-laden..." (Matt 11: 28) by the yoke of the Law. Jesus was promising that if anyone was willing to take up His version of obeying God's commandments, they would experience it as light, easy, and restful to the soul. (Sound familiar? Check out Jeremiah 6: 16 again.) Does that sound like strange language for a discipleship program? Aren't discipleship programs supposed to be hard, narrow, and strict, requiring very high commitment and perseverance? So, let me ask you something. Please think long and hard before you answer. Is that the kind of discipleship program you would enter? Many would say yes and sign up immediately!

The Hard, Painful Yoke of Obedience

At other times, Jesus said things that seemed even more extreme than the Pharisees' view of obedience such as, "If anyone comes to Me and does not hate his father and mother and wife and children and brothers and sisters, he cannot be My disciple. (Luke 14: 25) "He who saves his life will lose it and he who loses his life for My sake and the gospel's, will save it. (Mark 8:35) "He who does not take up his cross and follow Me is not worthy of Me." (Matt. 10:38) "If anyone wishes to come after Me, he must deny himself, take up his cross and follow me." (Matt. 16:24) In these passages, Jesus doesn't just invite followers to take up a yoke, He calls them to take up a cross! Does that sound light, easy, and restful to the soul? Is that the kind of discipleship program you would feel good about joining? Many would say no, immediately cross their name off the sign-up sheet and walk away! Many do!

Keep in mind that in Jesus' day, taking up a cross was not a metaphor for living a disciplined life. You were on your way to execution by the Roman government, and you were carrying the very instrument that would kill you in a terribly brutal and painful way. That is the only correct meaning for this phrase in the Scriptures. It never means, or implies, just starting to live a more disciplined life, like a New Years' resolution to give up something that is not good for you.

So, let me ask you again. Once again, think long and hard before you answer. Which is it? Was Jesus offering His followers a light, easy, restful way of life, or a narrow, strict, deprived, and painful way of life? Was Jesus unaware of the apparent contradiction or was He confused or deliberately misleading His followers? How do we reconcile things that seem so opposite? If you walk the path of discipleship, you will discover that both are true, and the seeming contradiction is only resolved by the actual experience. Let me explain.

Easy and Hard

Pick one of Jesus' commands that seems difficult for you. If called on to obey this command, would you expect to have an experience that is easy or hard? Will you be experiencing a light, easy yoke, or a brutal cross that kills you? As you are trying to keep that very difficult commandment, you may be saying (perhaps to yourself), "This is so hard! How can Jesus expect me to do this? This is impossible! No one can do this!" Sounds kind of like expecting to command a mountain to be pulled up and cast into the sea, does it not? (Matt. 21:21) Now imagine Jesus dealing with this same issue in His life. Was it easy for Him, or hard? When we read about it in Scripture, it seems like it was easy. Now remember that we are not talking here about miracles like healing multitudes or casting out demons or walking on water. We are talking about dealing with all the normal situations in life, both external and internal, that require obedience.

The ease with which Christ did these things did not come from His deity. They came from His complete sinlessness and His unshakable commitment to obedience to His Father. He was the Perfect Man, the second Adam. (I Cor 15:45, Heb 4:15) The temptations that He suffered were just like ours, and He experienced them in much the same way. (Heb. 4:15) They were genuine temptations and trials, but He was able to face them down and defeat every one of them.

Now come back to your difficult obedience issues. What if Jesus could come in as a substitute for you? It would not be significantly different than reading about these in Scripture. You would only see and hear the outward part of the obedience. If you could just have a connection with Him that would allow you to know not only the actions, but also the heart and mind that drive them. Maybe then you could truly grasp how to do this. Maybe then you could also grasp how to follow His commands with ease and joy. You cannot truly love others until you have a transformed heart that is filled with love that will instinctively flow out to them. This would take something miraculous because you know within yourself that you could not reproduce it on your own if your life depended on it. It requires a new heart and new mind. The current well-worn advice to, "Act like you love them, and the feelings will come along later," screams that we do not know how to love out of a transformed heart. This is what intellectual understanding of the Scriptures cannot accomplish, and it is why the evangelical church has not been able to guide Christians into the transformed life that the Scriptures clearly call us to.

Death and life

What if the only way to achieve this substitution was for you to die and then Jesus would come and take your place, posing as you? But the only way to truly make this substitution would be for Him to look like you, sound like you, and live your life in your place—and yet not your version of your life but His version of your life. Those who observe your life in this scenario would think they are observing you, but it would in fact be Jesus. And yet they would constantly recognize and remark that you act and speak like Jesus.

This is what Paul is describing when he tells us, "I am crucified with Christ, and it is no longer I who live but Christ lives in me...." (Gal 3:20) This is indeed something miraculous and you could not reproduce it on your own if your life depended on it; but you can learn to live in the reality that God has already created for you. It is a reality that you are not used to being part of, so you must learn to do it. It requires a new heart and new mind, but these too are gifts of the Savior. This too is what intellectual understanding of the Scriptures cannot accomplish. Being better informed cannot change your inner self. This is also why the evangelical church has not been able to guide Christians into the transformed life that the Scriptures clearly call us to.

It is right to see that Jesus is the dominant factor in each these scenarios, but not by "helping us to do our best", based on our goodness, strength or ability. Yet, we must also be careful not to mistakenly conclude that we can be completely passive in the obedience process. Jesus does not "take over and do it all" while we sit on the sideline watching, as we balance a cold drink and popcorn in our lap. We do not become a spectator as Jesus completely overwhelms us in some miraculously way to accomplish the obedience. Such an approach requires no real involvement on our part and no cost to us. This would not accomplish transformation and it does not develop love of obedience. It was not an accident that Jesus spoke of dying to truly live. Dying always requires your full participation and so does truly living!

Living the Mystery—Both Hard and Easy, Death and Life

Paul tells us that, "Your old man was crucified with Him (Christ) that the body of sin might be done away with..."; (Rom 6:6, parenthesis mine) "I have been crucified with Christ, and it is no longer I who live, but Christ." (Gal 2:20); "...having been buried with Him in baptism, in which you were also raised up with Him through faith in the working of God, who raised Him from the dead" (Col 2:12); "He made you alive together with Him," (Col. 2:13); "...the riches of the glory of this mystery (God's secret truth) is Christ in you" (Col. 1:27). These are among the truths that Paul described as, "...we speak God's wisdom in a mystery, the hidden wisdom which God predestined before the ages to our glory...for to us God revealed them through the Spirit." (I Cor. 2: 7, 10) These are all fine truths that are well-preached and well-taught from many sources, but they are only accepted as truth to be believed "by faith", with no clue as to how to live in them!

What Scripture tells us is that the miraculous substitution that we wish for has indeed been accomplished by the power of God in Christ. When Christ went to the cross, He did not merely take your sins to the cross like an old shirt you gave

Him to carry to the cross. It was also not only some small piece of you. He took your entire old you, the only you that existed before you turned to Him for your salvation, including the You that thought there was a lot of good in You! Before this work of Christ, the old You is all that could have existed. That's all You ever were and all You would ever be without Him. On the cross, He paid the price for your sins, but in the spiritual realm He also put to death the old You—the You without salvation, the You without Christ, the You without obedience to God. However, you did not just die. In Himself, He also took you to the grave, raised you in His resurrection, lifted you up with Him as He ascended to heaven, and seated you with Him in the heavens.

We must not erroneously conclude that we, as individuals, actually traveled back in time through some kind of weird time travel, to be joined with Christ in His death, burial, resurrection and ascension. We did not do these things ourselves, or for ourselves. It was all the work of Christ. It was all substitutionary. He deliberately did it all for each of us and for our eternal benefit and blessing. Then the full value and effect of each of those elements was granted to each one who chooses to believe in Him and follow Him. Each one is among, "those whom You have given Him to receive eternal life". (John 17:3). The full value and effect of His death was counted (assigned) to each one. The full value and effect of His burial was counted (assigned) to each one. The full value and effect of His resurrection was counted (assigned) to each one. The full value and effect of His ascension was counted (assigned) to each one. The full value and effect of His seating at the right hand of God was counted (assigned) to each one. To get the full impact of this substitution, imagine that through each moment of Christ's death, burial, resurrection, ascension, and seating, He specifically and deliberately thought of each and every person that would eventually receive the benefit of His substitutionary work—including you. As He thought of each one, He was saying, "This is for you, (insert your name), so that you may receive the Father's forgiveness and live in the Father's blessing."

Paul tells us, "Set your mind on things above, not on the things that are on earth. For you have died and your life is hidden with Christ in God," (Col. 3:2-3). Why does he write this immediately before he writes commands and exhortations for Christian behavior that are completely about things here on earth, not in heaven? (Col. 3:12 – 4:5, cf. Eph. 4-6) It is a "Bridge of Therefore". Paul is explaining that the source of living out this new life here on earth is not from here on earth. It is "from above"—in Christ. It is not locked up in a vault in heaven waiting for you to arrive there some day to have it. It is also for right now as you live out of your full resources in Christ. When you do this, it can result in a rich, overflowing obedience fueled by grace. Based entirely on grace, it is accessible to you. It is free to you, but it accessed by faith.

These and other declarations in Scripture are the basis for understanding that Christ is our all-sufficient source of a trans-formed life in Him, and this transformed life includes all of what we normally consider "just life" here on earth. This is the "walking in Him" that Paul exhorts in Colossians 2:6. Obedience comes from a free supply in Christ, accessed through personal and deliberate faith. The only limitation is how well you access it. Living out of all that Christ is for you is the fountain of life that allows you to, "…have life and have it more abundantly." (John 10:10) This is a lifestyle that lives, "just as if I had never sinned."

Spotlighting the Cost

Scripture tells us that the natural person that we are from birth is sinful to the core. In fact, the sinfulness flows forth from our core—our heart (Matt. 15:19-20). You could think of it as winding around our DNA like bindweed. It constantly pumps its poison into all that we are. It constantly ruins us from being who we were supposed to be with God. Just like many other defects, it was passed on to us from parents to children. This sinfulness (the old man) is what prompts us, and even controls us, to commit overt sin.

The real solution to sin is not rules or more self-discipline. It is death. This old you must die, and crucifixion is the best way to kill it! But instead of killing you, God takes the death, burial, resurrection and ascension of His Son and applies it to you. It is exactly the same as your salvation. It is an exchange—Him for you—and the benefit comes to you here in this life as well as on into eternity. This process requires you to be actively involved and willing, exactly as you were actively involved and willing in your salvation. You don't cause it or earn it or create it. You receive it as a gift which must be activated by your personal faith connection with Christ.

All that you are right now, including your thoughts, feelings, responses, attitudes, intentions, hopes and dreams, are what you believe is you. These are the things that define you (at least that's what you believe). Giving up of some part of who you are right now will seem painful and a bit scary. After all, who would you be at the end of this change? It is an invisible unknown to us, but there is no way to know unless you actually and sincerely make the change. You cannot make this change by self-reformation.

The "old nature/natural you" cannot be retrained by rules and discipline. The old version of you must actually "die".

This is unavoidably necessary to receive a much better new part of you, making a new version of you each time. It is painful and grieving at first, because a part of the living you must cease to exist. The you that existed must "die" to allow a new you to come to life in its place—usually in small increments. For each aspect of you that must be changed, that old part of you must die and the new version of you must be brought to life, take root and take full charge of who you are—your thoughts, your feelings, your intentions, your automatic responses and reactions, what you find acceptable, what you find desirable, what you hope for, what you wish to be rid of, etc. This must come issue-by-issue, piece-by-piece of who you are, and for this reason it requires your full participation and cooperation. As you learn to actively live in this provision that God has made for you, He works both death to the old you and life to the new you. It doesn't just show up under your pillow at night. *This is the cost of discipleship!*

For example, in order for you to change from a selfish person to a generous person, all aspects of you that have anything to do with this difference must change at the most fundamental level. You must become a person that truly enjoys seeing others receive more than receiving it for yourself. Having a rule that says, "Don't be selfish" doesn't get you very far or for very long. Something far more powerful is required. But how does a corrupt, selfish you make such changes? No version of human discipline will get it done. No version of self-punishment will get it done. Self-discipline and self -punishment may succeed for a short time, but not with a result that is very lasting or enjoyable. The only way is death to that selfish version of you, and God is the only one who can do it. But instead of killing you, He applies the death of His Son to the old you. As He does this, you suffer the pain of facing up to how you really are and admitting it to yourself and to God. This is the cost of discipleship, but it does not come without the painful death of the old you! Is it cost or benefit? Is it the elephant or the old sofa that needs to go to the dump?

When any aspect of the old you dies, you are going to experience genuine pain in your inner being. It is a living part of you, and when it dies, you experience a kind of inner pain. It's like emotional pain, or psychological pain. It can be like the death of a cherished dream. It is the pain of facing the truth of your sinfulness and agreeing with God that this sinful part of you is not pleasing to Him and destructive to you. Sometimes, it can seem just as hard and painful as cutting off a finger. This is why discipleship, spiritual growth and transformation can sometimes be so hard. Sometimes it is excruciating! *This is the cost of discipleship!* Is it cost or is it benefit? Is it the elephant or the old sofa that needs to go to the dump?

The death of the old makes way for the new to take hold and grow. The new you is, "...Christ in you." (Col. 1:27). From His living presence in you, He fills the empty space where the old you was once fixed, making that part of you alive and thriving in Himself. You experience it as a new you. You will sense that something within you has changed, and much for the better. Sometimes it is a very small piece, barely discernible, other times it is plainly noticeable, especially to others. You sense that the selfish you has become an unselfish and more generous you—perhaps only in some small way, but definitely there. You also recognize that this new, small piece of "generous you" feels better than "selfish you". More of this "generous you" will feel even better. You will also recognize that this change did not come from within yourself. It is as if it came from an outside source—because it did!

As you walk the path of discipleship with your Lord, He will lead you through a multitude of these experiences, each one addressing another issue of change that is needed. Repeatedly, He will circle back to a previous issue because He knows the change must go deeper. A bigger piece of you needs to be changed.

The new you will find obedience easier, in fact enjoyable. Over time, this transformation gets bigger and bigger, soaks in deeper and deeper, and the enjoyment also grows to be the dominant characteristic for you—joy in obedience. Obedience now becomes light, easy and restful to the soul, because your soul realizes that the old you, contaminated by sin, was not the real you at all. It was a poisoned, twisted, dark version of you that was no fun at all. You thought it was you, but it wasn't. Now you are set free! Free to be who you were really supposed to be! You were created to be in the image of God, and only that will deeply satisfy you. Now you hunger and thirst for righteousness. Now you long to feed on the bread of life and drink from the crystal spring of the fountain of life. Now you see and feel God all around you as your kind, loving Heavenly Father and Shepherd of your soul. You know the reality of having a pure heart that allows you to see God. (Matt 5:8) This is the joy of discipleship, but it does not come without the painful death of the old you! When you enter into the joy, you finally see the elephant for what it really is—just the big old sofa that has to go! *This is the cost of discipleship!*

Make no mistake, functioning in this new you can often feel awkward at first. This is natural for any human experience.

It is a learning process by a "learner" of Christ and His ways. Sometimes you will experience the change as if you were an unexpecting observer. You will come away saying to yourself, "What just happened? Where did that come from?" As you reflect on this, you must then actively choose the Holy Spirit's prompting to welcome this change and seek that it continues and grows. After some time, you will be prompted by the Holy Spirit to see this as illumination of the distinction between your old man (the natural you) and the new man (the transforming you). Once again, you will be challenged to embrace the new man and shed the old man because you want to become more like your Savior and each taste of that gets better.

Over time, these changes will make you a different person and establish a changing life pathway for you. In small increments, you become a new person on a new life pathway. Over time, you will see the old you and the old pathway fading into the past like a strange land from which you are escaping. Your every thought will be relief and gratitude for your rescue. This will fulfill what Jesus spoke of when He said, "Any man who keeps his life (what you had planned to become and do) will lose it (you will not achieve what you truly desire in your heart); and any man who loses his life (what you had planned to become and do) for My sake (to fulfill what He has earnestly desired and planned for) will find it (you will achieve what you truly desire in your heart)." (Mk. 8:35) *This is the cost of discipleship!* Is it cost or is it benefit? Is it the elephant or the old sofa that needs to go to the dump?

Suddenly, you lift your gaze to the horizon and see that you are nearing the top of the pass. Just over the rise ahead stretches the vast new land. It is the new land of transformation, and this quickens your pace.

CHAPTER 14

THE MISSING PILLAR OF DISCIPLESHIP

There has been a measureless effort by those who have served the Lord in bringing His truth to believers in many venues and many pastoral and teaching ministries. This has been faithful and dedicated labor which has certainly brought blessing to all of us who have learned the word of God through these efforts. No doubt, there will be rewards for those who have labored faithfully in what they knew. All these teaching efforts were aimed at achieving, "feeding the flock of God". We believed that if Christians were properly fed spiritually, they would automatically know to do what the Scriptures command, making them faithful disciples. This was incorrect. This chapter will tell you why.

An incredibly wise person once said: "*The difference between a great idea and great results is one word: how.*" [31] The command of Christ is to teach believers *to do* His commands. This is not only teaching them to *hear His commands.* This is not only teaching them to *read them* in their Bibles. This is not only teaching them to *understand them.* This is not only teaching them to *believe them*. This is not only teaching them that they should do them. It is teaching them to actually do them. This automatically requires, even demands, that we teach how to do them. It is quite clear that this essential element has been missing, or limited, in our teaching and discipleship—the "how" of doing what we teach and preach. *What distinguishes true discipleship from teaching and preaching is teaching Christians "how" to do what the Scriptures teach. Without this final step, we are not fulfilling the Great Commission. We must embrace this!*

> What distinguishes true discipleship from teaching and preaching is teaching Christians "how" to do what the Scriptures teach. Without this final step, we are not fulfilling the Great Commission. We must embrace this!

Teaching/Training

Again, we must remember that ancient Israel was not western. It was Middle Eastern, and it was far more eastern than western. Jesus was not born in Ohio or Georgia, or Minnesota or Kentucky, and neither was Peter or Paul. Jesus is the Messiah, King, and Savior of Israel in the Middle East. The entire setting of most of the Bible, prior to Paul's missionary journeys, is the Middle East. When Jesus commanded His apostles, "...go and make disciples...", He meant it in the way that was commonly understood and practiced by a first century Jewish rabbi in Palestine, not a western seminary professor or theologian. This is the understanding demanded by the claim of "literal interpretation", or more accurately, "historical-grammatical interpretation" to which nearly all evangelicals are anchored.

As described in Chapter 2, the Western concept of teaching is substantially different from the concept intended and practiced by Jesus and His Apostles for making disciples. To make certain we hear what Jesus truly meant by the Great Commission, it urges that we adopt a new word for this. In Western culture and mentality, it is *training*. Thus, the Great Commission becomes, "make disciples...*training* them to consistently do all that I commanded you." When Paul wrote about the value of the inspired Scriptures, he said it is good for both "teaching" and "training in righteousness" (II Tim. 3:16-17). A disciple is a "trainee" and "apprentice" in the ways of Jesus Christ. Thinking about discipleship in this manner is absolutely essential if we are to return to what our Lord commanded us to do! Without it, we will lose discipleship forever, if we have not already done so.

Thus, the Great Commission becomes, "make disciples... *training* them to consistently do all that I commanded you."

What would happen if we saw discipleship as a form of skill training? Have you ever taught a skill to anyone? Perhaps something like golf, or fly fishing, or painting, or photography, or using a computer or gardening, or making cinnamon rolls, etc. I have taken much enjoyment in sports, and baseball was my best sport. If I am going to teach a young pitcher to throw a good fast ball, I must show him/her how to stand, how to grip the ball, how to smoothly position the arm, wrist and hand to the correct position and alignment, how to rotate both the lower and upper parts of the body, how and when to transfer their weight from one leg to another and how to uncoil this whole mechanism to literally hurl the ball toward home plate, snapping the wrist and hand downward with the release of the ball. If they want the ball to have some movement, it must be held or released in a slightly different way. Then I must stand near them and observe how they do this, commenting, encouraging, re-explaining, re-demonstrating, in each correction and refinement until they consistently get it right. When they start doing it right, a cautious smile sneaks across their face because they can feel that they are doing it right. They have started muscle memory. Their smile gets even bigger when batters walk away from striking out, muttering to their coach something like, "He's really fast!"

To teach a young player how to hit, I must show him/her how to stand correctly, how to hold the bat correctly, how to swing correctly, how to balance their weight and transfer their weight during the swing, how to track the ball as it approaches the plate, how to read the spin on the ball and understand how that will predict the path of the ball, how to swing the bat to assure that the plane of the swing matches the plane of the ball as it passes through the hitting zone, and how to follow through completely after contact with the ball.

I never teach these things *to do* by just sitting them down in a room and preaching a great sermon about good hitting and urging them to do what I've said. I never sit them down in a big room and sing songs about hitting, then give them an emotional pep talk urging them to play well, followed by another song and prayer time. Such an approach would hardly be called skill training. If I attended a training for any other skill and discovered that this was the training approach, I would want my money back, and so would you! Why do we think that Christianity and discipleship are any different?

While coaching youth baseball, it was usually obvious when other coaches knew what they were doing and when they didn't. Those who knew what they were doing typically had winning teams because they were actually teaching baseball skills, tactics and techniques. Others were certainly dedicated, sincere and well-meaning, but just stood around shouting, "Come on Tommy, throw hard. Come on Tommy, throw strikes."; or "Come on Billy, get a hit! Swing level, Billy." I can tell you for certain that shouting "Come on Billy get a hit", but not teaching Billy *how* to actually hit, ends up with a very discouraged and defeated Billy who doesn't want to play ball very much. Are you kidding? Not enjoy baseball? It all depends on whether you know how to play well. (By the way, "swing level" is really bad advice.)

The Challenging Truth

I urge you to recognize and embrace this truth: *Teaching and preaching the Scriptures without teaching the "how" doesn't get to consistent, joyful obedience to all the commands of Christ. It doesn't get to Christians who act like Christ by having the life of Christ flowing up from within them. It is not discipleship!* If you don't teach the "how", you are only teaching them to be better

Teaching and preaching the Scriptures without teaching the "how" doesn't get to consistent, joyful obedience to all the commands of Christ. It doesn't get to Christians who act like Christ by having the life of Christ flowing up from within them. It is not discipleship!

informed, and perhaps to believe in a passive mental assent sort of way, but not in a doing way. Thus, is born the Christian who does not become like Christ.

Speaking on James 1:22, Chuck Swindoll once described the problem as, "…like there are giant erasers on the doors of the worship area." [32] This is extremely familiar territory for all pastors. Why won't Christians live out what we are sharing with them from the Scriptures? We are preaching our hearts out every Sunday and too little result is seen. A part of that answer is because the pew-sitting church does not see the Sunday message as being a kind of life-skills training session for today and tomorrow. It is an ill-defined exercise in listening to an animated talk about the Bible because that is what you are supposed to do in church. As long as you listen politely, maybe take a few simple notes, and then say something nice to the pastor and others on the way out, that's what church is all about. Christians don't see the sermon as life-skills training because, while it may inform them, encourage them or spur them, it doesn't train them *how* to do anything.

Here are just a few examples: How many sermons, lessons and devotionals have been produced over the years and centuries about the Scripture, "put on the Lord Jesus Christ"? (Rom. 13:14) What does that mean? How do I do that? What does it mean to, "clothe yourself with humility (I. Peter 5:5), as if it were as simple as putting on an extra sweater? How do I do that? How can I possibly just, "…put away all anger and disputing?" (Eph 4:31), as if it was a pile of old magazines I had forgotten to recycle? How about, "…walk by the Spirit." (Gal. 5:16) How do I do that? The answers are a whole lot more than, "Good luck. We'll pray for you." It is also not, "Brother, you must pray for the baptism of the Spirit." Most pastors and preachers would be loath to admit this.

It is not enough to preach to Christians that Jesus has *commanded* them not to worry. It is not enough to teach Christians that Jesus told us we *should not* worry, giving them a detailed exegesis of what that means in the original languages of Scriptures and then urging them to believe it. We are called to train them *to actually not worry*, and this automatically requires that we teach them *how not to worry*. It is not enough to preach to Christians that God has *commanded* them to "pray without ceasing". It is not enough to teach Christians that Jesus told us we *should* pray without ceasing, giving them a detailed exegesis of what that means in the original languages of Scriptures and then urging them to believe it. We are called to train them *to actually pray without ceasing*, and this automatically requires that we teach them *how* to pray without ceasing. It is not enough to teach Christians that Jesus told us we *should be a "cheerful giver"*, giving them a detailed exegesis of what that means in the original languages of Scriptures and then urging them to believe it. We are called to train them *to actually become a "cheerful giver"*, and this automatically requires that we teach them *how* to become a *"cheerful giver"*. This is true of every command that is urged on us by the Scriptures. Discipleship is not classroom. It is learning consistent and joyful doing.

How many Christian couples are struggling through lengthy marriage counselling right now because they do not know *how* to have and live a loving, committed, giving, kind, patient, forgiving and unselfish marriage relationship? If you learn to live by the other parts of Jesus' Sermon on the Mount, you will never need to know the meaning of His teaching on divorce. If Christians knew how to live in, "Blessed are the peacemakers, for they shall be called sons of God," (Matt 5: 9) and, "… seek peace and pursue it" (Ps. 34:14) the world would be asking Christians for guidance in the way to peace. Instead, we are most known for our petty and destructive bickering, infighting and schisms. Scripture itself condemns those who are divisive.

Now just to be clear, discipleship is not merely a normal training of "techniques" that you can learn at any competent training outlet. The unsaved person or the unspiritual Christian cannot train or be trained in Christlikeness. These are spiritual ways that must be learned on a spiritual level, that is if you can spare some time after softball practice. These are not matters that can be taught by professional counselors and psychologists. No church must hire an army of counsellors and social workers with degrees in psychology. God has a way that it is much bigger and more powerful. His gift is Christ Himself, given to the Church as its head and source of life. (Eph. 1:22, I. Cor. 1:26-31).

The Church is called to show the wisdom and power of God in Christ to the world that thinks they are too smart to consider God as important, or even real. The reason these things are not true in the Church is that so few know Biblical discipleship. Christ will make us able to do this, but we must stop turning a blind eye to the facts before us. We cannot continue to pretend that the emperor is beautifully dressed. We must stop counting our success by the number who enter the front door of the church on Sunday, but not those who steadily leak out the back door, unnoticed.

Take the Test

Ask yourself this question: If someone came up to you at church, or at work, or on the street, or in a store, and asked, "What must I do to be saved?" would you be able to answer them? Similarly, if someone came up to you at church and asked, "Can you teach me to pray?" could you do it? If someone came up to you after church and said, "I noticed that a lot of people were looking things up in their Bibles during the sermon. How do you learn to do that?" could you teach them? These are all teaching people *how* to do these. What we have woefully missed is that it applies to each and every part of following Christ. They need to know how to forgive an unjust wrong done to them. They need to know *how* to control their tongue and *how* not be overtaken with angry outbursts. If you know *how* to do these, it's probable that someone took the time to teach you. You should be able to teach others *how* to do them as well, and you should be delighted to do it!

All in the church who provide any preaching, teaching, discussion or facilitation about the Scriptures must fully embrace this truth. Then, you must honestly and deeply examine the question, "Do I know how to do what this Scripture is saying, and do I actually do it consistently?" If not, you must start there with yourself. Only a true disciple can train other disciples. As you start for yourself, remember you must be learning the "grace by faith" process, looking unto Christ as your source for transformation and obedience. This does not mean all preaching and teaching must cease until discipleship is thoroughly learned. With discipleship being lost for so long, we are all in the same boat—learning together. But you must be on the path ahead of your students, not vice-versa. We are called to lead the sheep, not herd the sheep. Embracing the need for "how" is absolute for true Biblical discipleship. There is a much higher truth that becomes the defining principle. This truth principle is what sets true Christian discipleship apart from all others.

Better belt up and rope up for the next part of the climb! And yet, you may be passed up by the children because they have a secret you may have lost years ago!

CHAPTER 15

LEARNING THE HOW— THEN AND NOW

I f discipleship requires that we teach "how" to obey Christ's commands, where do we find such information. There is precious little "how" in the Scriptures. They teach me what is true and not true, what God does because of that truth, and what certain people in the past did with that truth. How can I learn "the how" if there are no written instructions for this? The historical accounts included in the Scriptures imply a certain amount of "how" information within the narratives. However, that which is given is described in totally different times, cultures, and circumstances, sometimes making it difficult to wring out.

The lack of "how" information might tempt us to conclude that the Scriptures are incomplete, needing the augmentation of man. However, the Scriptures themselves tell us that this is not the case and warn us against seeking any doctrines of men or self-made prophets. It might also tempt us to rashly move back to some kind of Church dogma or tradition, believing that this is the best "how" available. However, the time periods in which these traditions and dogmas were being formed are the same periods in which the doctrines of the Church were being severely corrupted, fueling the need for the Reformation. This doesn't seem like a very hopeful or dependable solution.

Some have moved toward re-establishing the traditional "spiritual disciplines". These can be helpful, but if not done in the right way and for the right purpose they can easily be only another façade for legalism and ritualism. Continuing to call them "spiritual disciplines" instead of "spiritual privileges" are clues that we aren't on the right track with their use, but there is a much better way. To see that for ourselves, we must carefully review the map, all the way back to the first few steps at the beginning.

In the Training Yoke with Jesus—Then

As Jesus traveled around 1st century Palestine, preaching, teaching and healing, He developed a following. In order to hear and see Him during His earthly ministry, you had to go where He was. If you missed Him, you didn't get to see or hear Him. Over time, more and more people came to follow Him. Soon enough, we are told that, "...multitudes followed Him". (Matt. 4:25) This was far more than only the Twelve that we normally think of. (John 4:1, John 7: 2-3) These followers did not leave their homes, family and livelihood to physically follow Him everywhere He journeyed, but anytime He was in the area, they would travel to see and hear Him. Sometimes this was a significant distance. They were developing allegiance to Him and His message. (John 6:2).

At times, Jesus expressly called people to, "...follow Me". (Matt 4:19-20, Luke 9:59) As they followed Him around Palestine for over three years, they were becoming disciples.

This allowed them to both hear His teaching and preaching, as well as seeing the living example of the truth He was teaching them. It was the living portrayal of righteousness that exceeds the scribes and Pharisees, the living example of grace and truth, the One who explained God by all that He was and did (John 1: 18). They could even see things like how He chose His words, His tone of voice, His facial expressions, His body language, and most importantly, His heart for the people He ministered to— things that cannot be communicated in lectures, books and sermons. They even watched Him wash the feet of Judas Iscariot in the Upper Room while his plot to betray was already unfolding. Like all disciples of that day, they knew that He was training them to carry on with all of this, so they did not consider it as superfluous. They did not take a lot of notes and stick them in a notebook on the shelf, then hustle back to the boat for a good night of walleye fishing.

As we read the gospel accounts of our Lord's ministry, we marvel that there seems to be no pattern to follow for many of the situations in which He worked. If there was consistency, this could become the basis for a "handbook", but any such patterns would tell us only what to mimic. They would be superficial, ritualistic, not flowing forth from the innermost life with sincerity and power. It is quite clear that the gospels are not a record of all the teachings of Jesus, and they are not discipleship manuals. They are gospels, and we should not try to make them into what they are not.

Our Lord urged disciples to take on His yoke of obedience. (Matt 11: 28-30) Those in first century Palestine knew full well that a yoke was often used to train a young inexperienced work animal by teaming them with an older experienced work animal. Even today, it is common to use a similar technique to train work animals in a team, such as pulling a wagon, a plow, or a dog sled. An inexperienced and undisciplined animal is harnessed with an older well-disciplined animal. The experienced animal helps to train the younger animal in ways that the human owner cannot. Jesus was not inviting them to take up a yoke based on their own abilities and a new set of rules from Him. He was inviting them to come into the yoke with Him, allowing His strength and experience to train them in doing what He commanded. He clearly described this invitation as the call to, "...learn from Me". Any attentive reading tells us that those who followed Him in that day would have abundant opportunity to observe and hear not only His teachings, but also observe and experience His traits and characteristics. It was as if Jesus was telling them, "Do you want to learn how to forgive your enemies? Come into the yoke with Me and I will teach you. Do you want to learn how to love those who are undeserving? Come into the yoke with Me and I will teach you." They saw "what kind of man He was". Watching and listening every day, they marveled at what He said and did. They stood in awe of Him.

Any honest reading of the gospels tells us that the disciples often did not understand Christ's teaching and could not do much of what He taught them. Sometimes, this would lead to questions about the meaning, followed by further teaching by the Master. Jesus explained that this was because, "To you it has been granted to know the mysteries (secret truths) of the kingdom of heaven..." (Matt. 13: 11, parenthesis mine) This was followed by more complete up-close-and-personal instruction. This allowed the disciples to better grasp what He meant by the teaching instead of being stuck in the pondering, wondering and guessing of the crowds. Better understanding came from personal, direct teaching from the Lord.

Even with the tremendous privilege of having Christ as their personal Mentor, they struggled mightily to see any way they could possibly be like Him. I mean, who forgives seventy times seven? It's not hard to see Peter walking away from that conversation with his mouth hanging open in astonishment at such direction. They were trainees in the yoke, but at that point it was all external, and this would never do for creating a new holy people that are like Jesus.

In the Training Yoke with Jesus—Now

The disciples who followed Jesus around Palestine were able to learn much of the "how" by watching and hearing Him in personal contact. Disciples today do not seem to have the same opportunity to follow Jesus around to develop in discipleship. How can I become a faithful and competent disciple of Jesus now, when He is no longer walking the dusty paths of Palestine or the sidewalks of my hometown? I cannot follow Him around to listen, watch and learn as did the disciples we read about in Scripture. Jesus seems to be rather unavailable right now.

In similar manner, Paul wrote to the Philippians, "The things you have learned and received and heard and *seen* in me, practice these things." (Phil. 4:9) To Timothy, he wrote, "Now you followed my teaching, *conduct*, purpose, faith, patience, love, perseverance, persecutions and sufferings…". (II Tim. 3:10-11) However, we don't have access to the daily journals or videos of Paul nor any of the apostles. In the Book of Acts, we have narratives of the some of the experiences of the apostles and key leaders of the early church, but most of these are oriented toward major ministry or doctrinal events not adequate for any real training in day-to-day being like Jesus.

At first, this seems to deprive us of essential information about how to obey all Christ's commands and be like Him. Most discipleship programs emphasize the need for a mentor, but where do you get mentors who really know what they are doing? Most mentors will be limited to assisting the mental understanding and maintaining self-discipline, but not much heart and not much "how". Most mentors would be very reluctant to say, "Do as I do." All who have been trained in pulpit ministry have been trained to include some application at the end or sprinkled through the sermon. But this usually takes the form of two or three sentences and an illustration or two, and the illustrations typically focus on the mental understanding, not the "how". We must recognize that this does not teach very much "how". If the chain of knowledge was broken centuries ago, how do we restore it?

Christ In You

During His earthy ministry, Jesus' proclamation was, "The kingdom of God is at hand. Repent and believe the gospel." (Mark 1:15) Those who welcomed Him and His message followed Him because they believed that He was the Messiah that would bring the kingdom of God.

In the book of Acts and forward, a surprising change happens that seems to be missed by almost everyone. The message that was uniformly proclaimed by the Apostles and early church was not, "Come follow Jesus". It was, "Believe on the Lord Jesus Christ and you will be saved". (Acts 16:31) Only then were new believers brought into the experience of gathering as the church to, "…devote themselves to the Apostles teaching, (the) fellowship, (the) breaking of (the) bread and (the) prayers."

(Acts 2:42, parentheses mine). It was through this process that they would be trained to "follow Jesus" as disciples, learning to consistently live in His commands and become like Him. This is because something very important happened on the day of Pentecost, and it had everything to do with discipleship after Christ's earthly ministry.

On the night before His crucifixion, Jesus promised that, after He was gone, the Holy Spirit would come to the disciples. In fact, He said it was *to the advantage* of the disciples that He was going away so that the Holy Spirit could come and remain with them forever. (John 16:7) The clear implication is shocking but unavoidable. He said the Spirit would come as the Spirit of truth (John 14:7) to lead and teach the disciples in all the truth and remind them of all that He had said to them. (John 14:26) He said the Spirit would "...take of Mine and disclose it to you". (John 16:14) With the Holy Spirit's indwelling presence, the disciples would have an advantage that they did not have while Christ was actually present with them. The Holy Spirit who would be with them every single second as their Internal Teacher.

Scripture describes to us the multi-faceted ministry of the Holy Spirit. It tells us that the Holy Spirit indwells each and every true Christian. In Romans 8, Paul describes the Holy Spirit by several names, all of which are equally true. He is "the Spirit" (vss. 4-6), "the Spirit of God" (vs. 9), the "Spirit of Christ" (vs.9), "Christ in you" (vs. 10), and "the Spirit of Him who raised Him (Jesus) from the dead" (vs. 11, parenthesis mine). One of the ministries of the Holy Spirit is to fulfill the promises of Christ in John 14-16. One of those is to indwell us to teach, guide, mentor and enable us. This is the fulfillment of Christ's promises recorded in John's gospel.

It is astounding to read Paul's exhortation to the believers at Ephesus about their disobedience. He tells them, "You did not learn Christ in this way, *if indeed you have heard Him and been taught in* (or by) *Him...*" (Eph. 4:20-21, italics and parentheses mine) Jesus had never been to Ephesus. However, Paul clearly implies that as these believers had heard the teaching of the early church, they were "learning Christ". He states it in a manner as if they had heard Jesus teaching them. This is the experience of being in the yoke with Jesus so we may learn His ways well. We are urged to, "...walk in Christ" (Col. 2:6) and "...walk in the Spirit" (Ga. 5:16, 25). As we do this, under the direct tutoring of the indwelling Christ, we learn "the how" of keeping His commandments; and as He teaches us, we become increasingly transformed to be like Himself.

When Paul writes to the Corinthian church, he chides them for not being able to understand more mature spiritual truth. (I Cor 3: 1-2) In doing so, he explains that more mature truth can only be grasped by those who are "spiritual" (thus the essential role of the Holy Spirit). But once again, there seems to be very little direct information in all of Scripture that tells us *how to become spiritual.* The four historic approaches have been tried do not accomplish the goal, yet we continue to promote them. It should be quite clear by now that church rituals, legalism, intellectual explanation of the Scriptures and Pentecostal/charismatic practices all fail at making Christians who are spiritual. Those who are willing to listen to many lengthy, carefully reasoned, intellectual explanations of Scripture grasp only an intellectual understanding of what the Scriptures say. They learn to be a sort of "mini-scholar" instead of being faithful doers of the word. Eventually, they can join into discussions and debates and defend the doctrines of Scripture intellectually, but they do not learn much about how *to do* them. They are just well-informed non-doers of the teachings of Jesus.

When you properly understand the complete unity within the Trinity, the presence of the Holy Spirit is the same as the presence of Christ Himself. However, the connection is no longer external. External teaching and guidance is conveyed through the abilities of the mind. Now, His presence is internal. Now, through the indwelling presence of the Spirit of Christ, Jesus rides around inside of each Christian. This makes His connection with you even more powerful and direct, even better and more complete that the personal and direct tutoring given to disciples during Christ's earthly ministry. Internal teaching and guidance is conveyed to you "in the spirit of your mind". You "get it", but you cannot necessarily explain it (just yet). Best of all is that "getting it" this way includes the personal tutoring, prompting and empowering of "how" that only Christ Himself can give. He seeks to bring you into such connection with Him that it is like the branch abiding in the vine. Through this connection, He teaches you all the how, and it includes every aspect of yourself that is needed in learning. This kind of learning is much more wonderful and powerful than could ever be given by written instructions. Jesus really is alive, and He wants to be your personal mentor and life coach. He teaches you the new life walking in Him! He is your personal discipler!

You won't need to learn artificial and pretended externals because Christ will teach these to you —from the inside out. Externals like words, tone of voice, gestures, and body language all develop naturally from within. You will actually feel His internal presence molding you and urging you from within. His own life will be flowing forth from within you (John 7:38), bringing you along for the ride. Each time you yield to Him, you will feel His presence as He teaches you, and you will feel the reforming of yourself into a new you. The yoke is succeeding! This involves no charismatic/Pentecostal doctrine or experiences, no cultic teaching, no secret formulas, slogans, chants, no pre-packaged presentations, etc. It is simply learning to be spiritual, as Scripture commands and urges you to be.

To fully embrace and activate this, you must follow Him as a disciple, and proper discipleship has not been done very much for a long time! This leaves most Christians in a state of not really understanding or knowing how to do. *We must come into the vital reality of the indwelling presence of the Spirit of Christ.* Only Christ can personally teach you the "how" of obeying His commandments in every situation and scenario of your life. It is part of learning true Christian spirituality. It does not just show up under your pillow some night. You must develop it to use it properly. As Paul states it, "Work out your salvation with fear and trembling." (Phil. 2:12) Unfortunately, for most Christians, including most pastors, this is merely another fine doctrine to be believed by faith, but never understood or experienced! Welcome to intellectual Christianity = churchianity! Discipleship no longer requires you to leave your job, your home, and your family to be with Christ for training. He is with you, and in you! (Heb. 13:5, John 14:18)

We must come into the vital reality of the indwelling presence of the Spirit of Christ.

Without discipleship you will not make much headway in the Christian life, and all these wonderful truths will remain as shadows in the fog of correct doctrine and church activities. Correct doctrine is essential, but it is for a lot more than simply cannon fodder for the pastor's "powerful sermons". Without learning *the doing*, you will constantly struggle with the shortcomings described in Groeschel's book, and you will cheat yourself out of the blessings of transformed living. You will find yourself regularly saying, "Being a Christian is so hard!" That is not the Christianity that Jesus Christ brought to His church, and we have no reason to cling to it like a prized possession! Instead, learn the Christianity that is so wonderful that "it is to die for", like your most favoritest food.

The Church—a Culture of Discipleship

We must be cautious not to conclude that the discipling ministry of the Indwelling Christ is sufficient for the Christian. That is a recipe for a multitude of schisms and cults. If this were the case, the Great Commission would never have been given. Our Lord's instruction to make disciples was given to a group of men who were to carry it out. This is not in conflict with the role of Christ Himself as the Internal Teacher. John clearly speaks of both the Internal Teacher and remaining faithful to that which they had received from other true sources ahead of you on the path. (I John 3: 20 – 27, II John: 9) This is no different than many works of God. It comes through the direct work of the Spirit of Christ, as well as the indirect sources of the gifts of the Body and the fellowship of the Church.

The beginning disciple must learn from other more mature Christians around them, supporting encouraging and nurturing them—those who can say, "Do as I do." This level of mentoring also requires teaching the "how". As they learn from others, they will also learn "how" to receive more and more directly from Christ Himself. This is a normal function of the

Body of Christ as we, "teach and admonish one another..." (Col. 3:16) "...until we all attain to a mature man, to the measure of the stature which belongs to the fulness of Christ" (Eph 4: 13) (Once you have achieved all that, you can spend time running church activities.)

In order to disciple others, the disciple-maker must go beyond intellectual words and mental explanations. It must go beyond theology. It must be more like teaching someone to putt a golf ball or make homemade lasagna. Whatever tools, methods or techniques are used, it must actually put the learner in touch with the spiritual truth that is before them, and with the Lord who gives

> In order to disciple others, the disciple-maker must go beyond intellectual words and mental explanations. It must go beyond theology.

the truth. The students must develop the "spiritual muscle memory". As much as possible, any illustrations, stories, parables, tools, methods or techniques should be genuine—from the mentor's own experience or the experience of others they trust. The disciple-maker must be able and willing to say, "Do as I do", "Try it this way", or "Here's how I do that." Then, if you are paying attention, you can see it happen. The light bulb suddenly comes on! This is the moment the student grasps the insight in their spirit—their inner self. This is the spiritual equivalent of "muscle memory". Along the entire learning process, it is always the teaching of the Holy Spirit that will make the connection for the "aha" moments. This is true spiritual mentoring as modeled for us by Jesus and others who followed Him. From this point onward, they will never be satisfied with a Christianity that is only mental concepts and correct doctrine.

By being part of a spiritual fellowship of other Christians who also focus on these purposes and priorities, you can see and hear of their efforts, successes and struggles. The church is called to be a culture of discipleship. This culture puts discipleship front and center in everything else going on. Every activity or focus must be based on the central core purpose of, "How will this help me to become more like Christ?"

If we would finally properly grasp the function of the Body of Christ and the spiritual gifts, we would see that discipleship is a ministry of the entire Church. Each member must see their responsibility to teach others, as exhorted by Paul. (Col. 3:16) Each and every member of the Church, which is His body, must see it as their responsibility to be fully involved in the spiritual lives of other believers around them. If you know anything that someone else does not know, it is your responsibility to share that knowledge with them. You do not have to be a scholar or be elected to a church office or ordained, or, or, or…. All you must know is how to do even one thing that someone else needs to know. All you need to do is share with someone, "This is how I do that". Then leave the response and fruit to the Lord, but come back to them in follow-up to keep them moving forward in growing. We must be discipling each other as the normal routine in the church fellowship.

You can always tell the culture of any group—it's what you find them talking about all the time, because it is the center of their personal life as well as their corporate life. If you go to the coffee shop in a farming community, what is everyone talking about? Farming! If you go to the coffee shop in a fishing village what is everyone talking about? Fishing! The Church is a community! A church which has a culture of discipleship will be the same. When you come to church, the main topic of conversation is their walk with Christ, their journey with Christ, their path in discipleship. In this culture of discipleship, we must have the shared commitment that "no one gets left behind". This kind of culture and fellowship is so far superior to playing in the church volleyball tournament that it is ridiculous to even compare!

This is the "culture of discipleship" that the church is called to, and it is sorely needed. It is so desperately missing because we do not see discipleship as a kind of skill training. Have you learned to forgive others? Teach someone else how to do the same. Have you learned to speak words of encouragement? Teach someone else how to do the same. Have you learned how to persevere under testing? Put a loving arm around someone else who is struggling and teach them the same. This is what Paul labored for endlessly amongst the churches of his day. (Gal

Would you rather improve your nine-iron shot or learn to have abounding joy?

4:19, Col. 1:28) Why are we satisfied to settle for far less? A successful golf tournament is not a substitute! Would you rather improve your putt or learn to hear the voice of the Master as He teaches you how to be like Him? Would you rather improve your nine-iron shot or learn to have abounding joy?

Only true disciples can teach and mentor other disciples. However, since we haven't been doing true discipleship in a very long time, it is undeniable that we must start where we are and learn together—unless you want to die on this drifting space station. There are, for certain, some amongst us who know this life. It's time for us to seek them out and listen to them. Because of the terrible absence of this knowledge in western countries, we may have to consult with Spirit-filled Christians from churches in developing countries. It is better known in primitive churches there. We must swallow our pride and invite their help. "We must become like little children". (Matt 18:3)

"Unless you become like little children…" (Matt. 18:3)

We like to turn this verse around backwards to make it more useful for evangelism. But it is actually more applicable for discipleship. It does not say, "Unless you become like children and are converted…". It says, "Unless you are converted and (then) become like little children…" (Matt 18:3, parenthesis mine) Conversion is to make one existing thing (or person) into another thing (or person) that does not yet exist. Even though the existing thing (or person) already exists as it always was, it must fully yield to becoming something it has never been before. It is like being "…born again, even when you are old" (John 3: 4). Becoming like a little child is the first step in learning how to joyfully live in His kingdom and His family. You will be learning to be a brand-new person and live in a brand-new way, including a rock-solid Biblical spirituality. Discipleship teaches you all these things.

Because this kind of discipleship and spirituality has been largely absent from the western church for nineteen centuries, it is easy to doubt that it even exists. But it has existed in limited locations and times, and still exists in some small out-of-the-way locations. One of those times and locations was the ancient Celtic church of Ireland and Scotland before the Roman Church returned to the British Isles. Their remote locations or minimal significance granted them protection from the subsequent fallacies of the Roman Church, the Church of England,

and the later modernization of the Church. For many centuries they remained faithful to, "the faith delivered once for all to the saints". (Jude 1:3) The few historical records that still exist (usually word of mouth traditions within these small communities) reflect a rich spirituality that revolved around everything in normal daily life, not just church and church activities, and not theology. They did not all have their own Bibles, and their churches were simple wattle and mud huts. Yet they developed prayers, praises, poems and songs about everything, weaving their simple, but genuine, faith throughout their daily life. Through these, they expressed their deep devotion and fellowship with God in all of life, not only religious life. They learned the true meaning of the word "sacrament", as a "sacred moment", fellowshipping with the God of all grace and love in the most everyday things, all created and given by Him for our blessing.

The quality of these meditations, prayers and poems was in every way equivalent with Deeper Life teachers and writers. (More of this will be described in later portions of the book.) The anglicized viewpoint of the researchers of these ancient traditions may have a diminishing effect on our understanding of how rich and wonderful this spirituality really was. Some of this spirituality carried over into more modern Gaelic culture. In traditional Gaelic culture, a greeting is still spoken as you enter someone's home, "May God bless all in this house". Try it sometime and see what kind of response you get!

You can also still find this sort of experience in locations such as China. Cut off from nearly all the resources and assistance of the "western Christian world" by severe communist persecution, the Chinese church was cast entirely upon the few Bibles they had and the living witness and work of the Holy Spirit. We would find it difficult to describe this experience as anything better than barely surviving; but they would describe it as "thriving", because God used this situation to purify and empower these Chinese Christians to do astounding work. It gave us some of our most valuable resources about living a spiritual life and living out of our position in Christ, such as those by Watchman Nee. These are things we do not know much about in the land of churchianity.

It has been my great blessing to meet a few Christians still like this. One was somewhat like my god-grandmother in the rural Midwest. Later, years later, while taking some seminary courses, I was privileged to meet a fellow Christian who had lived through some of the years of communist persecution in eastern Europe. It was only a brief conversation, exploring development of spiritual maturity in Christians, but a powerful testimony of Christ shone out from their face and in their voice that I have seldom encountered in any American or Western Christian. This is also something we do not know in the land of churchianity—the glory of God in the face of Christ Jesus shining out through the face of believers. (II Cor 4:6, cf. Acts 7: 55-56) Only those who come truly close to the Living God go away with glory in their faces. (Ex. 34:29-35, II. Cor. 3: 7-8, 12-13) This is real Christianity lived out in all of life, not the heavily programed, produced and controlled Christianity of the west.

A dear Christian friend and brother of mine from past years sometimes said, "If you don't know how to worship in a pig pen, you don't know anything about true worship." Been to any worship services in pig pens lately? Your designer apparel won't impress them very much, and Christ is even less interested than the pigs! He doesn't need any of your "stuff". (Luke 16:15) He calls disciples, not fashionistas!

CHAPTER 16

OBEDIENCE THROUGH TRANSFORMATION—PART I

I f you look carefully at the specific commands given to Christians in the New Testament, then compare them to the traits and characteristics of Christ, you will see that they are nearly an exact match. To be sure, there were unique things about Christ due to His complete deity, but if you had followed Jesus around Palestine during His earthly ministry, you would see for yourself that He was the kind of man that He also commanded His followers to be. Being like Christ is the proper goal of every disciple. However, we cannot become like Him by following rituals, ceremonies, rules, intellectual belief or charismatic experiences. Transformation flowing from God's grace is the only way, and this is the way held out to us by the inspired Scriptures. However, for most Christians, it seems that the connection between our grace standing/status and our transformation is blurry at best and invisible for most. At least part of this is caused by our seeking to understand the Scriptures only mentally rather than in a way that allows us to robustly do what they tell us to do.

Transformation is never a thing unto itself. You cannot seek it, nor will God give it for its' own sake. It is not a technique or process. Discipleship is a way of life and transformation is the constantly growing result. Transformation may seem invisible at first, but this is a great misperception. It is consistently manifested in your changed thoughts, feelings, attitudes, intentions, reactions, words and behaviors that are gladly obedient to the commands and teachings of the Savior. This is both visible to others and experienced by you. Transformation is also inseparable from true Biblical spirituality. Thus, Paul writes, "Walk by the Spirit and you will not carry out the desire of the flesh," (Gal 5: 16) and, "…so that the requirement of the Law might be fulfilled in us who… walk according to …the Spirit." (Rom. 8:4) As others see and hear these changes, they will recognize that something hugely important is happening within you. You are being transformed in a way that cannot be explained on the human level! (John 3: 8)

It is not an accident that, when Paul describes all that God has provided for us in Christ, He prays that God would grant to his readers, "…a spirit of wisdom and revelation in the knowledge of Him". (Eph. 1: 17, Col. 1:9) Paul is not speaking here about the Holy Spirit whom they had already received at conversion, nor any kind of second baptism of the Spirit subsequent to conversion. It is the spiritual enabling to more fully understand God's revelation. It is the equivalent of what Christ spoke of as "ears that hear and a heart that understands" (Matt. 13: 15-16). Paul also speaks of this in I Cor. 2: 10-14. It is the spiritual enabling to receive the illuminating instruction by the Spirit of Christ who indwells each one who sincerely believes in Christ. This prayer should be regularly on the lips of each true Christian and especially each church leader. Just keep in mind that it is not a request aimed at intellectual understanding, but for consistent and growing transformation in your life as the reality of God's truth opens up within and through you. If this prayer is not on your lips on a regular basis, I urge you to begin doing so—right now!

Current Terminology

To be sure, others have certainly sought to explain how to live in the truth of our grace standing. They often use the terminology that the believer must "appropriate" what Christ has provided for you. This is intended to mean that you must actively and intentionally draw on Him in faith to receive what He has for you. Some have described this as "living out of your new identity in Christ". This intends that you make deliberate choices for all of your thoughts, feelings, attitudes, words and behavior to bring them into complete alignment with what you intellectually believe (by faith) about being in Christ. A few years ago, a movement/fad swept through the evangelical church prompting that you should ask, "What would Jesus do?" Knowing what Jesus would do is no different than knowing what the Scriptures command and teach us to do. It still leaves the matter of, "How do we achieve that?" All these are sincere suggestions and could be helpful once you truly grasp living out of Christ.

However, based on the observed and reported behavior of most Christians, this terminology does not seem to connect very well until after you have learned it. It seems to elude the understanding of nearly all Christians, including pastors, teachers and leaders. (In confidence, they will express doubt that it is real or even possible.) The severe shortage of true discipleship for nineteen centuries nearly guarantees this result. All too often, these suggestions prompt the same sorts of Christian legalism and human-based self-discipline described in earlier chapters. It still leaves us in lots of "should" and very little "doing".

The terminology of "appropriating" what God has provided for us in Christ seems too nebulous to develop changed thoughts, feelings, attitudes, words and behavior; and it often reduces to blind use of some approved formula. It seems to imply that we get these changes suddenly in one big chunk. It also implies something that is too one-sided on our part, as if Christ were some spiritual vending machine. "Living out of your new identity in Christ" for changed thoughts, feelings, attitudes, words and behavior is also too intangible, especially when there are so few around to allow observation and experience of what this is like. This is like asking us to live out another culture that we are not even familiar with. Most of us have never even touched living out of some alternative or new identity or culture.

Numerous dramas in literature, movies and television portray a character who has suddenly found themselves in a different place, time and/or culture—often not by choice. Sometimes sociologists or students of culture have intentionally placed themselves within an indigenous culture to learn more about it by simple, non-obtrusive observation/participation. Often, missionaries have done this as well. In most of these, the "visitor" had to learn to be part of a different culture, at least briefly. But in the end, they leave and return to their home culture. It was only an experiment.

If we were able to travel back in time to visit an ancient Christian Celtic community, we would be able to see and hear the external expressions of that Christian tradition; but it would not put us deeply in touch with the sources of that spirituality that flowed forth from the heart and soul. It would only be the shell of the life that is within, not the life itself, and many of the traditions that currently survive are limited to that. This will not do!

If you were to abandon your own culture and enter another with the express intention to become permanent part of that culture, you would need one or more personal trainers/tutors to properly mentor you. We would call this "learning their ways". This would be a new reality for you to live, involving not only your actions, and words, but also your thoughts, emotions, and intentions of the heart. This is what Christ comes to do in each and every one of His disciples. He wants you to learn His ways. However, His presence is not external as during His earthly ministry. It is internal, by His indwelling presence in you. Each sincere Christian is called to become an ardent student of the ways of Christ to become like Him. This is discipleship. Let us see if we can find a better way to understand living out of Christ as our resource for obedience and transformation.

Past, Present, Future

When we study what God has provided for us in Christ (summarized in Chapter 12), the time factor described in these passages is one of the most confusing elements to our minds. To our minds, we see some of these things as what God did in the past, and other things that will occur yet in the future. It connects what Christ has done for us with both past eternity and extending forward into what we consider as the future eternity. Yet, they are described as things that are already done or accomplished by God's actions, and the basis for obedience for all those who follow Jesus in all times. They applied to Christians in Paul's time, those living thereafter (including us), as well as those who will live in time yet future from us today. However, nothing in the passages seems to be about right here and now—for anybody in any particular moment of time. How can that be?

These statements do not align with our normal thinking and are genuinely mystifying to us. They appear to us as either nonsense or something that can only be understood by "the experts", therefore of no real interest or value to us. This has been a grave mistake which obstructs the spiritual growth of those who follow the Savior. All the existence we know is inseparably interwoven into time, and we think of time only as linear. To most of us, past, present and future are separate realities altogether; however, as Einstein has explained, time is variable. It can speed up and it can slow way down. It can even stand still!

When the Scriptures tell us that God is eternal, it means timeless—beyond time—unbounded by time in any manner. God is both inside and outside of the constrictions of "time", and yet fully present in all moments within time. He is the "Alpha and Omega, the beginning and the end" (Rev. 21:6). The viewpoint of God is timeless or "eternal". It is only one attribute of God that makes Him "wholly other" from anything in creation, including time. Our position, status and privileges in Christ are seen and described from the viewpoint of ultimate reality. Even though they happened in our past and extend into our future, it is just as easy to speak of them all as in the past, because God made the sovereign decision in eternity past that these would be true. (Eph. 2:4-6, John 5:25) They are absolutely guaranteed. This same language was often used in the prophetic writings of the Old Testament—what would happen in the future is spoken of as if in the past. (e.g. Isa. 53:4)

Even though we greatly wrestle with these concepts, you do not have to understand Einstein's theories to understand how God works in your life. It is far simpler than you think because

God deliberately made it simple, just like the gospel. Do you remember what Jesus said about becoming like little children? (Matt. 18:3) Children can believe that something is true even when they cannot grasp it mentally at all. If a trusted adult tells them that something is true, they are quick to believe it and reticent to give it up later. This is how we get such enduring belief in characters such as the Easter Bunny, Santa Claus and the tooth fairy. When they put on their magic cape, you have to watch them closely to make sure they don't jump off the table or the roof!

The Scriptures do not command us to think in fantasies or a pretend existence. They command us to live out these wonderful provisions and promises by simple faith, even though it is truly beyond our ability to understand. Some may see this as "blind faith", but only faith in a great truth that we cannot fully grasp with our limited mental understanding. It is "as if seeing what is not seen" (Heb. 11:27) It is, "seeing dimly" (I Co. 13:12a) As you live in that truth, by faith, you will gradually begin to understand more than you might think, but it is spiritual understanding, explained by the Holy Spirit who is functioning in you. As the Holy Spirit reveals it to your spirit, your spirit will gradually explain it to your mind. In discipleship, you come to understand by doing. You come to understand the great value and ease of forgiveness by forgiving as Christ commanded. Trying to understand before you do will never get you there. *You must believe before you can see.* (John 20: 29) *Humans always do what they*

> Humans always do what they truly believe! Saying you believe it but still not doing it is an utter contradiction.

truly believe! Saying you believe it but still not doing it is an utter contradiction.

We are accustomed to thinking of a benefit provided to us because of the actions, or inactions, of someone in the past. For a sincere Christian, you know that your salvation was accomplished only by the perfect sacrifice of Christ on the cross in the past. His sacrifice provided forgiveness of the sins of those who had not even been born yet, including you. Yet to have the value of that sacrifice in the past counted to you in the present, you had to decide to fully trust in Him (faith/believe) and His sacrifice in the present. You became convinced that He was the only source of God's forgiveness and eternal life, and you deliberately trusted Him for this gift. The disciple learns that there was more than one gift in the box of salvation! There are many gifts in this box, and yet it is all one big gift—Christ Himself.

In Colossians 2:6, Paul writes, "As you have received Christ Jesus the Lord, so now walk in Him…". Paul uses the word "walk" in this way to mean, "Live your day-by-day, moment-by-moment life in Him". This is another way for Paul to tell us to live our day-by-day, moment-by-moment life out of all that Christ has provided for us. He is the source. That same Savior who saved you by His death on the cross also rose from the dead and ascended into heaven to the right hand of the Father, and is now the living Source for all that you need to become a new person in Him. As you walk in Him, you become more like Him. Receiving these further gifts requires nothing more than your decision to look to Him and actively trust Him as your source for each and every change He wants to make in you—just like you did for your salvation.

You cannot earn or achieve your own salvation, but you can receive His free gift. You cannot earn or achieve your own transformation, but you can receive His free gift. You receive these in exactly the same way that you received His gift of salvation—by earnestly asking Him and fully trusting Him and His promise. They become like receiving the stream of living water and living bread into your whole being, changing your heart, mind, and behavior. It's like receiving a gift card for a free meal at your favorite restaurant and on the way out you discover that the card also provides a free meal every day for the rest of your life. What a gift!

This has been the great secret of many primitive Christians such as the ancient Celtic Christians. Parts of their pre-Christian spiritual beliefs included a version of non-linear time, therefore they found it easier to grasp some Biblical teachings brought to them by early missionaries. When they chose to believe in and follow Jesus Christ in accordance with true Christian teaching, their simplicity empowered them to "just live it". There was no huge array of versions of Christianity from which they could choose; nor did they think of Christian teaching as a theology (i.e. theory) to be believed, professed, but not practiced while they fill their lives with church activities and pursuit of the American Dream. Even though we consider it as vague and confusing, they grasped it more easily than we poor westerners. They did not understand these concepts from a modern scientific viewpoint, but they were comfortable functioning in them as the ultimate reality that was pressed into each moment of their own individual past, present and future. We can also learn to live in that grasp of reality by simple faith. That's all it takes as long as that faith is real! It is not fantasy. It is simple, child-like faith, which means you just do it, and you do it without doubt or hesitation!

Complete In Him, But Still On the Way...

Understanding this time factor in our grace standing also allows us to grasp the reality of how it is woven into each moment of time and life as we actually live it—what we think of as "the present". It is especially pertinent in this era of, "I'm under grace so it really doesn't matter." By not understanding it, nearly all levels and versions of Christians have been shut out of the reality of what they have in Christ. If known at all, it is only a theology, not a living reality. This has resulted in all versions of Christian atheists and all Christians that only believe (by faith) but have far too limited Christlikeness.

The plaguing question seems obvious and genuine. If we are completely forgiven and accepted by God through personal faith in Christ, how can it be necessary to give up sin and change? If God sees me "just as if I had never sinned", why give up sin and change? This is the question at the heart of every discussion, debate and dispute about eternal security and sanctification throughout the history of the church. What did Paul mean that, "...you are complete in Him"? (Col. 2:10) If we are already complete, how can there be commands and exhortations to change our thoughts, feelings, attitudes, intentions of the heart, words and actions? Complete and perfect doesn't need any change!

The status of "complete and perfect" describes what we will have when we reach heaven, fully clothed in the righteous robes of salvation by grace. It is described in terms of "ultimate reality/ absolute time", so it is stated in the past even though it is yet in your future. The essential matter to embrace is that the only reason we can look forward to this future is because God has determined to give this as His gift to each and every sincere Christian. It is grace! It is a guaranteed future because it is established by God's sovereignty as He chose to place you in Christ. (I Cor 1:30)

> "What kind of moment-by-moment life do you want here and now?" Do you want a moment-by-moment life still controlled by the poison and ruin of your sinfulness or controlled and fully alive in becoming like the Savior?

Until that day of "complete and perfect", we are "on the way". On the way is where we live in moment-by-moment life here and now. If a Christian dies, they are immediately ushered into the presence of the Lord in the condition of "complete and perfect" through Christ; but while we are still living here, we are still "on the way". Then the only important question is *"What kind of moment-by-moment life do you want here and now?" Do you want a moment-by-moment life still controlled by the poison and ruin of your sinfulness or controlled and fully alive in becoming like the Savior?*

What the church has missed so badly is that each step "along the way" is custom designed by God as an opportunity for you to embrace and possess part of His "complete and perfect" while you are yet here on earth. Each step of "on the way" is an opportunity to partake of who you will be in the "complete and perfect" future, but you get to have some of that here and now. You are not partaking of the "future you". You are partaking of Christ Himself, who is eternal in the heaven. He alone is the Source of that which will be the "complete and perfect", both now and the future. This enables you to move up and out of the poison and ruin of your sinfulness and into who you were supposed to be—like God. This is one of the elephants in the room that everyone tries to ignore. Over time, most of the church has made considerable effort to deny this truth, so the elephant has continued to grow to the size of a mastodon. Getting this beast out of the room and on its way to the dump is a real task!

The terribly misguided fear that seems to drive this severe avoidance and denial is that it would somehow open the pandora's box to salvation by works, but this is an illusion. You cannot stop needing God's grace, but you can get better. Getting better is not from you but by God's grace in Christ. You cannot stop needing transformation and this is by grace through faith, not of yourselves! Scripture places no limit on this progress! (James 1:2, I. Peter 4: 1-2) It is like the universe—finite, but unbounded. Even Paul said he had not reached perfection, but he also says that he presses toward the goal of having the righteousness of Christ that is *by faith*! (Phil. 3:8-12) The context makes quite clear that he is not speaking of the imputed righteousness that he had already received in salvation, but the righteousness that is imparted as he walked the pathway of Christ. Paul had once believed that in meticulously living according to the Law, he could find the personal righteousness that his heart truly longed for. Now he realized this righteousness is only drawn from Christ Himself, and that is the only thing that brings the personal righteousness that your heart truly longs for. It is an underserved gift, and it is fully available to each and every sincere Christian!

Over and over, Christians have heard that we are incapable of obeying Christ's commandments and teachings because we are so sinful. This is completely true of those who have not come to Christ for salvation. That is why we boldly declare that salvation is by faith alone, not of works. The average pew-sitting Christian repeatedly hears this and concludes that seeking to live according to Christ's teachings is not possible for anyone and certainly is not necessary. However, what Scripture also tells us is that, once you sincerely come to Christ and learn to live out of Him as your resource, you can learn to live out His commandments and teachings! That is why He gave them! He is not so foolish as to waste His time telling people to do what they are incapable of doing. Would you? You will not become perfect while "on the way", but you can get better!

Whether you realize it or not, deep in your heart you also yearn for this righteousness. It is what you would have been before sinfulness so severely damaged the human race. Ancient, imprinted memory lets you remember this righteousness in a faint, dim way and you can't shake it. Before you came to Christ, your sinfulness made righteousness distasteful to you. But you are never truly happy until you have it back, and Christ is the only one who can give it. You must want it with all your heart and seek it earnestly from Christ alone. While still here and "on the way", you can have bite after bite of getting better as Christ makes you more like Him. Once you get a taste of it, you will never be happy with either sin or unrighteousness. This is the life path of a disciple. You must press on to that goal which will one day be finally satisfied in heaven when you are fully "complete and perfect" by consummated grace.

To make the transformation that God desires, you must truly believe that you can be different through the power of Christ. You do not need to remain locked into what you have been. You can get better, step by step, bite after bite! Then, you must deliberately choose and welcome it so that your will is also changed in this regard. Changing your pattern of choices is part of the transformation that God desires. As a disciple of Jesus, you truly have the ability to choose that which is good and right, as well as the power to actually do what you have chosen, because He will flow the grace to you to fulfill all of this. You can and must choose, so choose what you really want. Each step along the "way of Christ" is a step of freedom and transformation as you shed the effects of sin upon you. The change and transformation that is urged upon us is for the glory of God, but it is also for our own benefit and blessing! (Matt 5:16) That's why the teaching we call The Beatitudes begins, "Blessed are those who…". (Matt 5: 3) As Dallas Willard has made clear, these are not how to qualify for heaven, but how to have a blessed life.[33] They come to those who choose to enter the Kingdom of God. You get to decide! Do you want a blessed life? Following Christ as a disciple is the only way to get there!

The Role of Faith

Throughout the Scriptures, God has established the principle that, even though He was providing blessings by grace, receiving these blessings required faith. This is the ingredient that I find routinely missing from the existing ways to understand living from Christ as our spiritual source of becoming like Him. The fall of the human race was precipitated by a failure of faith. Throughout the rest of Biblical history and human experience, God has acted to move those He chooses back to unwavering faith in Him, His word, and His goodness. Obedience flows out of truly believing that God's commands are the path of goodness, and it remains thus to this day.

Chapter 11 of the book of Hebrews gives us a sampling of individuals who took a definite and deliberate action of faith in their life and experienced God's blessing in return. Some of their faith actions involved great miracles, and others involved ordinary things. Some were only a single event, while others spread over many years. Some experienced immediate fulfillment of

God's blessing. Others never did receive complete fulfillment in this life, and this chapter tells us that they still anticipate the complete fulfillment yet to come. (Heb. 11:13) The biggest lesson of all from this passage is that what God brought them through on this path was never easy. It was often very difficult, painful, and sometimes deadly.

Note carefully that these faith experiences required a deliberate and active role. There are no examples of faith as a mere intellectual assent which carried no action. This is because faith is defined here as "assurance" and "conviction". (Heb. 11: 1) They were absolutely convinced. There was no doubt in their hearts that would cause them to waiver. (James 1: 6) It takes real conviction, and conviction is the true basis of deliberate action!

Note also that these faith experiences focused on a specific act or result. There was no fuzziness in the intent or purpose of these heroes. Growing as a disciple cannot flourish in such vague intention as "growing spiritually". No one knows what that really means, and neither do you. If hard pressed, your pastor would probably list a few things, but they usually center on becoming more "well-churched" instead of becoming more like Jesus. Your employer, your coach or your instructor would never accept such a goal from you. Learning to climb mountains cannot be achieved with a goal of "learn to be a better climber". If you don't narrow the focus, you will never achieve anything meaningful, and it is the same in discipleship.

The average Christian sees the experiences of these faith heroes as unattainable, far beyond what they are capable of— hence they never even try. After all, doing some great thing that ends up in the Bible must be only for special people who have special favor from God. When this is coupled with the belief that they cannot, and maybe should not, become like Christ, it immediately stalls any meaningful effort. But God does not call on you to save the human race by building a great ark, to begin an entirely new nation, to part the Red Sea, to lead a new nation across the desert of Sinai, or to put foreign armies to flight. Instead, God calls on you to become like His Son here in your everyday world. This is even more of a miracle than any other described in Scripture. It is not by your own ability, goodness or self-discipline, but entirely by faith in what He has already done for you in Christ. This is clearly what Scripture asserts over and over again. You can and should become more holy, sanctified, loving, kind, forgiving, good, faithful, wise, patient, joyful, gentle, self-controlled, peace-seeking, peace-making people. You can and should become the kind of person that prompts others to think you have been hanging around Jesus—all by the miraculous power of *grace by faith*!

Living on the basis of fully believing what God has said is really true is the entire basis for your salvation. It is also the basis of entering into obedience and transformation in Him. Faith is the element that crosses time, connecting your present to all that Christ has done for you in the past and all that Christ will do for you in the future! That is why those who become like little children do best in the kingdom of God. You might not think that flipping up the switch on the wall will make the lights come on, but you will discover its truth when you just do it! Then you become convinced without mental understanding. Over time, you can learn all about electricity and electric lights, but you don't have to learn it all to operate a light switch. Most of our Lord's commands are quite simple and straightforward. They do not require a complex theology to do them, but they do require willing and persevering faith. They require that you truly believe and trust Him for doing them.

CHAPTER 17

OBEDIENCE THROUGH TRANSFORMATION—PART II

The descriptions and metaphors presented to us in Scripture about transformation are like precious jewels left in plain sight but unnoticed by those who seek the treasure. We miss them because we are either not looking or are looking for the wrong things. The words of John, Paul and Peter all join together to form a wonderous picture of what the disciples of Jesus are meant to be—and can be. However, if we are approaching these passages primarily as doctrine, theology, or "great preaching material", we will never see the picture.

All the passages tell us that we have a great and living Source for becoming who we should be—those like Christ Himself. They tell us that it is His determined will that we be like Him, and that He has done a powerful work to make it happen, starting from eternity past and extending to eternity future. This work joins us with Him in His death, burial, resurrection and ascension in a manner that completely transcends time and space. This work flows His life into us like the vine flows life into the branch. Eventually, this leads us into a life that is described as, "It is no longer I who live but Christ who lives in me." (Gal. 2:20) His life into and through us produces fruit in good deeds and a changed life.

These passages also tell us that we have a personal role and responsibility in choosing, joining and partnering in this work He is doing in us. We must present ourselves to Him. (Rom. 12:1-2) We must build upon the foundation, being attentive in how we build. (I Cor. 3:10) We must be deliberate and assertive about it. (I Pet. 1:5-8) We must embrace, and even welcome, the painful trials that burn out the old man to prepare for the new man. (I Pet. 1: 6-9, 4:12-14) In all this, we must fully believe, trust and receive His grace as we walk in each step. It is a walk of grace (free gift) by faith (believe, trust, align, live).

Living and Growing in the Mystery

Paul tells us that, "The mystery (secret truth) of godliness is Christ." (I Tim. 3:16, parentheses mine); and "the riches of the glory of (God's) mystery in His saints (His Church) is *Christ in you*," (Col. 1:27, italics and parentheses mine). The reason discipleship has been so difficult for the post-apostolic Church to grasp and communicate is that it is based on, and stems from, a Mystery —a living Person who indwells you and stands ready to infuse you with transformations from within Himself. This is a secret truth, not because it is omitted from Scripture, but because it is beyond human understanding unless God reveals it to you and implements it directly within you. This is something that cannot be taught like a course or communicated by a lot of preaching. It does not matter how enthusiastic and energetic the preacher is, or how much s/he waives his/her arms and shouts. It can be spiritually perceived, but may not be logically explained, at least not at first. You can absorb understanding through your spirit (or the spirit of your mind), and then your spirit explains it to your mind, eventually leading to a mental grasp. As Paul put it, "...they are spiritually discerned." (I Cor. 2: 14) It requires Biblical spirituality, but Biblical spirituality has not been taught for centuries.

Remember, true discipleship is life based. The Scriptures play a vital role, but not a focus unto themselves. The ultimate focus and purpose of all the theology and doctrine set forth in the Scriptures is life based. Just because you have taken some notes during the sermon, doesn't mean you have accomplished what the Lord intended in this. Just because you have looked up all the verses and answered all the questions in the "study book" doesn't mean you have accomplished what the Lord intended in this. His purpose is to teach you how to consistently and richly live in the realities of what is described in Scripture! It is wholistic and complete, not only a small "religious" slice of your life. The whole point is to connect with Christ in a way that allows Him to infuse you with His traits and characteristics. It is His gift to you, based on the grace that He purchased for you. It is the birthright of every true Christian!

To choose the pathway of a disciple requires that you *learn* to see all your life in this way, and that God is involved with each and every part. Why else do you think Paul would write things such as, "...whatever you do, do all to the glory of God" (I Cor. 10:31); or, "Whatever you do, in word or deed, do all in the name of the Lord Jesus..." (Col. 3:17); or, "Whatever you do, do your work heartily, as to the Lord rather than men..." (Col. 3:23). These are only a few of the commands of Scripture, but most Christians have no idea how to do these. Have you ever seen any classes on these topics at your church? Every time you take in the Scriptures, your immediate response must be, "How can I learn to consistently make this part of my essential life?" To start, focus on the commands that are general and straight forward. That avoids any complication or confusion about whether it is God's will for you to do these.

As you go about your normal life of "whatever you do", you experience all sorts of thoughts, feelings, words, actions, and intentions of the heart. Each part of ordinary life is an opportunity to live the reality of such things as, "do all to the glory of God", "do all in the name of the Lord Jesus", "do it heartily, as to the Lord", "rejoice always", "give thanks in everything", "always praying", etc. Many things that fill your life are rather mundane, allowing you to focus on more than just the mundane thing. Instead of allowing your mind to wander, daydream or worry, turn your mind to the Lord who is right there with you. Talk with Him in meditation and silent prayer about what He shows you in this "mundane thing". Other things require focus and attention that do not allow this at the time. To properly link each of these to the Savior who walks with you and in you requires careful attention beforehand or afterwards. This can be connected to your morning and evening quiet times with the Lord, with more focused study times, or as you ponder sermons or teachings you have heard. It can become part of reflection on your day or even a single experience or situation in your life. It can come even as your focused prayer, especially when your prayers are focused on God Himself. In each of these moments, be attentive to the voice of the Spirit of Christ indwelling you. He will be seeking to mentor you in living out His word in your daily life.

Instead of responding by initiating some sort of self-reform, you must fully look entirely to Christ, not only as your Savior, but also as being your sole source for becoming a new person. He is your Sanctifier, and He delights in doing this for you. It takes some mental adjustment, but you must see all His commandments and teachings as His offer to build new and wonderful things into who you are. Step by step, issue by issue, this brings you into obedience. As you get a taste of obedience, you also get a taste of what you are supposed to be. You will find it more and more satisfying and fulfilling. Most of us know the experience of feeling good about doing the right thing. How would you like to feel good all the time? You will love it and you won't want to go back!

This is not a place for a lot of guilt trips, self-criticism or self-punishment. It is simply an honest facing of the issues within yourself that are not what they ought to be in order to become more like Christ. As indicated earlier, becoming more like Christ is the true way of becoming a happier and more fulfilled person. I can't think of anyone who doesn't want that. Do you?

In James 1: 5-8, we read a promise that if we need wisdom, we should ask God, asking in sincere faith. James tells us that if we do not ask in faith, we are double-minded and will not receive the answer we seek. A great many evangelicals would be tempted to read this verse as if it said, "If anyone lacks wisdom, let him study the Scriptures", but this is not what it says. James is telling us that even when we have the wisdom of God in the Scriptures, we still need His wisdom to grasp the full and true application for living it out each day. Sometimes this wisdom is found in the Scriptures as we read about the lives of other godly people, but it is within the examples and illustrations of their experiences, not ours. In order to be a faithful "doer of the word" we need God to deal it out directly and personally to us in our own experience.

This simply means that you recognize and fully embrace that God is the giver of every good and perfect gift, and that He gives these by grace when you earnestly seek Him and truly believe for them. James describes it in connection with receiving wisdom, but it applies to every virtue and element of godliness. Do you need patience? God will give that. Do you need strength? God will give that. Do you need courage? God will give that. Do you need kindness? God will give that. Do you need faithfulness? God will give that. Do you need the right words to say something important? God will give that, etc. Along the way, God will do all sorts of things, great and small to prepare you to develop that trait or characteristic. He will confront you with all sorts of issues related to it, including why you want it. An expanded way to move through this, issue-by-issue and day-by-day, might be as outlined in "The Grace by Faith Process" in Appendix 1. As you apply such principles, you must keep in mind the upward spiral of learning and the Principles of Discipleship summarized below in Chapter 18. Remember, this is a way of life, not a seminar or 30-day program.

It is vitally important that, in each of these, you heed His voice rather than deny, avoid, or ignore it as some kind of false guilt response. You must respond to His voice with yielding and cooperation. If you respond correctly, He is going to use all sorts of tools and the circumstance to apply both death (to the old self) and life (to the new self), hard (to the old self) and easy (in the new self). If you do not learn and yield, it assures that the lesson must be repeated again later, extending the pain and delaying the transformation and the joy—and the elephant will remain comfy-cozy at home in your life.

Think about simple people such as the ancient Celtic Christians. If you were to travel back there among them, how would you swing the sickle to cut the hay to the glory of God? How would you milk the cow in the name of the Lord Jesus? How would you catch the salmon for dinner, doing it heartily as to the Lord? How would you gather wood or fetch water to the glory of God? How would you rejoice always as you smoor the fire just before getting into your bed? (This had nothing to do with chocolate, marshmallows and graham crackers.) None of this is "churchy stuff", but it is part of the life of a disciple of Jesus. None of this requires in-depth Bible study, but it is the life of a disciple of Jesus. It is living in His clear commands. Does any of this require that you die to self and live to God? Most Christians, including most pastors, would say it does not, but it truly does! It's all about what you are thinking and feeling toward God, others and yourself as you do them. The way the old you would do these is truly different than the way the new you would do them, and the difference makes all the difference. It is part of the life of a disciple of Jesus.

Now, come back to your own normal life here. How will you clear the dishes and load the dishwasher to the glory of God? How will you drive to the gas station to gas up your spouse's car in the name of the Lord Jesus? How will you unload a truck full of concrete blocks on the jobsite, doing it heartly as to the Lord? How will you churn out a report at work, doing it heartily as to the Lord? How will you turn down the furnace and then the bedcovers to the glory of God? None of this is "churchy stuff", but it is part of the life of a disciple of Jesus. None of this requires in-depth Bible study, but it is the life of a disciple of Jesus. It is living in His clear commands and in His rich fellowship in each of "whatever you do". Does any of this require that you die to self and live to God? Most Christians, including most pastors, would say it does not, but it truly does! It's all about what you are thinking and feeling toward God, others and yourself as you do them. The way the old you would do these is truly different than the way the new you would do them, and the difference makes all the difference. It is part of the life of a disciple of Jesus.

It is both true and normal for you to respond that you don't know how to do these. However, these and many more things that are spoken of by the Scriptures can be infused into you by receiving them as gifts from the Savior. He knew them and He wants to teach you to do them as well. This is part of the mystery of Christ in you and received by personal, sincere and deliberate faith in His secret working in you.

Developing Christlikeness is very real, and it will be real to others as well. There is no such thing as silent and invisible fruit of the Spirit. The spiritual fruit of kindness will be expressed in words, actions, attitudes, intentions, tone of voice and facial expressions that are kind. The spiritual fruit of joy will be expressed in words, actions, attitudes, intentions, tone of voice and facial expressions that are joyful. You will sense, feel and observe these differences as they happen. As others observe and hear these changes, they will recognize that something hugely important is happening within you. You are being transformed!

All this transformation process requires that you develop your relationship with Christ. Developing relationship with Him is very much like developing a relationship with anyone else. You need to spend time with Him. You need to talk with Him. You need to open your heart to Him. You need to share life with Him because He wants to share life with you. You need to listen to Him and seek to understand from your spiritual connection with Him. Because of your position in Him, He is always looking for chances to spend time with you. He is always looking for a chance to interact with you. He is always looking for a chance to flow grace and transformation into you. He is never interrupted when you come to Him or talk with Him. There are no exceptions. You are under grace!

Your relationship with Christ is a spiritual connection that goes along with you every moment of every day, but you must learn to consciously live in that reality. It allows you to receive and enjoy His forgiveness, enjoy His presence, enjoy His love, enjoy His peace and wisdom; but it also allows you to draw on Him for all that He has provided for you out of Himself. This will develop your spiritual senses and functions. This is a vital spiritual connection with Christ which is essential to your discipleship.

The book, *Practicing the Presence of God,* [34] by Brother Lawrence has been a favorite for many Christians over the years. It is quite simple and general, and when we read it, we are automatically drawn to a life that reflects his life focus. Unfortunately, it contains no instruction in how to start taking this approach in your own life. I found the more recent book, *Practicing God's Presence* by Michell and Diane Cook [35] more helpful for a basic tutor and guide for those who seek to start walking this path. It is designed to be used as a thirty-day experience, but I recommend that you stretch it out over a much greater time, taking only one exercise and example per day or even one per week. Another good source is the daily devotional guide, *Jesus Calling* by Sarah Young. [36] This will help you follow the essential principle that discipleship is deliberate and intended to be a consistent experience with Christ as your mentor. It is not merely for the "religious", "spiritual" or churchy moments. After all, discipleship is about consistent doing in all of life, not only the "religious" or "spiritual" part of life. This is the kind of vital spiritual connection you must seek with Christ.

The Wonderful Surprise in Discipleship

Work your way through the following thoughts. Think carefully, deeply, honestly.

1. Do you think that Jesus Christ was a very unhappy person?
2. Do you think His life was a drudgery of unfulfilling things, day after day? (After all, all that religion stuff eventually gets boring.)

If that were the case, how could He possibly, in good conscience, say something like, "These things I have spoken to you so that My joy may be in you and your joy may be full"? Praying to the Father the night before His death, He would pray, "... these things I have spoken in the world so that they may have My joy made full in themselves". (John 17:13) He told the disciples, "Peace I leave with you. My peace I give unto you." (John 14: 27) Does Jesus offer false or misleading promises? No, Jesus was perhaps the happiest man that ever walked the earth, and He wants to give it away to those who follow Him. Yes, I mean give it away to you!

Christ was also called "Man of sorrows and acquainted with grief", so He was not happy all the time. He did say that He had no place to lay His head. (Luke 9:58) He had His Garden of Gethsemane where He said, "My soul is now sorrowful unto death." (Matt 26:38) He suffered cruel torture and death on the cross crying out, "Father why have you abandoned Me?"

(Matt. 27:46). But those were not what primarily defined Him or His life other than at certain times. Most of His life was full of joy, full of love, full of forgiveness, full of kindness, full of creativity, full of knowledge, full of wisdom, full of peace, full of strength, full of courage. This is the kind of person He wants you to become as well. He is the only one who can give you these things, and He wants to. What reason could you possibly have for not wanting to be like Christ? Discipleship is the only way to get there. This is His promise and determined will for you.

A surprising and wonderful benefit from the transformation process is that Christ wants for you is to become a person of happiness and peace. This does not depend on your temperament or personality or personal background. All that you inherit genetically, as well as all you experience in life and how you respond to your experiences, are what makes you who you are. This means that all the sin within you, and all the sin that has happened to you from other people and the situations that you have encountered are very big factors in shaping you to be you. We were never meant for sin. We were meant to be in the image of God. That is how the human race started, and we are never truly happy and satisfied until we recover to that now distant shore. We are all victims of sin, both internally and externally, and it warps us into what we were never intended to be.

What many do not realize is that our inherited sinfulness (our sin nature) creates within us a deep internal conflict which functions constantly, even though you are minimally aware of it. This is what Paul describes briefly in Gal 5:17, Romans 2:14-15 and more completely in Romans 7. Whether we are talking about the moral person who wants to do right out of the instinctive/internal moral law within us, or the Jew who wants to do right based on the Mosaic Law, or the Christian who wants to do right based on the teachings of Jesus and the Apostles, there is always conflict within us about doing right and doing wrong (and enjoying it). These internal and competing impulses torture us and tear us apart, turning all moral choices and actions into an internal war. And let's face it, moral issues are woven into far more things in life than we might think. No matter what we propose to do or not do, part of us is saying, "No, don't do that"; or, "Why did you do that?" This is just like living with someone who constantly criticizes you. It's terrible! This conflict makes us deeply unhappy on many levels and prompts us to "act out" on other issues because of the struggle that is going on within. I can assure you that abandoning objective morality will not solve the problem or the conflict. It just drives it deeper underground, makes it more painful, and makes it harder to overcome. This internal conflict cannot be escaped except through Christ and His indwelling Spirit.

When you start making progress in overcoming sin in your life, you discover that you didn't really like sin in the first place. It makes you feel terrible. It contaminates you, poisons you, twists you, and makes you dysfunctional in numerous ways. It ruins your life, and yet it is very difficult to escape no matter how you try; but Christ can bring you out of this! This is one of the most wonderful parts of discipleship, and you will see for yourself how wonderful it is.

The Perfect Family Tree

Try to imagine who you would be right now if sin had never occurred in the world, but your family tree was exactly what it is. Your family photo album would have all the same faces in it. You would have all the same genetic inheritance, but with absolutely no effects of sin whatsoever. What would that version of you be like? It would be a sinless you. You might not even look the same because sometimes the effects of sin can produce noticeable changes in your appearance. What would a free-from-sin you be like? What would a free-from-guilt you be like? What would you be like if you were free-from-internal turmoil? That is what you were meant to be. That is God's wondrous goal and plan for you. This would be a version of you that is like Christ. You would not be deity or supernatural, you would just be a sinless you, a sinless human, and this would make you feel incredibly free of internal conflict!

Discipleship under Jesus brings you into this wonderful reality! You will find yourself saying, "At last, something that really changes me! At last, I am becoming who I was supposed to be—one who is in the image of God—one who is connected to my Heavenly Father in a deeply satisfying and fulfilling way! I feel His love! I feel His beauty! I feel His peace! I feel His joy! I feel His power! This is the wonderful freedom gifted by Jesus to His disciples.

My prayer for you is Ps. 4:6a-7, "Lift up the light of Your countenance upon us, oh Lord. You have put gladness in my heart, more than when their grain and new wine abound." Do you believe that God wants to bring you into such overwhelming joy and blessing that you can barely stand it? True discipleship is the only way to have them. I hope you will decide to walk that path. You too will become a new traveler on an old pathway. You will be amazed at how the ancient footsteps will seem to fit your stride, as if they were made just for you. In a mysterious way, they were meant just for you!

Feel like you are hanging on with only five fingertips yet? Time to learn to fly!

CHAPTER 18

THE PATHWAY
FOR DISCIPLESHIP

Some basic principles

The long imagined secret pathway for discipleship is just that. It is imagined. On the other hand, the pathway that does certainly exist centers in the issues and principles set forth in the Scriptures by Christ in His commandments and teachings. These are absolutely the pathway that He established. Even though He arose from the grave and ascended into heaven, the Holy Spirit continued to give His, "…whole truth" (John 14: 26) to His apostles and prophets. This what He promised, and this is exactly what He did. They then passed this complete body of truth to the church to complete what we have as the New Testament. It is the work of the Holy Spirit taking the full truth of Christ and revealing it to His church. (John 16:14) Thus, the entire New Testament, is the "word of Christ". (Col. 3:16) The pathway for discipleship is laid down in these commandments and teachings and in no other way. Christ Himself taught that the Old Testament Scriptures also speak of Him (John 5:39,

Luke 24: 27). Thus, in a larger sense, the entire Scriptures are the word of Christ. The only reason it has seemed like a secret pathway is because we have pursued our Lord's teachings and commandments as doctrines rather than a way to live by committed obedience and transformation.

Firmly securing the outer border of these magnificent truths, beyond which no one is to transgress, is the clear statement from John that once these writings were completed by the Apostles, "going on further" was "…not abiding in the teaching of Christ". (II John 9). It is only our neglect of obedience, the narrow focus on theology/doctrine and the erroneous pursuit of churchianity that have obscured our eyes from this path, even though it lay before us quite clearly. It will always remain obscured to those who continue to take the wrong path. The way of obedience always follows the principle of, "I will obey as much as I know and then eagerly wait for more of the pathway to be shown to me." The pathway for each individual takes living shape in our daily lives as we follow Him in all of our moment-by-moment experiences.

This does not cast us backward into some Christianized version of the Mosaic Law. Instead, it springs us forward into the fullness of God's administration through Christ and the fulfillment of living fully and joyfully to glorify and enjoy God in all things. Sometimes this leads us into green pastures and alongside quiet waters, munching and drinking our fill while we lounge about in comfort. Other times, it leads us through the Valley of the Shadow of Death. Even there, "His rod and staff comfort me"; and, "He prepares a table for me in the presence of my enemies" (Ps. 23:4-5). This teaches us to display His transforming presence in our lives and to meet not only the Mosaic Law, but the far higher, "…requirement of the Law." (Rom. 8:4) in ways which vastly exceed the righteousness of the scribes and Pharisees, but without the Mosaic Law as the basis. It is entirely by faith in this transforming Savior and Sanctifier. It was God Himself who promised, through the prophets, that a New Covenant would be established by God to accomplish His ultimate purpose and plan for Israel and, "… all the Gentiles who are called by His name" to inherit salvation and equal citizenship in the Kingdom of His Christ. (Amos 9: 11-15, Acts 13:47, Act 15:16-17, Rom. 15: 12)

There is no inspired "instruction manual" which teaches us how to, "walk in Him (Christ)" (Col. 2:6, parenthesis mine). Every time we seek such, it reveals that we seek only a legalism that is superficial and more comforting, yet unsatisfying. This may seem very disheartening and confusing for those who believe they must understand it before they can believe it or live it. In order to implement the commands and principles in Scripture, each sincere Christian must seek the mentoring of Christ as their own personal Teacher and Shepherd, and He invites and welcomes this relationship. However, this will not simply be more theory/theology/doctrine and head-knowledge. *Disciples must embrace that living it is the path to understanding it.*

Disciples must embrace that living it is the path to understanding it.

In some ways, the exact pathway for each disciple will be as unique as each individual. I have had to face the truth that our wish and search for a simple-to-follow, dot-to-dot pathway springs from our sinful desire to marginalize God and keep enjoying our worldliness most of the time. This follows a church culture that has lasted many centuries and wants to continue as long as possible. "I would like three dollars-worth of God, please." [37] I urge you to confront this in yourself and fully embrace true discipleship. Despite the variations of differing individuals and cultures, basic human nature is largely uniform, therefore the basic principles and matters for discipleship will be quite similar for all. It is only the application of the principles that may tend to be somewhat unique. There is more than sufficient commonality that easily allows mutual interaction, discussion, guidance and prayer with other Christians around you as they are also pursuing discipleship.

These matters ought to be the common interaction and fellowship amongst Christians, not the weather, sports, politics, or the stock market. This is what would constitute a culture of discipleship within the churches. There is no reason or basis for hesitance, reluctance, embarrassment, avoidance, or carefully guarded secrecy as we pursue these absolute essentials together as the body of Christ. This is what we are supposed to be about—nothing else, nothing less. Is that a church culture you could fully embrace and be glad to be a part of??

Patterns of Progress

All human learning tends to be cyclical, much like an upward spiral. You cannot learn anything in a complete and perfect way the first time. You must initially learn to the extent you can, move on, then come back when you are ready to learn more. Don't try to learn to do hard things from the beginning. This is an almost certain recipe for superficiality and legalism—head knowledge, not life knowledge. However, what is hard or easy for you may not be the same as for another, so each person must take the approach best suited for them. In baseball, you cannot learn to hit a really good curveball until you learn to hit generally. Once you develop good form and skill hitting an average fastball, you can then learn to hit an average curveball, then an average slider, then a better fastball, and curveball, etc. In mathematics, you don't learn trigonometry before addition and subtraction. In piano, you don't learn to play Mozart until you first learn a great many basics. The first song you play is likely to be something very simple; but if you persevere, you can eventually play Mozart.

I have likened discipleship to skills training, and there too, you learn first things first, then move on to other things. It will be similar with Biblical discipleship. Once you learn a basic at the entry level, you can move on to the next basic at the entry level, then the next, etc. At the same time, you will also be moving upward along the learning curve. You will find that each matter strengthens the others, moving you onward and upward along the learning spiral. This is why you cannot learn discipleship in a thirty-day journey or week-end retreat.

Always remember these six principles. You must be ruthless in application of these:

Principle #1:

Biblical discipleship is based on, and flows out of, the inspired Scriptures of the Bible, the word of God. You must see the Scriptures as the powerful flow of the heart and mind of God, living and effective if you sincerely seek to obey it. This will not demand that you understand a lot of really complex theology. You will be surprised at how simple it can be as you learn to become like a child in the kingdom of Christ.

Principle #2:

Biblical discipleship must be deliberate. There are two ways to implement this principle. Some aspects of discipleship can be structured. This is specifically true of taking in God's word. There are many good sources for taking in the blessings of the Scriptures as instruction, encouragement, strength, support, and to express devotion. It is truly as Paul stated, "It is the power of God to salvation for everyone who believes…," (Rom. 1: 16) It is also, "…profitable for teaching, for reproof, for correction, and training in righteousness, that the man of God may be adequate, equipped for every good work." (II Tim. 3:16-17)

However, discipleship is about genuine daily life. All the teaching, reproof, correction, training, nurturing, comforting, etc. will be about you in real life. As such it will often seem unstructured or "serendipitous". Even though it seems that way to you, you must keep in mind that it is all part of a very deliberate plan by your Savior and Mentor, Jesus Christ. Pay attention, learn well and learn to journal so you don't forget and don't lose your place.

Discipleship is about a changed life, not a process or program. All that the Lord will do in discipling you is entirely about molding you into that new person who is like Him. It is about changing you at such a deep level that you live a new and different kind of life because you are becoming a new person. You will be developing a new lifestyle that will be permanent, not temporary just because "you are doing discipleship right now." You don't "try discipleship for a while" to see what it is like and then move on to something else that catches your fancy. This is churchianity at its worst.

The best news of all is that there is no need for you to quit your job, sell your house and car and go off to some secluded place to learn all this. It can, and must, be learned along the path of your normal life. Christ will use all the events and situations in your life as tools and opportunities to teach you what He wants you to know and be.

Principle #3:

You will look constantly to Christ Himself to be your teacher and mentor through His indwelling Holy Spirit. He is the only one who can properly and fully disciple you because He has direct access into your heart, mind, soul and spirit. The many tools and resources now available as well as the guidance and support from other believers who share this same road are only tools to help you along the way. They never become a substitute for the Living Master, thus avoiding the pattern of, "I am of Peter", I am of Paul", "I am of John". (I Cor. 3:4) You will always look and listen for the voice of your Teacher through His indwelling Holy Spirit. He will guide, open, explain, illumine, and give the connections we would describe as "ah, now I get it". As the Holy Spirit teaches you all things, He is taking the things of Christ, your Savior, Lord and Teacher, and revealing it to you in direct illumination of the word of Christ. It will be a common experience that as you are doing something by faith, He will suddenly instill in you a new insight and a new piece of transformation to match. You will suddenly realize that you understand and grasp something in an entirely new and better way. One of these subjects will be a better understanding of yourself and you will look forward to seeing the changes in yourself. Others will too and be amazed.

Principle #4:

Discipleship is a life-long journey. I promise you there is no end in what you can learn in becoming like your Lord. You will not "run out of material". There are no "glass ceilings", except those falsely imposed by churchianity. The only boundary is the full truth of the Word of God, stated this way, "...until we all attain to the unity of the faith, and the knowledge of the Son of God, to a mature man, to the measure of the stature which belongs to the fullness of Christ." (Eph. 4: 13). (Once you finish this, you can spend time running the church softball tournament.)

What is Deliberate Discipleship?

Since discipleship is very life-based, it can seem disturbingly random, serendipitous and mystifying. This can seem frustrating to a systematic thinker. It is downright unsettling to those who think that Christianity can be reduced to a ritual or canned programmed. You can rest assured that, since God is actively and deliberately working all things for your good (Rom 8: 28), and since His version of "good" is, "...your sanctification" (I Thess. 4:3), it will not be random on God's part. There is no such thing as "random" or "chaos" for the infinite knowledge and wisdom within the mind and heart of God. After all, we are dealing with the Living God who really exists, infinite in both knowledge and wisdom. If you struggle with "random and serendipitous", it probably means that God wants to teach you how variable real life actually is, and that you cannot control it to fit into "your program" or plan. You must learn to surrender into His hands, allowing Him to carry you along. Each moment and step is a step into a new and unknown future.

Sports gives us a helpful illustration of deliberate improvement. When players arrive at pre-season training, managers and coaches already have very specific skills that they know you need to improve in the coming year to continue developing your skills and effectiveness. This is based on statistics on how you performed last year and the observation of other more seasoned veterans of the sport. The statistics and observations tell them where improvements are needed. Any player who wants to assure their place on the team better arrive with their own awareness of how they need to improve. Better yet, they would have worked on those skills in the off-season. A second baseman might say something like, "I need to turn the double-play better when the throw is coming from the shortstop in a deep position." Left fielders might say, "I need to improve my throw to third base from deep right-center field." During spring training and into the season, they would spend extra time working on improving those skills in addition to their general skills. This is deliberate skill training, and disciples of Jesus must also have it.

Discipleship skills and training cannot be programed and tracked like other skills. It would be most foolish to develop a computer software that guides you in doing this, along with daily prompts to remind you and a graph of your results. However, your mentor, Christ, has a very deliberate plan for your discipleship. Simply living your normal daily life and walking with the Lord will reveal a variety of things that you need to improve to be Christ-like. It is essential that you pay attention to these, using them as prompts to see what God is doing in your life and how you should respond.

Your everyday life combined with the witness of the Holy Spirit should make you aware of what you need to work on to grow in Christlikeness. This tells you what you need to improve, and Christ stands ready to work with you in making these improvements. Do you need more patience? He will tutor you in that if you genuinely seek Him. Do you need more openness and acceptance? He will tutor you in that if you genuinely seek Him. Do you need more self-discipline? He will tutor you in that if you genuinely seek Him. This must be deliberate!

If you are paying attention, you will begin to realize that your life is becoming a long string of "God things", both large and small. God's plan for you is to unfold His will in your life one moment at a time. Little, if anything, will seem "miraculous". The unique and most important thing about Biblical discipleship is that you must *learn to do*. Otherwise, it just becomes another learning of theoretical concepts (theology) and will not transform you or make you like Christ. This path can still be deliberate on your part by your determined decision to walk in each "random" step as God leads you into and through it. This makes your whole life a bit like what is pictured in the Christian classic, *Pilgrim's Process*.[38]

No matter how serendipitous or deliberate each step of change is, it must all be pursued in faith- focus on Christ as the only one who can send these changes into you out of His riches of grace. He is your source and mentor. Many of the steps may seem small, but you must take these steps of small obedience. Over time they will build to become large changes. This is the only way to build real change in human beings. This kind of change is permanent and changes the entire person. This is what God is interested in, nothing else, nothing less.

The first deliberate step you must make is to step onto this pathway of discipleship with the full resolve to never turn back! As you do so, you also become a new traveler of the ancient path. Oh, hear the voice of your Savior and Shepherd calling you to this path! Start now!

CHAPTER 19

CENTERING YOUR LIFE IN GOD

What was the center of Jesus' life?

As a disciple, you will be learning to become like your Master. Of course, Jesus knew the Scriptures perfectly, and quoted them routinely to explain His teachings, responses, actions, reactions and plans. Therefore, most discipleship programs consist of learning the content of the Bible more thoroughly, starting with techniques for daily Bible reading/study/memorization, and prayer in a daily quiet time with God. Then they proceed to studying the basic theological issues such as Salvation, the Bible, God, Christ, the Holy Spirit, Sanctification, the Church, and sharing the gospel with others. To be sure, these are all important matters to include in discipleship, but it is not the place to start. There are good resources already available for such studies, as well as guides for your daily quiet time/personal time. However, as a disciple of Jesus, you must know more than what the Scriptures say and mean. We must know the "why" and "how" of doing what they teach, and I have yet to see any such studies or guidelines that teach you much of the why and how. Without the why and how, the "what" will only become something to fill up your head and notebook, rather than filling up your life with transformation. We must start at a much more foundational level.

If you had been walking the paths of Palestine with Jesus in the first century, day in and day out, you would not start with Bible study. Even though His first disciples began to follow Him very shortly after His baptism and temptation, (John 1: 35 ff) there is no hint in the gospels that Jesus started them in discipleship by teaching them basic Biblical theology. He didn't even teach them how to pray until Matthew 6, which scholars tell us was at least six months after they met Jesus. It is clear that Jesus taught His disciples in private (Mark 9: 30-31, Matt. 10:37). We don't know the extent or frequency of this private teaching. The teachings that are included in Scriptures are almost entirely those given in public, but there was a lot of time spent walking the roads of Palestine and sitting around in the evenings. They certainly did not sit around in silence all these hours and days. I suppose you could speculate that this private teaching and discussions included what we would call theology, but it is an argument from silence, which doesn't hold much water or certainty. Approaching discipleship as teaching basic Biblical theology automatically produces intellectual Christianity—knowing and believing what you should know and believe, but not knowing how to do anything with it, and quite frankly not really, really believing it either. This has always been the biggest problem for the Church, and still is.

Based on Christ's teachings that are recorded for us in the gospels, we see that the teaching and training by Jesus was very life-based, not theology based. The few such conversations with the disciples that we have in the New Testament clearly demonstrate this. Why? Thorough and regular instruction in doctrine seems essential to training disciples, however record of such instruction seems extraordinarily missing from the gospels. As I pondered this, there appeared to be no answer. But suddenly it dawned on me that, as McDowell had said, the disciples learned the "theology" and "the answers" to many of their questions just by following Him around, listening and watching (and marveling). As they did this, they consistently saw a number of fundamental truths in His teachings and portrayed by His example. The truths came wrapped in the clear portrayal of how to live them out. They saw that these truths went all the way to the core of His being. He lived in these truths as naturally as breathing. In fact, they seemed to flow forth from His whole self. He wasn't only repeating the teachings of others or giving them "His view" of certain theological interpretations. He knew the absolute truth from within His being. He was the Truth in human flesh. As part of these core beliefs, He knew the absolute truth that if you really, really believe something, you will consistently implement it into your life. It is an absolute fact!

> To say that Jesus lived all of life on the basis of really, really, believing that what God says is the absolute truth is the same thing as saying He lived a life of absolute real faith. God's truth defines reality!

To say that Jesus lived all of life on the basis of really, really, believing that what God says is the absolute truth is the same thing as saying He lived a life of absolute real faith. God's truth defines reality! For some reason, we have always talked about how hard it is to have faith like this. Once again,

Brian Burson

for our purposes here, we are not talking about faith healing or performing miracles, but the ordinary day-in and day-out issues that He faced during His life and ministry. However, it can, and should be, just as easy for us as it was for Jesus. What we experience as difficult and arduous is our sinful nature fighting back against obedience, not against having faith. We know within our own minds and hearts that, if we admit we believe something as God's absolute truth, we really must do it. So, we play a little manipulation trick on ourselves and God to avoid guilt. (Sin is always deceitful.) We cast the blame on our inability to have faith rather than our unwillingness to obey. "Has God really said...?" Sound familiar? (Gen. 3:1) If you confront this duplicity within yourself, refusing to co-operate with it anymore, you will take a giant step forward in living out your faith.

Do a quick check within yourself right now. What prompts your sense that obedience is hard once you know what God really says? For example, take the command, "Give thanks in everything." (Eph. 5:20) How many interpretations could there possibly be of that commandment? So, if what it means is clear, do you do it? Why not? If you have good self-awareness, you will quickly discern that the real problem is the obedience part. Down deep inside, you really don't want to give thanks to God in everything. This is your sinful nature fighting back against obedience. It is exactly the same attitude that drove the lawyer's question to Jesus, "Who is my neighbor?" (Luke 10:29) As any good lawyer knew, if he could obfuscate the meaning of "neighbor", he could excuse dis-obedience. Even though you may be surrounded by much evil, you can also find good things in most situations. Those good things are all from God, and you can give thanks for all of them with an open heart. He is the Giver of every good thing. (James 1:17) Even if you think your circumstances and surroundings contain absolutely nothing good that prompts you to give thanks, you are also surrounded by God and all He is doing. Do you really believe that God is not doing anything in evil circumstances? You are wrong! (See Habakkuk 1: 5 and John 5:17) This alone can be the basis of giving thanks. (Rom 8:28-30) This cannot be superficial mouthing of words, or pretense, but must be completely sincere and real.

For Jesus, living in the truth as the factual reality was the only thing that made any sense at all. All other approaches to life would be some kind of insanity. Others who listened and watched Him live this out sometimes concluded that He was either insane or demon possessed. (Mk. 3:21, John 8: 48, 10:20) It was a classic example of, "Those who danced were thought to be quite insane by those who could not hear the music."[39] (If you decide to live a life of absolute faith, you may also be thought to be insane.) It was Jesus' deliberate determination and decision to be in complete cooperation and obedience to absolute truths, and it mattered not to Him that others did not understand or agree. He was merely walking in the truth. To Him, this was normal human behavior based on true faith. As the disciples watched this over a period of years, they could see for themselves that living this way is what made Him so happy, satisfied, fulfilled, calm and confident. They would automatically want to learn to live this truth, but that would mean they need the same kind of faith. Jesus tells them that if you have faith the size of a mustard seed, you will do mighty acts. However, miraculously moving mountains is not the issue. Not even Jesus did that! The issue is that the *amount* of faith is not what counts—it is the *purity and reality* of the faith.

Centering Your Life in God

Although missed by most scholars and theologians that I have ever read, there was something truly unique about Jesus that differed from other teachers and masters that the disciples might have followed, and it didn't take a bunch of scholars to discover or define it. The average person who followed, watched and listened to Jesus for very long would have noticed this rather quickly. *Jesus knew and believed, to the depth of His heart, the core truth: His Heavenly Father is at the center of everything. Everything!* Here are some of Jesus' statements that declare this:

> Jesus knew and believed, to the depth of His heart, the core truth: His Heavenly Father is at the center of everything. Everything!

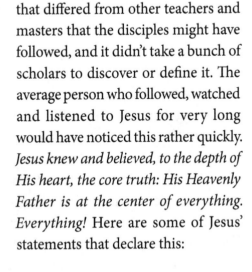

Matt. 6:4 – God sees everything, even what is done in secret

Matt. 6: 25–God feeds the birds

Matt 6.: 30 – God clothes the grass with its blossoms, and such glory is greater than the expensive clothing worn by Solomon.

Matt 10: 29–Not even one sparrow falls from the sky, "…without My Father."

Matt 10: 30–The individual hairs of your heads are numbered by God.

Matt. 10:40 – God will reward giving even a cup of cold water to someone in His name.

Matt. 12:36 – God hears every idle word spoken and will require an accounting for it.

Matt. 17: 27 – God knows exactly where, when and how to catch a fish that has swallowed a coin.

John 4:34–His entire purpose in life was, "…to do the will of My Father."

John 5: 19–He could only do what He saw the Father doing.

John 6:38–He could only do what the Father had sent Him to do.

John 8:26–He could not say anything except what the Father gave Him to say.

John 19:11–Pontius Pilate could have no power over Him at His trial unless it had been given to him from above, i.e., from God.

In addition, throughout His life and ministry, He clearly declared that He believed that the Hebrew Scriptures (what Christians call the Old Testament) were the inspired word of God that are absolutely true and authoritative, cannot be broken, must be fulfilled, and are the life-giving spiritual bread by which man must live. As such, He also believed the many things that are spoken in the Old Testament about God's omnipresence, sovereignty, and power. Here is a very brief list of some of these:

Ex. 4:11 – God decides who has normal physical function and who has physical dysfunctions (cf. John 9:1-3)

Ex. 8:22 – God decides and controls where and when plagues occur.

I Sam. 2:7-9 – God decides who will live and who will die, who will be rich and who will be poor, who will be exalted and who will be brought low.

I. Chron 29:14-16 – All things come from God and anything we give to God is simply returning what He has given to us.

Ps. 50: 10 – God owns the beasts of the field and the cattle on a thousand hills.

Ps. 95: 4-5 – God owns and controls the depths of the earth, the peaks of the mountains, the seas and the dry land.

Ps. 104 – God is the creator, manager and caretaker of all of creation, from the most powerful forces to the smallest detail, and all these things are His possessions.

Ps. 139:1–16 – God is omnipresent, knows when you sit down and stand up, He knows every word you are going to speak before it comes to your lips, God formed you and "weaves you" as you are developing within the body of your mother. No matter where you go, near or far; in the dark, in the light; God is there with you. He is there with you personally. In fact, He was always there. He was where you left, and He is where you arrive. He ordained every day of your life and your eternity. He alone knows your heart, if you are anxious, if you are fearful and if you have ways of pain in you.

Ps. 147: 8 – God makes the grass grow on the mountain side.

Prov. 16:4 – "The Lord has made everything for its own purpose, even the wicked for the day of evil."

Isa. 45: 7 – God formed the light and the darkness and causes both well-being and calamity.

Isa. 46: 10-11 – God declares the end from the beginning. He calls even a bird of prey or an individual man from a distant land to do His purpose and it gets done as He wishes.

Ezek. 18:4 – All souls belong to God, both human and animal.

Dan. 2: 21–God removes rulers and establishes rulers.

Dan. 4:17 – God rules over all mankind and bestows rulership on whomever He pleases.

Hosea 2:8-9–God is the giver of grain, new wine, oil, silver, gold, wool and linen; and He has the right to withhold it or take it back if it is misused.

The difference between Jesus and others in these matters was that He really, really, really believed it. He knew it to be absolutely true and He understood how to balance these in complete wholistic truth. He lived in complete accord with this absolute truth. He was living in the reality of what He knew to be fact! This motivated Him, drove Him and empowered Him to live His life centered in God. His Heavenly Father was the entire focus of His life because God is at the center of everything. Even at the age of twelve, He stayed behind in Jerusalem after His parents had left for home because He wanted to, "… be about My Father's affairs/things." (Luke 3: 41-50) This is not because He was anticipating, "going into full-time ministry". It was because He knew it to be true. This viewpoint is not strange or unique if you really, really, really believe that God is at the center of everything. This is what any young Jewish boy would do if they believed, at the core of their being, that God was the center of everything. Whatever path lies ahead of them, where they would live, what they would do for a living, who they would marry, how many children they would have, whether they would have personal conflicts with the Romans, all would be centered in God. God would be at the center of all of this, directing and enabling them to do what they should. Succeeding in life would only come from God. (Rom. 8: 28-30) The sincere prayer of their heart would be, "May Thy will be done, not mine." (Matt. 6:10) This is far more than just learning the theology of the sovereignty of God. Most Christians would have a hard time describing how to make the sovereignty of God practical to everyday life without giving up their free will and becoming a depressed determinist.

This topic is typically offered within Christianity as a high-level course entitled something like, "Developing a Biblical World View". It is almost always approached as a theological, intellectual, philosophical course, which it is not. It is truly practical and based entirely on absolute realty. Since it is so vital to becoming a growing follower of Christ, there is no reason for delaying this or avoiding it. It is an essential for all of normal daily life. Quite frankly, this is one of those subjects that are handled far better by children than "educated adults." Learning to be like Christ in this matter only requires that you too really, really, really believe that what God says is, in fact, absolute truth, and it should be the basis for all of your life.

Recognizing that God is the center of everything and then living in energetic, glad-hearted full adoption and co-operation with that ultimate reality is part of becoming like Christ. It will allow us to fully function in such commands as "Give thanks in all things." (I Thess. 5:18) "Pray about everything." (Eph. 6:18) "Rejoice always." (Phil 4:4) "Whatever you do, do it to the glory of God." (I Cor. 10:31) Only our unwillingness or hard-heartedness will interfere with this. Paul worded it this way, "From Him, and through Him, and to Him are all things." (Rom. 11:36, cf. I Cor. 8:6); and, "He Himself gives to all people life and breath and all things." (Acts 17:24-28) James tells us that, "Every good and perfect gift comes down from the Father of lights." (James 1:17) How many good things did you have in your life last week? It's probably a lot more than you think. How many of these did you recognize as being a gift from God to you? Did you give Him thanks?

As I sit here writing this, I am listening to some very beautiful music. To me, it is definitely a good and perfect gift from my Father in heaven. God created music. The entire concept of music and how it impacts human experience was planned and created by the One True Living God of the Bible. If all matter and energy resonate at various frequencies, then all matter and energy make music if you could hear it. We can only hear a certain range of frequencies and those are used for all of what we call music. God can literally hear all of His creation as if it were music. (Job 38:7) God created me to be able to hear and enjoy many kinds of music. God created the kind and source of music that I am listening to right now, and He created in me the ability and privilege of greatly enjoying it. God is hearing the very same music right now and He enjoys that I am also enjoying it in fulfillment of His purpose. My joy in the music is hugely multiplied knowing this is a gift of God and that He is sharing it with me.

At the beginning of this book, I talked about how I enjoy tiramisu as a favorite dessert. To me, it is definitely a good and perfect gift from my Father in heaven. God created every ingredient in tiramisu and how those ingredients would combine to get the delightful flavor of tiramisu. He created me to enjoy its flavor and texture, and I enjoy celebrating His goodness to me. He enjoys sharing such moments with me and His presence makes my enjoyment of tiramisu even greater.

I have always been a wildlife lover. In our part of the U.S, we see many wild geese flying over at low altitude during certain seasons and weather. Since we have lakes and ponds nearby, I see more than my share. I love hearing the geese overhead, honking back and forth, almost constantly shifting their V-formations to accommodate geese behavior and instincts. I love rushing out onto the driveway to watch group after group swiftly flying overhead in the last two hours before sundown. To me, it is definitely a good and perfect gift from my Father in heaven. God made geese. He made their behavior and instincts and how they fly and honk. He enjoys geese. He made me to enjoy seeing and hearing them too. He enjoys sharing such moments with me. All these are part of His great goodness and grace to me, and His presence makes my enjoyment even greater.

These are very small examples of the distinction between knowing the theology and knowing the living reality that God wants us to have; but it can be extended to everything around

you. Everything around you is not God, and God is not everything around you. That would be some sort of animism or pan-
theism. God is separate from all that exists in creation, but He
is the creator of it, the owner and active manager of it, and
He delights in it. (Ps 104:31) Everything around you can be an
experience of delight for you too because God is at the center
of it, and it all expresses His glory.

Living as Spiritually Alive

The reason Jesus found it so natural to live out what He
knew to be God's truth was that He was completely spiritually
alive to God. His spirit was fully alive, active and vibrant toward
God. He never knew anything else. Since Christ was without
any sin, either inherited or His own, He was fully alive to the
Father in His spirit. He could sense the presence and activity
of God all around Him in everything. He could see what the
Father was doing. (John 5:19) He could hear what the Father
was saying. (John 8:26) This does not mean that He had some
kind of special physical vision or physical hearing ability. He
could see and hear these things from within His spirit. It was
like an additional wavelength of His awareness. However, by
illustration, it would be like having the ability to see ultra-violet light as part of the color spectrum or hear intra-sound and
ultra-sound in addition to all the normal sounds. (Some helpful
examples are Matt. 4:1, Mark 2:8, Luke 10:21, and John 6:15.)

In contrast, in our natural existence before salvation, we
were spiritually dead. We are described as being "dead in sin"
(Eph. 2:1-2) before we come to Christ. As part of being born
again through faith in Christ, we are made "alive in spirit and
alive to God". (John 3:5-8; Rom, 6:4, 11; Rom. 8:9-11; Gal

2:19-20, 5:25; Eph 2: 1-5) However, for us this is something entirely new and we must learn to live in, and correctly handle this new reality. We are babes in Christ who must grow. As we grow, we can become accustomed to this new level of awareness. We are told to "walk in the Spirit" (Gal 5: 25). We are told to "pray in the Spirit. (Jude 20) We are told we must "worship in the Spirit" (John 4: 24). We are told to have "fellowship in the Spirit" (Phil 2:1) (None of these involve charismatic doctrines or practices.) If we don't grow, we never develop the ability to live in this new greater reality of being alive to God, but the reality is exactly what God wants us to live in. This is not living in a fantasy, nor in some self-created alternative realty. It is the absolute reality of the One True God who really exists. Examples such as the ancient Celtic Christians can be quite helpful if we are willing to hear their testimony without undue prejudice. Living in the reality that you are alive to God in the Spirit allows you to center your life in God. It energizes your relationship with God.

As part of living in discipleship, You must come to grips with the fact that You are not the center of the universe, and You have no right to live as if You were. In fact, it is extremely foolish and mis-guided to think or live this way. Believing and living as if You were the center of the universe is part of the twisted, poisoned You that resulted from the sin of Adam and Eve. It's part of considering Yourself equal with God. By centering your life in God, not in Yourself, you will see many opportunities and reasons to naturally express thankfulness, love, and fellowship with your Heavenly Father who is, in fact, the center of the universe. It is truly a wonderful and deeply satisfying way to live.

Look around you right now (assuming that you are not driving or operating dangerous machinery). God has told you that He is always present around you and within you, always loving you, always forgiving you, always accepting you, always giving every good gift, always giving life and breath to all things, always working everything for your good, etc. etc. etc. You don't have to analyze everything for yourself to see if you agree that it is good and works together for good. You don't have to embark on a lengthy study of the sovereignty of God versus the free will of intelligent beings. God has said it is so. You can respond and interact with God right now on the basis of His absolute word. You can relax into the arms and guiding hands of your heavenly Father that is making it so. You can thank Him and praise Him and adore Him and accept His gifts and assurances with glad-hearted gratitude. Relax into His presence and His purposes. This is part of centering your life in God, and this can be your experience every moment of the day and night.

What would have to change if you started living all of life on the basis of really, really, really believing this, and started just living out what God says is true? (For a hint, take a look at I. Sam 2: 1-10, Luke 1: 41-45, 1:46-55, 67-79, Luke 2: 25-32, and 36-38) These were individuals who did not know the full reality of being born-again and having the full time indwelling and filling of the Holy Spirit; yet they energetically expressed their relationship and response to the One True Living God who really exists, and they did so in a manner that was completely normal to them, because to God everything is normal. After all, He is the One who created these normal responses in them. What would change in your experience with God if you started living all of life on the basis of really, really, really believing this? Lukewarm Christianity and all forms of churchianity would disappear. It would be far less likely to find Christians who were not like Christ.

In churchianity, there is little to no reality in these matters. They are only doctrines to be understood and believed mentally, not a living reality to live in. In the evangelical church, having a functioning spiritual relationship with God may be considered as charismatic or Pentecostal, but it is not. For the purposes of this chapter, the primary result is that we can develop a life that takes God at His word. Taking God at His word automatically creates the opportunity and wide-open invitation to live in the reality of what God has said. However, since these subjects are not taught or practiced to any real degree, they become stunted and non-functional. Since they become stunted or non-functional, the expectation of a reality becomes lower and lower, until the reality becomes so close to zero that it doesn't matter. "Sola scriptura" comes to mean they are taught only as doctrines to believe. If you say you believe them, that's all there is, and you are good to go! Reaching "spiritual maturity" is based on extensive head knowledge of the Bible, not in functional spirituality with God.

Now, let's take a big bite of the true reality that God offers in Christ. If you really, really, really believe that God is a real Being, that He is your loving heavenly Father, that He is always with you and around you every moment (omnipresent), sees everything, hears everything, knows everything (omniscience) and always accepts you in full connection (fellowship), never rejects you, never fends you off with a stiff-arm, never turns a deaf ear or a blind eye, never ignores what you are thinking or feeling, never feels that you are not important, always gladly hears your prayers (communication), THEN how would you interact with God through your normal day? Would you "practice the presence of God" through your day? Would you welcome God's presence in your personal world each moment through the day? Would your life be so full of joy, peace, confidence and strength that you could hardly stand it? Would you limit your interaction with God to only your wish list and needed miracles?

This is one of the very positive contributions of the ancient Celtic Christians. They still understood living with a spiritual awareness and focus and adapted it over very well when they became Christians. They knew and felt the full impact of centering their lives in God and being fully alive to Him. As they lived their simple lives, full of much labor and what we would consider much hardship, they celebrated and praised their Heavenly Father, their precious Savior and the Holy Spirit as the giver all of these simple things as gifts. They wrote, recited and prayed many poems and prayers and sang many simple songs about the blessings of each of these simple things, from milking the cow, to harvesting the oats, to shearing the sheep, to catching the fish, and even the kindling and "smooring" the home fire. They sang and recited as they worked, as they milked the cows, as they herded the sheep, as they pulled the weeds from the kale garden, as they pulled the nets to catch the fish, as they swung the scythes to cut the hay or the oats and pitched them into piles with the fork, as they hand-milled the oats for cooking. They didn't wait for Sunday church to turn it into a performance. They didn't have to depend on Christian radio for music written and performed by professional musicians. They made up their own music and sang it with an open heart. They fellowshipped with God and enjoyed His presence in all things. It was the living fulfillment of Scriptures such as Eph. 5: 18-20 and Col. 3:16-17.

Historical sources tell us that these simple Christians lived a rich spiritual life true to the Scriptures, and without any of the resources that we think are necessary in intellectual western Christianity. They were not smothered by a sense of entitlement like we are. After all, we think Americans have the right to pursue happiness, and we expect it to be fulfilled as our rights. Rights don't prompt very much thankfulness. It also breeds neglect. They were not smothered by a burden of programming and production to make their spiritual lives meaningful or their church gatherings a glowing experience of the Living Christ amongst them. It seems clear that, for some, their Christian beliefs were unduly mixed together with vestiges of their ancestral tales and pagan traditions that we would call superstitions. But if these are carefully distilled out in the clear light of the Scriptures, that which is true becomes even more pronounced as a wonderful Christian spirituality for daily life. That life is programmed and produced by God Himself. Learning to walk in it is the wonderful privilege of a disciple.

We can sit back smugly and assume these were legalistic rituals that meant little to them, or a contaminated carry-over from pagan beliefs. But that may also be an assumption of an arrogant people who think they are too sophisticated and intelligent to see such mundane daily activities in such a vitally spiritual way that richly incorporates all of life, both good and bad. Simple people use such expressions as part of genuine faith. This is how simple people experience and express their being alive to God in Christ. "There were not many wise, not many mighty, not many noble…" (I Cor. 1: 26) It has been the life of many simple Christians in all eras and all parts of the earth if they are willing to center their lives in God and live fully alive to Him in spirit. It is part of, "becoming like a little child" in the kingdom of God. (Matt 18:3) At one time, you could find these simple but powerful spiritual expressions amongst simple people in places like Appalachia and the Blue Ridge. You can still find a few believers around who know this reality, but they are rare these days. I have had the privilege of knowing only a few in my own life. You can still find this in primitive churches in under-developed countries like parts of Africa.

We are invited to give up our superficial and smug pretenses of being happy in the American Dream and learn the true happiness that only God can give, and He gives it liberally. It is wrapped up in each moment of your ordinary day. Jesus lived this way. Disciples learn to live this way as well. Your Lord invites you into it. Won't you come and enter into the joy of your Lord? It doesn't have to wait for heaven. Come, sit at His feet and learn from Him like a little child! (Matt. 11:29) Sorry, no smart phones allowed at the feet of Jesus.

CHAPTER 20

CENTERING YOUR LIFE IN GOD'S LOVE

If someone were to ask you, "What do you think is the greatest commandment in the Bible?" how would you answer? A disciple of Jesus would answer the same as He did, "You shall love the Lord your God with all your heart, all your mind, all your soul and all your strength." (Matt 22: 37-38) With a basic grasp of Scripture, you may notice two things: 1.) Jesus was actually quoting from Deuteronomy 6:5 in the Old Testament; and 2.) This is not one of the Ten Commandments, as found in Exodus. 20. Yet, in His very next statement, Christ said further that the entire law and prophets depend on the commandments to love God and love our neighbor. (Matt 22: 40) Notice, that loving our neighbor is also not one of the Ten Commandments. Christ said that loving God was the greatest commandment, and apparently the scribe who asked the question agreed. (Mk. 12:32)

Christ loved His Heavenly Father with all His being. He knew the Father fully and completely. He had uninterrupted fellowship with the Father, with the brief exception during His crucifixion. At all times, He was giving and receiving love from the Father. He knew all about it, and He wants you to know all about it too—in your heart, not just in your mind or your note-book. Because you are in Christ, you can know this same love directly from God who is already constantly streaming it to you.

In the New Testament, the Apostle John (sometimes called the Apostle of love) quotes Jesus saying, "He who has My com-mandments and keeps them is the one who loves Me..." (John 14: 21). Years later, in his first letter, John writes, "For this is the love of God, that we keep His commandments, and His com-mandments are not burdensome." (I John 5:3) Does it surprise you that there is so little difference between the Old Testament and the New Testament? It might seem that John has added a phrase, "...and His commandments are not burdensome". However, if you look carefully, you will see that this is the same sentiment as in the second commandment in Exodus 20: 4-6. Those who love God will obey His commandments and in turn, receive His lovingkindness. John is simply saying that when you really, really, really love God, obeying His commandments will not seem burdensome at all because it will be an expression of your great love for Him. It has been true throughout the ages for all of God's people, and it has nothing to do with legalism. In fact, it is the exact opposite of legalism! Love motivates obe-dience, not the hope (or demand) of earning some reward from God in return for your obedience. Love delights in pleasing the one you love. Is delight ever hard? I never feel that eating a nice big serving of a great tiramisu is a terrific hardship. Its light tex-ture and intense flavor always make me feel like I can never get enough. Love and delight are very addictive!

If the Son of God said this is the greatest commandment, who has authority to change it? No one! If this is the greatest commandment, and one of the primary roles of the Holy Spirit is to, "...fulfill the requirement of the law in us, who...walk according to the Spirit", (Rom 8: 4) how important is it? What do you suppose the Holy Spirit is constantly prompting us to do? If this is the greatest commandment, how much focus and attention should be given to it? Would it be fair to say it should occupy a very significant part of our time and attention? Should we see it and keep it as the "main thing"? Perhaps we should keep the main thing as the primary focus of our lives, just as Jesus did.

So, how much time did you spend this past week, loving God with all our heart, mind, soul and strength? Not doing your duty, but simply loving Him. When you attended church recently, how much time and attention was given to loving God with all your heart, mind, soul and strength? When you had your quiet time with the Lord lately, how much time and attention was given to loving God with all your heart, mind, soul and strength? When you took part in small group recently, how much time and attention was given to loving God with all your heart, mind, soul and strength? Next time you go, ask others this question and see what they say. Most will be completely bewildered, not knowing how to respond. Others may want to disagree that it is important, or they may say that you shouldn't be so judgmental. Yet, all you did was ask an honest question. How can we believe we are disciples of the Jesus who said this, and yet we don't focus on doing it? Is He our Master, or do we just like to say He is? This is what churchianity has done to us. Churchianity will tell you that devoted faithfulness to your church activities is the most important!

In both the Old Testament and the New Testament, the Scriptures command and teach us that we are to love God with all your heart, mind, soul and strength. How can God just command us to have a particular emotion toward Him? We typically think that love "just happens", just like spiritual growth and transformation "just happens". Worse yet, secretly, deep down inside, we don't think that God has done what He must do to earn our love. He hasn't answered our prayers like we wanted or expected. He didn't get us that new job we wanted. He didn't get us that house we wanted. He didn't get us that vacation we wanted. He didn't keep our new car from being stolen, etc., etc., etc. Disappointment doesn't motivate much love from fallen creatures. Fallen creatures also don't have much ability to love based on choosing to love, and even less to love automatically and instinctively. They think something outside of themselves must prompt them to love, almost compelling them to love. Someone, or some circumstance must enter "the secret code" to prompt us to love. In the romantic realm, we talk about someone "playing on our heart strings" or "having the combination to our heart". Giving love as an instinctive reaching out to others is almost unheard of. However, this is the whole focus and meaning of the parable of the Good Samaritan. Love as an instinctive reaction does not pause or hold back to ask silly theological questions about "Who is my neighbor?" It just loves! It reaches out with compassion and help. It takes transformation to do that, and only Jesus is in the business of transformation. No other religion, philosophy or spirituality can do this.

God knows exactly why this is so hard for us, just as it was hard for ancient Israel. They too were commanded to love God and keep His commandments. (Deut. 10:12-14) So, He takes the initiative in exactly the right way to prime the pump. The Scriptures consistently tell us that God is the initiator of love toward us. God is love. (I John 4:8, 16) Love flows out of the essence of who God is much like light flows out of the sun. It was out of His love that God sent His Son to save us. (John

3:16) Jesus was the embodiment of God's love. It was because of His great love for us that God placed us in the status/standing/position of grace, and this is the basis of, "...all spiritual blessings in the heavenly places in Christ Jesus." (Eph. 1:3, 2:4-7) We only respond to, and return, His love. This is true in both the Old Testament (Deut. 7:7-8, 10:15; Isa 63: 9) and the New Testament (John 3:16, I John 4:10). It is receiving God's love that makes it possible for us to finally become free to love Him and others. This is why John also says, "The one who does not love does not know God" (I John 4:8), and "The one who abides in love abides in God." (I John 4:16) John is not equating love with God, but anyone who has come into such close fellowship with God to say that they "abide in God" cannot possibly not know how to love.

God's love is so overpowering and wonderful that anyone who comes close is saturated by that love and it automatically prompts and enables them to also love. It's like saying that anyone who comes too close to a nuclear reactor will automatically soak up radiation. This is one of the reasons Jesus attracted so many people to Him during His earthly ministry, especially by those who felt like they were never truly loved by anyone, like tax collectors and prostitutes, and other sinners. All you had to do was get close to Him and hear Him speak, and you were drawn by powerful love. Your pretense of denying your sinfulness was melted away, you knew He was the only one who could love you as you needed to be loved, and you were compelled to give up your resistance and come to Him. Those who think about salvation and forgiveness as if it were a business contract with God are not likely to know this love.

The essential concept of love cannot be understood intellectually, so no matter how good the theology, it can only declare that God loves, and describe the ways by which God has demonstrated His love to us. Scripture itself does this. (Acts 14:17, 17:25, John 3:16, Rom 5:8) But an intellectual/theological explanation of love is not what we long for, nor is God satisfied with such limited communication of His love. *Mental assent to the fact that God loves us is not all that God wants. God wants us to experience His love.* Experiencing the outward demonstrations of love is supposed to link us to the love that is behind it and prompts it. We get to receive and enjoy the demonstration (the outward sign), but we are called to look to the source and experience that love that prompts such demonstration. It is to be experienced in our hearts as a river pouring out within.

> Mental assent to the fact that God loves us is not all that God wants. God wants us to experience His love.

(Rom 5:5, cf. John 7:38) The One True God who really exists pours it out into us through the indwelling presence of His Holy Spirit. It was God's love that prompted Him to provide all of His grace to you, including the way of salvation through His Son, and including all you have available to you by your position in Him. (John 3:16, Eph. 2:4-9, I John 3:1) We so poorly understand unconditional love!

We have developed some very misleading notions of what God's love is. It has been explained and defined many times, but always in intellectual and theological terms. Many sermons and teachings have been given on God's love, but few Christians seem to be enthralled by this great love that the Father has for us. It is far more than only a commitment to your well-being. It is far more than undeserved acceptance. It is not a kind of feigned love from an infinite being who really has no emotions, nor any need of them, but feels sorry for humans who do, so He tells us that He loves us. God does not grit His teeth and say, "Well I guess I have to love them because no one else will." God's love is not distant, stiff, formal or administrative. It is not like the powerful king who stands on his balcony high above, looking down over his people far below, saying, "Oh, how I love my people", but remaining high above, having no contact or concern toward them and their misery.

The proper definition of this kind of love is "to treasure, to consider as precious, to greatly value". [40] God's love is rich, warm, enthusiastic, up-close-and-personal, face-to-face. His love is expressed by such things as "gathering us together under His protection like a mother hen gathers her chicks." (Matt. 23:37, cf. Hos. 11: 3, Mk. 10:13-16, John 14: 9) His love is like the father of the prodigal son who runs to his returning son, embracing and weeping with joy. God's love is a "cuddling" kind of love. It's a jumping up and down in glee sort of love. These are the attributes of God's love, and they go far beyond theological or intellectual description. When we read the attributes of love in I Cor. 13: 4-7 we are not only reading the attributes of human love. First and foremost, it is God's love that is kind, gentle, patient, not arrogant, not selfish. If we bathe in that great love, we are automatically prompted to give love to others, starting with God.

The quality of the love you give to others does not reflect the quality of the love you receive from God. It reflects the quality of love *you experience* from God. We only learn to copy Him, based on our experience with that great love. In spite of what you have been told, these are emotional words. These are heart words, not mind words. God doesn't want you to merely *know about* these attributes of His love. In Scripture, knowing something requires experience. God wants you to know these by *experience,* so He pours out His love in your heart where you can experience it the most.

Unrequited Love.

Ah, but you may say, "I am confident that I have Christ as my Savior, but I don't experience God's love in this way." This may be because everyone who has explained God's love to you has only told you about the intellectual or theological side of it. You never even considered that God's love might include the major emotional aspect that *is to be experienced.* You may only believe in Gods' love *by faith.* This makes it an intellectual understanding, not a heart understanding. It may be that you have never received this kind of love from another person, so you don't even know how to find it or recognize it. However, it is equally likely that the "short-circuit" is caused by something else, and it is likely that the Greatest Commandment will provide the solution.

Have you ever been on the receiving end of unsolicited love? This may have been something like middle-school puppy love. You were an eighth grader and some sixth grader confessed undying love toward you, but frankly you could not be less interested and found it rather irritating. You probably tried to avoid them at all costs. Or perhaps it was your mother's elderly aunt who took a great liking toward you, and you simply felt nothing in return. After all, you hardly knew who she is. Someone else expressed great love for you, and since you felt little or none toward them, it prompted you to fend off their expressions of love. It remained superficial, not really touching your heart. No matter how much it was expressed, you did not really feel anything, and perhaps you felt repulsed. You didn't

297

feel any of their love because you did not reciprocate it. It is only when love is fully reciprocated that love is truly experienced. It is only when we have both received love and *given* love that we experience its power and wonder.

If you have trusted Christ as your Savior and Lord, it is a fact that God's love is being poured out into your heart by the Holy Spirit (Rom. 5:5), so the problem is not on the supply side. The blockage is on the receiving and giving back end. Because you don't return love back to God, you do not enjoy the love given, and may even be fending it off. You have tried to avoid God emotionally. You have put a lot of comfortable emotional distance between you and God. You have deadened your emotions toward God. This results in being unable to experience God's overwhelming love and reduces it to a mental idea—a doctrine to be believed "by faith".

Perhaps you have often, or routinely, taken this kind of emotional posture with others as well. It is possible that you have cut yourself off from the realm of love, perhaps due to some very serious and painful experiences. We often don't even realize it, but at the subconscious or semi-conscious level, it was intentional. This will rob your life of the wonderful experience of love, from all sources, including God. Perhaps you have been told, and/or concluded on your own, that this is just because you are not an emotional person. You see yourself as more of a mentally oriented person. But there is absolutely no reason why a smart person cannot have the full spectrum of both giving and receiving love. The lack of love or avoiding love, as if it were "illogical", is a part of learned personality, even if it is self-taught. It is not normal human response and God can overcome it like no other.

Another possible scenario for why you don't experience God's love this way is that you don't really think you need it. It's like when you were twelve years old and you fall and hurt yourself a little bit, but you want to prove to everyone that you are not a child anymore and you don't need any consoling. You don't need anyone to treat you as a hurt child who needs to be picked up, brushed off and comforted in front of your friends, especially by your Mom. You want to be a grown-up, so you fend off the need for love. This kind of fending off God's love is a form of pride, coming from your sinfulness. You really do desperately need God's love and you will never truly be happy or fulfilled until you embrace it for all that it is.

The great news is that this can be reversed, by the power of God's love and your choice to receive it fully and give it back as well. Christ will teach you this because He wants you to know God's love in the same powerful way as He did. Christ wants to return you to "just as if you had never been affected by sin". If sin had never occurred in the human race, we would all be completely comfortable with, and deeply enjoy, the full range of healthy emotions, including rich, warm love. This is who God intended us to be—like Him. Accepting and embracing love is not a sign of weakness. It is not a sign of childishness. It is the sign of wholeness—a sign of great maturity.

We thrive best when we know we are loved with an abundant and powerful love. In chapter one of his book, *Anam Cara, A Book of Celtic Wisdom*, [41] John O' Donohue writes rich words about what wonderful blessings come to us by sincere, committed love. His words are mostly concerning the love of a true friend, which in Celtic tradition is called "the anam cara"; but he also speaks of the love of God as the highest giver and source of this kind of unswerving, committed love. The most powerful

words about love are that this kind of love makes us feel free—
not free to do wrong with no consequences, but to be all that we
were supposed to be—free from sin and all its effects. We were
meant to be the kind of beings that love simply for the pure joy
of it and for the joy and release it brings to others!

All of these scenarios can be solved by starting to obey the
Greatest Commandment. Start right where you are and ask God
to make you like Christ, someone who receives and gives love
freely and openly. Ask Him to forgive and cleanse away all the
reasons that prompt you not to open yourself wide open to His
love and fully reflect His love. This must come first as God's
love flowing into your own heart from His inexhaustible supply.
If you do not receive the great flow of His love, you will find it
impossible to reflect back that love to Him and to others. It may
not come suddenly as in the form of a miracle cure. It's likely
to be a series of small doors opening to allow more and more
love to enter your heart. If it came all at once, it might over-
whelm you beyond your ability to cope. In order to bring you
into this full experience of His love, God may have to "meter it"
over time—like opening a number of doors that gradually allow
the full flow to enter. Each of these doors will be connected to
one or more reasons in you that prompt you to refuse or fend
off His love. You may even fight against having some of these
doors opened because you don't want to face the issue that is
involved. But when the flow reaches the point of "the bathtub
is running over", you will be only beginning to experience all
the love that God has for you right now, all because you are in
His child. Once you are there, it is nearly impossible to go back.
You will be addicted!

You may not realize it, and you may be hard to convince, but
you always love because you choose to love. This is how God

made you, because He intended you to be in His image. You always have it in your power to love, you just don't realize it. The sinful nature within you always tries to damp and stamp this out. Lies, anger, criticism, division, hatred, blame and isolation are what the old nature likes, and it doesn't want You choosing to give love, ever, unless there's something in it for You. If you will simply choose to start loving God, loving Him with all your heart, mind, soul and strength, love will be reciprocal, and it is very likely that you will begin to experience the love of God poured out in your heart. It may come in like a flood!

To love God this way you will treasure Him, highly value Him, consider Him precious, and give Him your up-close and personal love. You will have genuine affection for God. You will see your times with Him as face-to-face, smiling, delightful encounters of the One True God who really exists. It is loving God with all your heart, all your mind, all our soul and all your strength = with your whole self and with everything in you. That's how He loves you! He wants you to have all the fulfillment of living a life full of love, but you must love God back in order to make it all work. You will only experience God's love in direct proportion with how much love you express for God. That does not turn this love into a mental activity, which is how it is often described. It is an emotional activity that is in your power to choose, to choose releasing love. God is this way, and you were made in the image of God. Once ruined by sin, Christ can now restore you to this wonderful experience and way of life. This is part of "the way of Christ".

There have been many descriptions of heaven, some valid, some not. We have heard numerous accounts of near-death and after-death experiences. There will be many things to see and experience in heaven, but one of the most powerful will be that it is a place that is truly filled to overflowing with love. Love will be like a delightful fragrance in the air all around you. It cannot be any other way since God is the center of heaven, and God is love. Since we were made in the image of God, we were made for love. We were meant to naturally have love as the basis for all relationships and interactions. In heaven, this will be our perfect experience. Eternity with Him will be a constant feast of love from your Heavenly Father and all others there with you. However, God does not desire or intend that you wait for heaven for a very large measure of His love. However, since we still carry the severe damage of the sin nature, something is needed that we cannot produce for ourselves. The solution is to provide the miraculous transformation that changes us to be like Christ.

One of Paul's prayers for the Ephesian church is that, "… being rooted and grounded in love, you may be able to comprehend… what is the breadth, and length, and height and depth (of all that you have in Christ) and *to know the love of Christ which is beyond knowledge.*" (Eph 3:14-18, italics mine) In this prayer, Paul clearly speaks of knowing a love that "surpasses knowledge".

The two words translated "comprehend" and "know/knowledge" are two different words in the original Greek language of the New Testament. The word in verse 18 ("comprehend") means to grasp the fact of love mentally. The words in verse 19 ("know/knowledge") are the word that means knowledge that includes personal experience. It would be beyond the purpose of this chapter to completely explain this passage. To make certain you work from an accurate translation, I recommend Kenneth Wuest's expanded translation. [42] However, Paul is clearly saying that, once you are "rooted and grounded/founded in love", it allows you to move upward to know a much greater love than you knew before. How do you come to know something that is beyond knowledge? By the full experience of it! This is what Paul was praying for the Ephesian believers, and his prayer was that the Holy Spirit would grant these believers the power to grasp this and come to know it. This is what the disciple learns to know—the overflowing love of God that becomes a flood of love toward God and others. You can always tell if someone is experiencing this overflowing love of God. You can see it in their eyes. You can hear it in their voice. You can hear it in their prayers. And you can witness it by the way they reach out to others.

The Prize of Love and Obedience

How is this related to learning to obey all the commands and teaching of Christ? In John 14: 21, Jesus told the disciples, "He who has My commandments and keeps them is the one who loves Me; and he who loves Me will be loved by My Father, and I will love him and disclose Myself to him." How can Christ and the Father love me on the basis of obedience when He already loves me enough to die for me? The Scriptures are not contradictory. Some have tried to explain this away by a theology that relates this teaching to the Law and the Old Covenant. It is impossible for me to believe that only hours before Christ was going to shed His precious blood as the basis of God's grace, He was still talking about arrangements under the Law where you supposedly earned something by obedience! Isn't His love based on grace? Yes! He was talking about a greater experience of knowledge that can only be disclosed by direct personal experience. This heightened experience of love is based on the greater commonality reached when we consistently obey

His commands. Obedience motivated by your love for God puts you on a wavelength that allows you to more powerfully receive and know the love of both the Father and the Son. That increasing stream of His love will empower you more and more to love Him back, which will then automatically empower you to obey His commandments. The "This is so hard" syndrome will fade away and become, "This is so wonderful, I can't believe it! Why did I wait so long to start?"

Beware of Obedience Not From Love

If you sense that you don't love God as you should, the solution is not necessarily more obedience. Obeying God's commands does not always spring from love for Him. The Pharisees meticulously obeyed the Mosaic Law (at least they thought they did), but Jesus condemned them for not loving God. (Luke 11:42) The Pharisees thought they were meticulously obeying Gods commands, but they were neglecting what they themselves believed to be the greatest commandment! Legalism tends to blind you to that.

We must not make the same mistake as the Pharisees who opposed Jesus at every turn. Obedience out of legalism does not require the motivation of love for God. It's one of those things like "all squares are rectangles but not all rectangles are squares". It is very important you do not conclude that increasing obedience automatically increases love for God. More heroic legalism will not achieve great love. It truly doesn't work that way. It's just the opposite—more love will prompt more obedience. You can easily check out your basis for obedience by checking your feelings toward God before, during and after your obedience.

So, how much time will you spend this past week, loving God with all our heart, mind, soul and strength? How much time will you take to allow Him to clear out all the reasons, all the obstacles, all the interferences to building this kind of love relationship with your Heavenly Father who is the ultimate giver of such love?

Some Obstacles

There are two big issues related to centering your life in God and loving God with all of your being. They must be recognized, faced, and fully resolved before you will make any real progress in these matters. Both hindrances like to hide in the shadows to avoid detection. This allows them to survive and thrive for as long as possible. They are often still around after years of being a Christian, and churchianity is completely comfortable in allowing them to do so. Churchianity is content to just let you say you believe it, without much concern about whether you truly live in the reality as your normal experience. Churchianity is not looking for the starry-eyed wonder in your face from being in Love's presence!

The first obstacle is your perception of the seriousness of your sin. In Luke 7:36-50, Jesus encountered a woman who interrupted His dinner because she wanted to pour out her heart in speechless, repentant tears and anoint Him with perfume. Whatever else you may conclude from her actions, Jesus focuses them all as being the woman's expression of her great love prompted by "forgiveness of her many sins". The Pharisee host had deliberately insulted Jesus by withholding the normal cultural expressions that were appropriate for welcoming a respected guest into his home. On the other hand, the woman entered, without any invitation and breaking all cultural bounds, pursued Jesus to the dining room in order to wash His feet with her tears, wipe them with her hair (the symbol of her glory), kiss His feet, and then anoint them with perfume. John the Baptist, the greatest prophet of all, (Luke 7:28) said he was not worthy to stoop down and loosen Jesus' sandal strap, yet this woman was kissing, washing, and wiping His feet with her tears and hair. (The language here indicates this took some time, and Jesus made no effort to stop or hurry her. Meanwhile, the Pharisee's indignation is growing by leaps and bounds.)

Responding to the criticism of his Pharisee host, Jesus tells a parable to explain that forgiveness of little sin (or none) prompts little love (or none), but forgiveness of much sin (as displayed by the woman's actions) prompts great love. Like the Pharisee, those who consider themselves as upright and respectable (self-righteous) recoil from the woman because she was a great sinner and acted in a very socially unbecoming manner in public. Like the Pharisee, we have a hard time loving God very much, and certainly have no intention of displaying even our little love in a manner that is socially inappropriate in public. This is because, like the Pharisee, we don't feel like God had to forgive us of much or anything truly serious or scurrilous. After all, we are upright and respectable. After all, isn't this what God wants of Christians—to be respectable? To be a "nice person"?

If we love little, it can be an automatic signal that we consider ourselves as needing little forgiveness. This betrays our utter failure to recognize that we are also failing to obey the very greatest commandment, and every minute is a separate offense. Once the full weight of this fact strikes you with full force, this will change. Your sins are many, just like this woman in Luke's gospel. Once you come to grips with this in your heart of hearts, you will find it easier to love with all our heart, mind, soul and strength.

Reconciling to God

The second obstacle is also hidden deep within the underground caves of our souls. It is the obstacle of reconciliation with God. Reconciliation is a two-way street. We often speak of reconciliation from God's side of the equation, but we miss the other half of the equation. On His side, God has completely reconciled us to Himself through Christ. There is absolutely no remnant or shred of anything that once constituted us as "enemies of God" (Rom. 5:10, II Cor. 5:18). We are in His Beloved Son, fully accepted and loved, and we have the wonderful privilege of a completely open, free and unhindered relationship with our Heavenly Father, just like Christ.

Paul writes on two levels about this reconciliation. He is writing to Christians when he described his ministry of reconciliation, and he finishes by saying, "Be reconciled." He is not inviting these Corinthian Christians to get saved again. He is urging them to enter fully into the reconciled relationship with God. This is reminiscent of John's writings in Revelation when he describes Jesus as outside the house, knocking at the door to seek entry and fellowship. (Rev 3:20) He was writing to Christians. Even though you have accepted Christ as your Savior, you can still treat Him as an outsider in your life. This automatically creates or reflects emotional distance between you and God, and you can never center your life in someone who seems distant and disconnected. This assures that You can center your life in Yourself which is exactly what You want in the first place. That is, until You finally decide that You are not God, and You are not the center of the universe.

On your side, you also considered God as an enemy, and you treated Him as an enemy. It's been that way since Adam. Adam's first response to God after the fall into sin was to deflect blame for his sin onto others, including God. Read it for yourself in Genesis 3:8-24. You can almost picture it, as it might be portrayed in a drama. God calls upon Adam to recognize and confess his sin, and Adam's response is to blame God. Even though it is not described in detail, you can well imagine the rest of the scene. After getting the whole story out and hearing all the blame shifting, God foretells the terrible results that will unfold from that point, then drives Adam and Eve out of the garden, posting an angel with a flaming sword at the gate. All the way out, Adam is complaining, "But it's not my fault! It's not my fault!" Once outside, Adam looks back, shouting in angry pain toward God, "It's not fair! It's not fair! It's not my fault. It's your fault!" He picks up a stick and hurls it back toward the guarded gate. Then, barely holding back the defiant tears, he kicks some dirt back in the same direction as he watches the gate disappear, as if into the mists of Paradise lost. Finally, he yells in angry defiance, "Go ahead and leave! I don't need you anymore anyway!" The animosity, pain, blame and avoidance has continued ever since in the heart of every human. We are estranged. We avoid God. We've got a grudge against Him, and we won't soon forget what He did to us.

Your great sinfulness automatically prompts this in you. It is important that you recognize that, even though you no longer consider God as an enemy, you still have a very large accumulation of thoughts, feelings, and automatic/instinctive reactions to think of God as an enemy, someone to avoid, someone that's not fair. In your inner-most mind, you can still react to God as if He were your enemy. You can act as if He is estranged from you. If He is estranged, it is entirely on your side of the fence.

God has done nothing wrong and does not need your forgiveness at any time or in any manner. God has told you the truth. His ways are always, just, right and perfect. (Ps 18:30, 119:75, 145:17) Our choice was our choice, not His. However, you are vulnerable to the lies of Satan, and you can easily swallow down a lie that God did something that wasn't fair or right. You must determine to abandon all unfounded enmity toward God from your heart, mind and soul and be fully reconciled to God on your side. (II Cor 5:20) On your side of the fence, you must completely change how you think of God. Stop thinking of God as an enemy and enter into the reality of being fully reconciled. A person who is fully reconciled never treats the "former enemy" with suspicion, never doubts his/her motives or intentions, never rejects, excludes, avoids, marginalizes, ignores, or denies. You never respond with distancing or sidelining. You never push God out onto the outer edge of your life. You always welcome every opportunity to come up close and embrace, look at each other with up-close-and-personal, face-to-face relationship. You never treat that person with, "Oh, I'm busy now. Come back later when I can fit you into my busy schedule of higher priorities."

God is already completely reconciled toward you on His side. Until you completely reconcile on your side, you will find it difficult to love God with all your being. Even more sadly, since love must be reciprocal, failure to reconcile and love God back, you will seriously interfere with experiencing the full power of His great love toward you. You will not experience the great river of His love pouring out into your heart. Taking this step may require you to face your pain, blame and anger toward God for allowing painful events, times, or circumstances in your life. Your ancestors chose to know both good and evil and all of these painful matters in your life are the result of that choice. Good has had its presence in your life, but so has evil. Evil has entered your life because various individuals, groups of individuals, categories of individuals, or intermittent streams of individuals used their power of choice to bring evil into your life. It was not God's fault and to blame Him only confirms that you are a child of Adam.

In a subsequent chapter we will learn how to take up your citizenship in the kingdom of God and learn to be an overcomer of evil. It comes with the territory of being a disciple who follows Christ, the King of a new kingdom, the Overcomer of all evil, and the second Adam. However, none of this will happen if you choose to merely stick this in your head, in your notebook, in your drawer, or in your large collection of "minimally important things to pay attention to". You must choose to live in it as your new life. However, this will not be possible if you have not learned to center your life in God's love and goodness. You will still be distancing yourself from Him and blaming Him for the evil that attacks you, almost relentlessly. Abandon your response and instinct to distance yourself from God and His love! Choose instead to bathe yourself in the great river of His love and love Him back with all your being. I promise, you will never want to go back!

CHAPTER 21

GLORIFYING AND ENJOYING GOD

The Search for Meaning and Fulfillment

I have always enjoyed observing nature and all the activities that go on in that realm. Everything in nature seems more-or-less predictable, based on all we know about it. In the Rockies, we have a few large predators, including bears, mountain lions, coyotes and occasionally wolves. Although not predators, animals like moose and elk can also be dangerous at times, and visitors to the forest must be mindful and careful. Any time you are planning to go camping, hiking, fishing, hunting or even birdwatching, you are always advised to be on the watch for these animals and know what to do if they are near. If you do the wrong thing, you might evoke an aggressive response by these animals, and they can be dangerous. Their behavior is not always completely predictable, but there is a narrow range of behaviors to anticipate and be prepared for. You can bet that a mountain lion will not invite you into its den to watch the sports channel. If you are there, it's probably because you are the lunch special.

Each species also appears to have a defined purpose and role in the overall scheme of nature—all except humans. We don't seem to be able to discern or know our purpose very well. It would almost appear that our purpose is to go around life wondering what our purpose is. Sparrows seem to know their purpose and they live well within it. It seems to be instinctive. Wolves seem to know their purpose, and they don't spend much time guessing at what it is. It seems to be instinctive. Trying to modify it or train it out of them is very difficult and never guaranteed.

It would seem that knowing your purpose in life is a wonderful thing; but on the other hand, once we humans think we know our purpose, we aren't very happy about it and often want to change it. When we allow unavoidable circumstances to dictate our purpose, we feel we have been forced into it. We want to self-define our purpose, but all too often we are not happy even when we think we have discovered and pursued it. We aren't even happy about the choices available, including the idea that there is no purpose. In fact, concluding that there is no purpose is the most depressing and unhappy conclusion of all! It's like finding yourself floating in a lifeboat alone with no compass, no oars, no sail, no rudder, no map, and no land in sight in any direction. How can we be so fundamentally disconnected from our purpose? Is this some gigantic failure in evolution? How can we be the most highly developed species on the planet without this inner knowledge? Perhaps we are the least-developed species?

The most tragic thing of all is that most people, including most Christians, struggle through many years of life, and perhaps reach the end of life still wondering and grieving whether their life had any purpose or meaning other than simply existing and dealing with the circumstances as best they could. This is hardly a meaningful life, and it is far less than God intended.

Glorifying God

One of the best-known historic confessions of Western Christianity is the Westminster Confession. This was a summary statement of belief by the Church at that time, expressing their mutual agreement and official stance on certain teachings of the Bible and the Christian faith. Attached to this confession was a catechism to instruct others in the content and meaning of the confession. In both the shorter and larger versions of this catechism, the first statement tells us that the "chief end of man" (the ultimate purpose of each and every human) is to, "... glorify God and enjoy Him forever." [43] This was an excellent choice by the framers of the confession, and totally in alignment with the clear teaching of Scriptures. However, there is no content in the confession or the catechism stating how to go about fulfilling this purpose. Like all other commands and principles of Scripture, God gives them to us to obey (live out), not just formulate confessions that are to be memorized and recited to be accepted into the church.

So, how much time did you spend last week glorifying and enjoying God? What does that even mean? How do I do that? "Glorify God" is an action phrase. What do I do? What should I not do? Is this so general that it's only another way of saying, "Don't commit sin"? Surely there must be more than that! Living your whole life dedicated to *not* doing something doesn't seem very satisfying. More to the point of this book, what would our purpose be if we were to be like Christ? What was Christ's purpose in life? He clearly stated and demonstrated that His purpose was to glorify God. Did He pursue it adamantly? Did He accomplish that purpose? Despite popular current evangelical notions, the scope of that purpose was not limited to just dying on the cross and going back to heaven. To say your purpose in life is to die and go back to heaven also doesn't seem to be very satisfying. Sound familiar?

Jesus was committed to glorifying His Father in heaven. Only hours before His crucifixion, Jesus prayed what Christians know as His High Priestly Prayer, recorded in John 17. Near the beginning, He prays, "I have glorified You (the Father) on the earth, having accomplished the work that You gave Me to do." (John 17:4, parenthesis mine) It's as if Christ summed up His entire earthly ministry, possibly His entire life, as being to glorify God by completing the work that had been given to Him by the Father. Notice He said this before the cross, even before uttering the words, "It is finished." (John 19:30) This does not deny that the cross was a vital part of that work given to Him by the Father. He had clearly implied this in foretelling His ultimate rejection and execution by the Jews and Romans. (Matt. 16: 21, cf. John 12:27) But it assures us that the work He had been doing up to that point was also, "…part of the work you gave Me to do."

As you read the gospels, you come away with the unavoidable impression that Jesus was a fully happy, satisfied, and fulfilled man. How is that possible if you have dedicated your entire life to fulfill the wishes of another and to seek the glory of another? Perhaps if we felt that our life, so lived for the will and glory of another, would bring about a huge improvement for the entire human race we could embrace and endure that. But for most of us, no such opportunity or mission like this seems available or even on the far horizon. Most of us struggle through life hoping to find something that will make it all worth the effort. Many years later, the Apostle Paul writes to the Corinthian church, "Whether then, you eat or drink, or whatever you do, do all to the glory of God" (I Cor 10:31); and to the Roman church he writes, "...that with one heart and one mind you may glorify God". (Rom 15:6)

If you had followed Jesus around Palestine for over three years, you would unavoidably observe that He lived in fully committed harmony with the truth that He had come to glorify the Father, in other words to do many things that would cause honor and praise to Him as the originator and power behind all those things. Since a disciple seeks to become like the Master, this must also be a central motivation of your life, and *it has little relationship with what you do for a living*. Much confusion in this matter has been woven into the overall fabric of traditional Christian teaching. This confusion is more inadvertent than intentional, making it both powerful and subtle. Combined with the lack of teaching of the "how" of Christ's commands, it has produced a very minimal and superficial result in the life of even those Christians who wish to do what is right. It is usually thrown into our prayers when politely asking God's blessings on some activity we are about to start. This combination has been deadly.

Much is stated in the Scriptures about holiness, which simply means "separated unto the Lord". It is the same word translated "sanctified" and "saint". In Scripture, all believers are called saints (Rom. 1:7, I Cor. 1:2, Eph. 1:1, Phil. 1:1) because, in Christ, we have been set apart or "separated unto" God for salvation, sanctification and eternity spent with Him. If holiness means, "separated unto the Lord", how can there be no differ-ence between secular and sacred? This becomes quite confusing to the average Christian. How does "do everything as to the Lord" allow something, or multiple somethings, to be "sepa-rate unto the Lord"? We seem forced back to just not sinning. Talk about confusing! But this is the secret at the foundation of doing all things to the glory of God. All things are sacred if you do them as unto Him and to His glory.

There is a tremendous amount of Scripture devoted to the glory of God, and it can be a very complex subject. A large collection of Scripture verses can be assembled to express and describe that God possesses, and is fully worthy of, immense glory. No one else possesses, or is worthy of, such immense glory. The commonly used Hebrew word for glory comes from a root word that means "weighty or heavy". To our thinking, this seems like an odd term for God's glory. As with many ancient words, this is a vivid word-picture. It doesn't take much aware-ness to realize that humans have always been fascinated, and even enamored, by light. Numerous examples can be brought to mind, such as stars, candles, jewels and precious stones, Christmas lights and mobile phone lights at concerts. Light is dazzling, fascinating, and beautiful to our minds and imagina-tions. (How does evolution explain that?)

In ancient language and culture (as well as our own today), a person who had great authority and power was typically a person of great wealth, and possessions. Likewise, a person of great wealth was typically given abundant honor, respect and fear. (Times haven't changed much.) Wealth was measured in precious metal, gold and silver being the favorites. They would own a lot of gemstones and jewelry made of gemstones mounted in precious metal. They would possibly own and wear clothing woven with gold and silver threads. These materials and items tend to be heavy and very shiny. It would take numerous beasts of burden to carry around the wealth of a rich man. Ancient and contemporary rulers love to have furnishings made of gold and silver. This leads to the concept that a person of great power and authority is "heavy" and "shiny" or "glorious". (Rhinestones and "bling" are not a new idea, only a cheap version of a very old idea.)

As God reveals Himself in human experience and in the Scriptures, He takes this fundamental concept and heightens it to its extreme to express His immense power, perfection and holiness. God's infinite perfection and attributes are so great that they are super-dense/super-intense. He sometimes appears in the form of blinding light as an expression of His great glory. This is a visible manifestation expressing that God's infinite perfections are so intense that they become a blinding outshining of light. These characteristics literally flow from Him like the light shines from the sun.

We are told repeatedly that we are to give glory to God and that God is worthy of all glory. Giving God glory is not saying that we give Him something He does not already have. It simply means that we are fully recognizing and expressing that God has such glory. His glory is a visible expression of His immense power, authority and that He is stupendously wonderful. We are recognizing and expressing that God is so powerful and wonderful that He deserves all credit for everything He does, and we deserve none of the credit at all.

How can we understand Paul's urgent invitation that even things as simple and everyday as eating and drinking be done to the glory of God? To return to our overall issue, *how* does the Christian eat to the glory of God? Have you ever seen a class or

Bible study devoted to that subject? Paul's companion invitation and exhortation is, "Do all things as unto the Lord." (I Cor.10:3) Ever joined a small group to focus on that? The answer flows out of a combination of several streams of truth, all combined into a wholistic fabric of living reality (as long as you really, really believe all of them):

- recognizing that God is at the center of everything,
- recognizing that everything that exists is owned by God, and He has the right to do with it as He pleases,
- recognizing that every good gift comes from God,
- recognizing that even those things that are not good are allowed by Him to ultimately accomplish a good purpose,
- recognizing that all the ways of the Lord are right and just,
- fully embracing that there is no distinction between secular and sacred,
- fully embracing that being spiritually alive to God enables you to recognize these with a glad heart at all times and in all moments,
- choosing to gladly and freely give all positive credit, honor and praise to God for all that He is doing.

In their book and workbook, *Experiencing God*, by Henry Blackaby, and Claude V. King, we are urged to become aware that, "God is always at work around us" (in some way), and then, "God invites you to become involved in what He is doing." [44] The fundamental principle expressed in the widely popular book, *Practicing the Presence of God*, by Brother Lawrence [45]strikes a similar, but simpler chord. Brother Lawrence focused on the presence of God in his daily work, loving God and doing his work as unto God. All other things that might have drawn his focus was subordinated and directed to these two primary purposes of his life, whether it was in the kitchen or the sandal repair shop. However, truly doing all things "to the glory of God" and "as unto Him" is taking this principle to an even higher level, the level of a true disciple of Jesus.

Once you truly embrace that God is at the center of everything, you will see a great many things to become part of, or respond to, all in a manner that gives/brings glory to your Heavenly Father. Each unfolding moment, each event, and each circumstance in our life becomes an occasion to please, honor, and praise God. (Ps. 50: 23) This helps put you in touch with God in all moments and all circumstances. How you are aware, in touch, and responding will be somewhat unique to you, and that is how God wants it. God is the author of order, but not the author of sameness, monotony, vain repetition or making everyone respond in the same way to assure some kind of false order. He is not the author of cookie-cutter Christians. How you respond will be concentrated on God, what He is doing as the center of all things, and how you will glorify Him in this awareness. It is intentional.

Enjoying God

Despite the historic confession, I doubt if many in any church era, including this one, would say they have learned to truly enjoy God. You may enjoy the church service, you may enjoy the Christian song, you may enjoy the Bible study, you may enjoy a nature walk, but enjoying the God Who Is Really There in all those things may not have crossed into your awareness. You are not aware of it because you have not learned to see with spiritual eyes, hear with spiritual ears, and understand with a spiritual heart. The fact is that when you enjoy the church service, the Christian song or the Bible study, it may well be because the Holy Spirit is prompting that response in you. God is the source of your enjoyment. He is giving these gifts to you as elements of His grace in your life. However, beyond this, enjoying God Himself is what we are invited into as a child of God. In fact, Scripture tells us to, "delight yourself in the Lord." (Ps. 37:4) But alas, how many times have you joined a class or study or small group with the designated purpose of learning to delight in God? Enjoyment is the kind of language you use for enjoying your favorite dessert—like tiramisu. Can you enjoy God like that? To enjoy God requires you to be experiencing your spiritual aliveness to God and being aware of God Himself, not only the things He has provided for you in the visible world. It is looking beyond the blessing to the Blessing-giver and doing so consistently and joyfully. It is also looking beyond the trial to the Blessing-through-trial-giver.

The fundamental concept of enjoying anything means that you "enter into the joy" of experiencing that thing. If you don't "enter into joy" because of this thing, you did not "enjoy it". To enjoy God means that you experience joy because of your contact with God or your experience of God. The spiritual fruit of joy is called a spiritual fruit because it comes from a spiritual source with spiritual power. It is not natural. It is not due to your personality, or temperament, or your up-bringing, or your temporal privileges. It is the result of the prompting and life-giving Holy Spirit within you. The Holy Spirit indwelling the Christian produces in you the emotion of joy—and yes, it is an emotion.

The traditional distinction between joy and happiness amongst Christians really has no Biblical foundation whatsoever. It was created in an attempt to distinguish between the happiness that comes from "physical/worldly blessings" and "spiritual blessings". However, with the mind of Christ and guided by the Scripture, there is no distinction between "physical/worldly blessings" and "spiritual blessings". The only true distinction to be carefully made is between the pleasure from sin and pleasure from righteousness. God is the giver of all blessings. There is no other source for them and therefore He should always receive all credit and praise for them all.

Just as with experiencing love, this flow of joy can get choked off by your own internal control mechanisms. It is more likely that it is choked off by modern theories about origins and operation of the universe that do not include or allow God. Once learned, it takes work and grace to unlearn these. If you choke off your emotions because you think Christians are not supposed to have emotions, or not supposed to have positive emotions, you may not experience very much joy in spiritual things, nor God Himself. You have "quenched" the Holy Spirit who gives the joy. (I Thess. 5:19) If you have become so indoctrinated against Gods' presence in His universe and world you will be blind to it even as you are surrounded by it and walk through it all the time.

It is essential that you know that you cannot fake true joy. It can be pretended, and often is in Christian circles, but the distinction between real and fake joy is always discernible. Real joy just flows out through you like a fountain from within your heart. (John 7: 38) But to have this, you must absolutely become fully aware (spiritually alive) to God's presence and action in the world around you and within you.

To get you started on this, imagine what it would be like if you were able to spend the whole day one-on-one with your favorite real-life hero or heroine, along with your very best of all friends. The day would be spent doing together all the things that you really enjoy. You know that your best friend enjoys many of the same things as you, and to your great surprise and joy, you discover that your favorite real-life hero also enjoys many of those same things immensely. Because of the importance you assign to these individuals, you would never act or feel inconsiderate toward either of these individuals because they are very important to you, and you greatly respect and appreciate each one. Because you all have so much in common, you never feel or react in a way that makes you feel like you are holding back on enjoying anything in the day. You also do not fake your enjoyment simply to be polite or accommodating. What kind of day would that be? Would it be hugely enjoyable and satisfying? Would it be a day that you remember and cherish for a long time? Would you describe it as "feeling happy"? Enjoying God gives you the same emotional experience as being happy. Does it make any sense at all to avoid or refuse that? Of course not.

Because you are in Christ, God sees you just as His Son, and He loves to spend time with His Son. He loves to spend time with you. Because God is the giver of all good things to enjoy (I Tim. 6:17), you know that every good thing comes into your life from Him and is never in conflict with His will. He has promised you that He never leaves you or forsakes you, and that He will be with you forever, even to the end of the age. (John 14:16, Matt 28:19-20) God loves to join in with you in everything good you do, including when you refuse to do that which grieves Him or is against His will. He loves to see you have enjoyment and fulfillment in what you do. His great desire is to give you a blessed life by enabling you to do all that He designed you to do. In fact, He loves to see you develop a zest for life because you are learning to walk in all that He designed for you to do. He is truly your "Anam Cara". He is very frustrated when He sees you sitting around bored, stifled or unfulfilled. Now tell me, would you like to live that kind of life? Does that that seem hard, difficult, narrow, and harsh? Enjoying God never seems hard, difficult, narrow, and harsh.

None of this requires that you jump into the great error of the health, wealth and prosperity gospel that has left its poisonous mark on so many. How does Jesus say, "Blessed are the poor...," (Matt 5: 3) if only having wealth brings blessings? How does Jesus say, "Blessed are the gentle...," (Matt. 5:6) if forcing your way on everyone else is the only way to find fulfillment? (The favorite book of You is about getting your own way by intimidation.) It is because the children of the kingdom learn to enjoy God above all things, and God's love and wonderful presence is not dependent on things or power. He is always there. "He is there, and He is not silent." [46] You only need to turn around and look to Him for all things. How does Paul say, "I count all things as worthless trash in comparison with knowing Christ..." (Phil 3:8) if contentment comes only from having all the things that Paul gave up? Are Jesus and Paul fools, idiots, or shysters? No! They simply knew the secret that is waiting for all of those who truly follow this Savior who holds all things in His possession and control. God is the only source of enjoyment, and He gives it liberally to those who truly seek Him with all their heart. (Jer. 29:13) Does it make any sense at all to avoid or refuse that? Of course not.

This does not make Christianity some naive Pollyanna viewpoint. The world is full of many hard and harsh things, events, situations, and people. Jesus knew that as much as anyone. If you were poor and living in an underdeveloped country, or impoverished Appalachia, or impoverished inner city you would know this with even greater force. We do not live in denial or fantasy, but in the ultimate reality that transcends all other things. This is part of what Jesus meant when He said, "I have overcome the world". (John 16:33) When He said this, He was on the doorstep of being tortured and crucified by one of the cruelest political and military powers of the world. Was His boast an empty one? Did something suddenly turn out wrong? No! He knew that every stroke of the hammer that nailed Him to the cross was at the same time driving nails into the coffin of the power of evil and hammering open the doorway into joy for all who follow Him.

To live with your life centered in God, centered in His love, loving Him back, glorifying and enjoying Him in every moment, brings you into a life that is "lived unto God", and that is the most enjoyable life program you could ever buy into. Your whole focus is on your loving heavenly Father. This is the meaning of the devout life, and it is indeed available for all children of God, not only for some, not only for the favored, and not only for those in vocational ministry. Disciples learn to live in this realty rather than just sitting back and claiming to believe it but never experiencing it. Experiencing it, both here and in eternity, is the entire reason that God gives it.

Delighting in God

As if enjoyment is not enough to express, "...the riches of His grace which He lavished upon us" in Christ Jesus (Eph 1: 7-8), God takes the ultimate step in granting us the opportunity and ability to also delight in Him. The term "delight" goes even further, above and beyond "enjoy". It is possibly the highest level of enjoyment that could possibly be experienced. It's when you feel enjoyment even more deeply and more completely. It is the pinnacle of enjoyment. Delight is when your eyes widen, you lift your eyebrows and smile with pleasure. Your face kind of lights up when you have delight. You feel it all the way to your soul because delight comes from the soul. You feel all the resistance and attachment from anything negative kind of melt away, at least for the moment. It's how I feel when I am eating tiramisu, from the first bite to the last. If you could take delight in something every minute of the day, you would be the most relaxed, happy person on earth. This is what God calls us to all the time. It is part of His grace in Christ, and yet we know almost nothing of it in western Christianity.

Notice, please, that this is not something you understand by properly "exegeting the passages", or by application of any particular theology, or theological system. This is way beyond intellectual Christianity. It is also not something you experience by filling in some questions in a study book with the "right answers". It is enjoyment or delight in a Person. As with genuine love, the only way to truly know it is by experience. Just as with genuine love, taking delight is mutual. On His part, God takes delight in His people (Deut. 10:15), and if you delight in Him the river of joy and fulfillment flows bank full.

Beware false choices

I happened upon an interesting and thought-provoking article in "Knowing and Doing—A Teaching Quarterly for Discipleship of Heart and Mind", published by the C.S. Lewis Institute, dated Summer 2003. [47] The author, Dennis P. Hollinger, Ph.D., describes how various Christian students in His classes expressed a preference for either glorifying God or enjoying God. He describes the typical viewpoint, attitudes, and behaviors of each type of Christian, as he has experienced it. His brief analysis is easily recognized and quite common in a great many Christian circles. I've seen the same trends as well, and it is easy to agree with his analysis. The preference of each student would likely predict what kind of church is attended by each of these typical Christians.

What if we would all see and agree that these two are supposed to be joined together and they each drive the other forward. There is no choice forced upon us. There is no spectrum between opposites. Preferring to glorify God above enjoying God, or vice-versa, might be manifested in the early stages of discipleship, but how about glorifying God by enjoying Him? How about if we immensely enjoyed glorifying God? Would this be the legitimate goal for all disciples? If you can grasp and embrace this, you are on the road to discipleship. When you love God with all your being, you will absolutely enjoy bringing Him glory. The love for God that is prompted and energized by the indwelling Spirit of Christ is not an intellectual idea, nor is it an emotion that comes and goes, depending on how you feel at any particular moment. It is not controlled by your temperament or personality. It is unchanging and unstoppable. If every moment of your life could be experienced as enjoyable, would you call that hard and narrow? It is so addictive that you will want to do it more and more, and there is no end in sight!

God calls upon you, and urges you, to make this part of your personal goal as a disciple. It is the normal Christian life that He intended and that Jesus Himself knew fully without restraint, but it is not learned in churchianity. It is only learned in Biblical discipleship. The path lies before you. Step onto it and pursue it with all your heart! Your Savior and Mentor goes ahead of you and walks beside you to instruct you in the way! (Isa. 30:21)

CHAPTER 22

KNOWING AND FELLOWSHIPPING WITH GOD

Knowing God

Perhaps you have heard the following as a response to criticisms that Christianity is just a religion: "Christianity is not a religion. It is a relationship with God." Of course, I agree, but let me ask some similar questions as before: How much time did you spend this past week, having a deeply satisfying relationship with God? Have you considered that the center of your relationship with God should be loving Him with all your heart, mind, soul and strength? When you attended church recently, how much time and attention was given to having a deeply satisfying relationship with God? When you had your quiet time with the Lord lately, how much time and attention was given to having a deeply satisfying relationship with Him? How much time would you spend in simply standing, sitting, kneeling in the powerful glowing stream of mutual love—His love to you and your reflected love back to Him? When you took part in small group recently, how much time and attention was given to having a deeply satisfying relationship with God? If there were at least two believers there, His promise is to be there also, "in the midst". (Matt. 18:20) Did you sense His presence? Did you turn your attention to His presence? Did you make Him welcome? Did you involve Him in the conversation? Did you share your heart with Him in any moments other than during the official "prayer time"? If you would do that, how would that change your relationship with Him? Perhaps you noticed that the questions above added the qualifying phrase, "deeply satisfying". If you did not notice, go back over them again and reflect on whether your relationship was deeply satisfying in each of these scenarios.

I fear that the phrase "having a relationship with God" has come to be so commonly used that it has lost its meaning. It's like asking someone, "How are you?" The socially correct answer is always, "Fine." I am not convinced that most of those who use such phrase really know what they are claiming or advocating. All sorts of scenarios and experiences can be thought of as "having a relationship with" God. You might have a relationship with your neighbor, but it may be good, bad or mediocre. You may have a relationship with a friend or family member that is strained and awkward. It barely qualifies as a relationship, but it does exist. You may have a relationship with the people you work with, and each one is different. Relationship is such a broad term that it bears further defining. Relationships may be good, bad or ugly. They may be wonderful, painful or somewhere in between. So, what kind of relationship do you have with God?

As our Lord begins His High Priestly prayer in John 17, Jesus says that the Father had given Him authority over all humanity, so that He (Jesus) could give eternal life to those who had been given to Him. Then He states, "This is eternal life, *to know You, the only true God, and Jesus Christ whom You have sent.*" (John 17:3) One of the most prominent themes in the Gospel of John is this eternal life. Throughout his book, John tells us that eternal life is a gift of God by believing (believe/entrust/commit) in/into His Son. This statement by Christ is not a contradiction to all those other statements about the need to believe in Him for eternal life. This statement is an all-encompassing description of the ultimate outcome of believing unto eternal life. The highest meaning of eternal life is to know the eternal God. Receiving eternal life through Christ Jesus allows you to step into the reality of *actually knowing the real God*. You step out of the world of religion (or no-religion), with its ceremonies, rituals, formulas, rules, services, etc. and step into the world of actually having real-life contact with the One True God who really exists and really is as He has described Himself to be, both in the Scriptures and ultimately in His Son. You get to experience God, not with your normal five senses, but in your spirit, which is now alive to God in Christ. Paul speaks of losing all things but considering them as worthless trash compared to gaining the privilege of knowing Christ. (Phil 3:7-8) Paul did not say this out of theological or religious obligation. He had come to full terms with the meaning of Jesus' words that selling all you have in order to have the kingdom of God is well worth it (Matt 13:44). It is not a sacrifice. It is the best trade you ever made! In both Ephesians and Colossians, Paul prays for his fellow Christians that they would increase in their knowledge of God (Eph. 1: 17, Col. 10), as does Peter (II Peter 1:2). He could not have said this with any semblance of integrity unless he really knew this was the greatest gift that he could possibly give—to pray for others to have this knowledge of God.

Knowing God is not a blind reaching out in the dark of a pitch-black room or universe, hoping that someday you will finally touch something that might be real. It is not joining in some religious or spiritual ceremony or ritual, hoping to somehow find some eternal meaning in it that satisfies your soul. It is not enjoying the liturgy or religious ceremonies because it is somehow comforting. It is not enjoying a good Bible study. It is not knowing or enjoying your favorite Christian music. It is truly *knowing God and His Son, Jesus Christ.*

Knowing God, as Scripture invites us to, is not limited to *knowing about* God. It is not knowing all the Scriptures about God. God has given us the written revelation of Himself in the Scriptures. An important part of knowing God is to learn about Him from His inspired and complete word. By careful, thorough and prayerful study of the Scriptures, we learn things about God that we could never otherwise know, or at least not with the necessary certainty. These tell us the characteristics of God that are so far beyond ourselves that we cannot truly grasp them, even on the basis of inspired Scripture. His eternal attributes could never be fathomed by the unassisted human mind. His written revelation overcomes part of that and becomes the springboard to know them further than the superficial/intellectual knowledge of the Scriptures. Scriptures tells us that Jesus Christ is, "…the radiance of His glory and the exact representation of His nature…". (Heb 1:3) Jesus told the disciples, "He that has seen Me has seen the Father". Since the disciples had seen Him (Christ) they had also seen and known the Father. (John 14: 7) This is all part of the Scriptural record that helps us to know God and His Son.

However, even a comprehensive grasp of Scripture leaves us short on truly knowing God as a Living Being with whom we can have a relationship. We are reading and studying an ancient written record with the belief, large or small, firm or shaky, that doing so will somehow enable us to actually know God. When we are invited to have a relationship with God, it is the invitation to truly relate to Him, to have personal interaction with Him, not just the written testimony about Him. But it is essential that you understand what God tells us in that same inspired word of God. In order to have a relationship with God we must reach out beyond the inspired written record, as perfect and complete as it is, to the One True God who inspired and gave it and who wants us to know Him in close-up-and-personal relationship—the One True God Who Really Exists. We are invited and urged to stand on the solid platform of revealed Scripture and reach out further into the light of faith and actually know God in a living, vital relationship. He is here! He is real! He is not silent, and He is not withdrawn! This privilege is extended to us on the basis of grace. It is a gift!

Because we are in Christ, we are invited to kneel before Him and sit beside Him and talk our hearts out with the assurance that He is always attentive, always accepting, always loving and always delighted that we came. This is our standing in Christ. It is guaranteed because of all that Christ is and all He has done for us. Not only are we "accepted in the Beloved" (KJV). We are actually, "…highly favored in the Beloved One." (translation mine, compare Eph. 1:6, Col. 1:13 with Luke 1:28). This is the life to have that is worth selling all else. It is the life that follows in the footsteps of our Savior, Jesus Christ. Only you can determine not to have this by refusing to reach out or withdrawing into your own little shell of existence. Why would you do something so foolish? Yet most Christians have done this, but only because no one has taught them to do otherwise. With no one to guide them, (Acts 8: 30-31) they choose instead to stay within their own little American way of life plus churchianity. And God stands by the way, peering far down the road hoping to see your form—ragged, weak and starving—finally coming toward Him so He can rush to your side and embrace you...finally.

In speaking to the Christians in Laodicea, (Rev. 3:14-22) Christ described the grievous failures and errors that they had fallen into. His prescription for their recovery was not a new building, additional staff, a new leadership, or new computer simulation software. It was their need to invite Him back into their individual lives. He was *standing outside and knocking* to gain entry. We must understand that His offer was not to only stop by for a bite to eat then go on to the next one on the list. This wasn't like pastoral visitation. It was to have deeply satisfying relationship and fellowship with each one—then never leave. Sorry, no smart phones or tablets at the table while Jesus is present.

Fellowship with God

Paul writes, "God is faithful, through whom you were called into fellowship with His Son, Jesus Christ our Lord. (I Cor. 1:9) John tells us, "...and indeed our fellowship is with the Father and with His Son, Jesus Christ." (I John 1:3) Typically, this leads to other verses and accompanying comments that tell us that avoiding sin is essential to having fellowship with God and that having a faithful personal time or quiet time with the Lord each day is the way to have this fellowship. The role of reading/studying Scripture and prayer is certainly important, but then the Christian goes on their way off into the day ahead as if God had remained in the prayer closet, and He will be there again tonight or tomorrow when we return. Avoiding sin is truly important, as John himself tells us in later portions of his letter, but there is much more to the fellowship experience than just dealing with sin. There must be more to it, and there is. As indicated in Chapter 11, most Christians who lived prior to the printing press or even the middle of the eighteenth century did not have personal Bibles or the privilege and opportunity for personal Bible study each day. How would this great multitude of Christians have fellowship with God if they had no Bibles and/or could not read? Christians have always had the privilege of prayer. Did the lack of Bibles push them into spending more time in personal meditation, prayer and worship, simply being in His presence, instead of Bible study where it is all too easy to disguise a lack of relationship in the dress of intellectual Christianity? How do you like it when your child limits their contact with you to the obligatory ten-minute phone call each day, especially if the call is focused on something they want from you?

The Apostle John tells us that, "…our fellowship is with the Father and with His Son, Jesus Christ." He invites others to "… have fellowship with us" (I John 1:3). Then throughout his letter he states and describes the behavior and attitudes that always go together with those who have this shared fellowship with the Father and the Son. Fellowship is a level of knowing. It's a level of intimacy that is well beyond superficiality and formality. It goes far beyond "two fellows in the same ship" (also known as two shipwreck survivors). The term fellowship in Scripture always means "a sharing in". If nothing is shared, fellowship has not occurred. Fellowship with God only occurs when something is shared with God. It is not like being accepted into a kingdom only to never see or talk with the King.

In his gospel, John speaks of abiding in Christ, "...as the branch abides in the vine." (John 15: 1-11) No greater fellowship is possible than the fellowship of the branch with the vine from which it grew, and now, from which it must draw all its essential life nourishment. The branch is seen as if it is distinct from the vine, yet all it has for its existence and life is drawn from the vine. The branch cannot bear fruit of itself. It must draw all from the vine, even providing a space for the fruit to develop and ripen. The only purpose of the branch is to fulfill the purpose of the vine to bear fruit. When the branch bears fruit, it has completed its purpose. It is fulfilled, and it is how the branch lives out the principle, "It is enough for the student to become like the teacher." (Matt 10:25) In John's letters, he develops this truth to unequivocally state that when a Christian claims to abide in Christ, he will clearly live and be like Jesus. Sound familiar?

If having fellowship means to share in common, ask yourself how much, and in what way, do you share things with God? Centering your life in God and being spiritually alive to God must be more than just something you say you believe, but in which you have no living reality. When you center your life in God, it will result in rich, warm fellowship with God. This will be a fellowship with God in everything your life contains— everything you experience, everything you feel, everything you think, everything you do, everything you desire, etc. You must think of it in much the same way as sharing tangible things with friends or family. You share a sandwich, you share a dessert, you share viewing a beautiful sunset. It is something you do together. The fact that they are there sharing it with you is perhaps the most important part of the experience. In a traditional dating scenario, sharing things that you consider personal can be a big step in the relationship. It communicates something that might lead to kinship. It implies that you may have an interest in sharing life together.

But true fellowship goes far beyond that. It is a sharing of hearts, souls and spirits. You feel as if you are united in some deep way that is hard to explain. It is the fruition of Christ's words, "I in you and you in Me, just as the Father is in Me and I am in the Father." (John 14:20, 17:21) You don't become part of God or part of the Trinity, but there is a mystical adhering/joining, a spiritual level of hand-in-hand and arm-in-arm. The custom in some indigenous cultures of "embracing" with hands to shoulders and touching forehead to forehead is a powerful physical picture of this spiritual reality that is far bigger. This is the kind of fellowship God invites you to. If we think we don't share much in common with God, it is only because we are so dull of hearing, seeing and understanding. Everything that exists, except for sin, is created by God and shared with you by God, in the hope that we will come into face-to-face fellowship as we enjoy these things with Him and in the process learn to enjoy Him. After all, enjoying Him is part of the highest purpose for every human.

We do, in fact, have kinship with God. We are His born-again children who are alive to Him in our spirits by the indwelling of His Holy Spirit. God thinks of us in much the same way as human parents think of their dear children, with one powerful exception. Human parents prepare and seek to see their children launch out on their own for their own life. However, God does not. God prepares and seeks for His children to come closer and closer and closer. This is not a closer that is dimensional or spatial. It is a "closer" that is relationship, fellowship, sharing. It is the experiential side of, "...abiding in Him" as the branch abides in the vine. (John 15: 4-5, 10) The connection of the branch to the vine is at the cellular level. This is how close Jesus wants us to be with Him, no exceptions.

Being spiritually alive to God allows us to have the living reality of fellowship and enjoyment of God. It is not only a doctrine to believe or profess. He is inviting us into this moment-by-moment experience of living with such vital connection to Him that it is like the branch that draws all of its life from the vine. Paul said that, "It is Christ that lives in me…," (Gal. 2:20) and "…to live is Christ." (Phil. 1:21) Just understanding it mentally and saying you believe it is not all that Christ wants for you. Just having it positionally is not all that Christ wants for you. He wants you to know the living reality in moment-by-moment life—all of life.

This is the level of fellowship that our Lord invites us into, and it has seldom been known in any western church—not liturgical, not evangelical and not charismatic/ Pentecostal. It is not a level or type of fellowship that occurs only when you "serve the Lord". It is the ultimate of being one with God, through Christ. This is real. This is what God invites you to. It is part of a normal Christian life. Remember, "normal" means "as it was supposed to be" by copying the original pattern, not how it turned out after years of repeatedly copying flawed copies.

This is the kind of fellowship and enjoyment of the Father that Jesus had, and His disciples are seeking to become like Him. It is possible, and it is normal. However, this is only entered and experienced after learning to walk in the way of a disciple of Jesus. When you work through subsequent books and workbooks you will discover this is true. This is because it is so different from "canned western Christianity". If you want this blessed kind of life, you must learn each step of becoming a disciple. That's learning to *consistently do* as a new way of life, not merely learn to know, understand, and mentally "believe". I beg you to surrender to this step. You will never regret it and you will never walk away from it!

Recognizing the obstacles

There are a number of obstacles to seeing this fulfilled in your life, but none is bigger or more powerful than the belief that since you are not in "full time ministry/service", most of your time, energy, possessions, income and life belong to you. As long as you give God "His share", like attending church and church activities, giving/tithing/, and occasionally serving in some way at church, etc. you are good to go. This is the long-standing tradition of churchianity. In fact, if your pastor can get you to do this much, s/he feels like s/he has really accomplished a lot and will tell you that you are living a very dedicated life for God. But you will not experience the kind of fellowship that Jesus was speaking of and offering. The kind of fellowship He was speaking of is only available by centering your life in God, and it has nothing to do with quitting your job, selling your house and taking up the ministry. It is also more than refraining from lies, theft, deceit, gossip, laziness and occasionally sharing the gospel at work.

Not surprisingly, other obstacles include those matters that are described above and in Chapters 5-11. Choosing not to center your life in God, or not living in your spiritual aliveness will not put you on the right track to start fellowshipping with God as He desires and intends. The alternative usually chosen is centering your life in the American Dream and churchianity with all they seem to promise. Unfortunately, they do not pay off, and you eventually go away feeling like, "Why did I give so much of my life to those things? Now they don't seem that important. Did I waste my life?" Choosing to accept chur-chianity as the only valid version of Christianity will not put you on the right track to start fellowshipping with God as He desires and intends. Eventually it bares its soul as the American enterprise version of Christianity. That's why attendance drops when the pastor leaves. The forsaken church suffers a great blow, often struggling for years to recover, and may even cease to exist. Choosing to believe that obedience and pleasing God are versions of legalism will not put you on the right track to start fellowshipping with God as He desires and intends. Only true discipleship leads you to, "I have such a blessed life. I must tell others about this."

Your Heavenly Father is the only one worthy of being the center your life. He is the only one who can lead you into a deeply satisfying life and eternity. He seeks deep and fully sat-isfying fellowship with you, but you must choose it. Like love, fellowship is a two-way street and if you do not choose and pursue it, you will not experience it. Think of what a tragedy that would be if you were to find out how much you have been missing all this time. Think of what sorrow will fill your heart when you realize this loss. Only true Biblical discipleship will teach you how to grasp this firmly and never let go.

CHAPTER 23

ENJOYING LIFE
AND ALL THINGS

T he most wonderful surprises are waiting for all who enter
into the disciple's life. All are invited, all may come. The way
is full of blessings, based on grace, "…buy without money and
without cost." (Isa 55: 1-2) It is not any version of the health,
wealth and prosperity message, nor is it an invitation to live
a miserable existence with a long gloomy face or some bland,
boring sameness all the time. It is an invitation to a wonderful
and fulfilling life.

Psalm 119 is full of statements of the manifold blessings of
hearing, heeding, understanding and doing God's commandments, as expressed in the Law. We would be prone to attribute
these statements to the Old Covenant, as aspects of legalism, yet
the result expressed by the psalmist in Ps. 119:45 was, "…and
I will walk at liberty for I seek your precepts." If this is an attribute of the Law and the Old Covenant, how much more wonderful should the New Covenant be? Jesus spoke of the mandate
to enter the small gate and walk the narrow path to be a disciple. (Matt. 7:14) Yet He also described His yoke as "easy and
light"—something that would give "rest for your souls". (Matt.

11:30) How is this apparent contradiction possible? Questions that churchianity cannot understand much less answer. It's like asking whether light is a form of energy or a particle.

Various philosophies and religions over the centuries have promoted one or the other extremes of lavish living or frugal living as the path to contentment. In the American Dream, we easily learn to enjoy the prosperity, and we often think that more plenty will bring more contentment. We have sometimes passed through the "getting along" stretches. "Doing all things by His strength…" is usually assigned to the stretches of "getting by", but typically we are not content during these times.

Jesus tells us that He did not even have a place to lay His head…" (Luke 9:58) during His ministry years, but you never get the impression He felt terribly needy for more real estate and a designer bedroom. How much you own is not the point. It is how content you are! If I'm not mistaken, contentment is what we are all longing for after all. Jesus teaches His disciples how to have this. It is His promise for those who take up His yoke in discipleship. (Matt. 11: 28-30)

Paul tells us that he had learned an important secret in His service for the Master. He had learned how to be content and get along with little, as well as how to be content and get along with plenty. (Phil 4:2) How do you learn to be "content" in all circumstances? Yet, this is what Paul clearly says. This may sound like a feast or famine experience, constantly bouncing back and forth between the two extremes, but this is not Paul's intention. His point is that he has learned to live out a fulfilling life of a disciple and servant of Christ no matter the circumstances, even to the extremes of the spectrum. The emphasis is on contentment. He had learned the secret of being content. (Phil 4:11) Paul had learned his Lord's teaching that, "...a man's life does not consist in the abundance of things." (Luke 12:15)

Paul directed the rich to fix their hope not on uncertain wealth, but on God, who, "...richly provides us with all things to enjoy..." (I Tim. 6:17). He is not urging them not to put hope in their riches *for salvation*. He is urging them not to look to their riches as the ultimate source of *enjoyment and contentment*. The contradiction that forms the backbone of Paul's statement is almost shocking. Most who have riches, or even sufficiency, believe that their "all things to enjoy" comes from their wealth. "All things to enjoy..." comes from what is over and above having what is necessary.

Contentment is another one of those things that cannot be acquired or received by intellectual pursuits. Any honest reading of the Book of Ecclesiastes will confirm that. Although many try, you cannot acquire contentment by an in-depth intellectual knowledge of the Bible or how to exegete its most difficult passages. Contentment is an emotions word. It is a feeling word. It is a deep feeling that all is right and good things are ahead. It feels like safe and secure and warmth, peace, and rest and belonging. At the risk of going too far, it feels like the Garden of Eden, our original home before sin suddenly invaded. Even if you may disbelieve the Biblical record of the Garden of Eden, you cannot deny your longing for it. Interesting, huh? How does evolution explain that?

If you could return to Eden on the innocence side (before sin entered) what kind of life would you experience? Would it feel like safe and secure and warmth, peace, and rest and belonging? That's what we were made to be. That's how we were designed to live by our good Creator. It was sin that destroyed it all.

Contentment may strike you as too passive. If so, you can also think of it as deep enjoyment of life—all of life. Deep enjoyment of life is much like giving thanks for everything. On this side of the Garden of Innocence, life presents itself to us as a mix of good and evil. Each experience of pain, suffering, grief, sorrow, or loss is caused by sin. Sometimes this is our own sin and sometimes that of others, but it is always because of sin and its ongoing results. Each such painful experience is God's statement that sin never brings good or blessing. We are forced to learn this lesson over and over. The lesson is supposed to move us to abandon sin completely, once and for all. We do not enjoy what is painful, like suffering, grief, sorrow, loss of dear things and people in our life. However, in every such experience, we can rejoice that one day, God will destroy and remove all things that cause pain, suffering, grief, sorrow, or loss of dear things and people. In the meantime, He also places us in situation after situation that allows us to be His agents to minimize, soften, reduce, and even end the destructive results of sin. All too often, the Church has miserably failed this mission. This has led the unbelieving world to believe that we turn a blind eye to sin, even coddle it for our own advantages.

At the same time, we can deeply enjoy all that is good in the world that God has given us, and there is a lot of it, if we only pay attention, notice and respond to God with immediate thanks. This is far more than just "stopping to smell the roses" once in a while. It is noticing all good things all along the way, as we encounter them. As we live connected to God as the center of our entire life, we can see all good things and stop momentarily to thank and praise our Heavenly Father. He is there and

He is not silent. He is there and not absent to the person whose spirit has been made alive to Him.

The core problem is that all too often, we do not truly enjoy what is good. We take it for granted as what we are entitled to. Since we take these as entitlements, we also do not respond to God with thanks. We don't see the good things as good gifts given by a good God who gives us all things to enjoy *as we enjoy Him*. (I Tim. 6:17, James 1: 17) This would lend itself as nourishment to the soul, but we don't do that. It would also lend itself as an open witness to the unbelieving world. It would prompt them to earnestly ask us about this great hope that gives us such contentment. (I Peter 3:15)

Soul satisfaction

When you experience true contentment, you experience well-being in your soul. Even though it is often spoken of in Scripture, the well-being of the soul is not a very familiar matter with much of the church. It is pictured well in Psalm 23. This passage cannot possibly be truly understood intellectually, and it calls for far more than just acceptance as something to be believed by faith. All the word pictures wrapped into this psalm have one message: "It is well with my soul". You could also call it the Old Testament version of, "I have learned to be content in all circumstances".

John Ortberg's fine book *Soul Keeping* [48]is well worth reading. It uses a somewhat traditional basis for well-being of the soul. Most of the principles are also taught by numerous traditional sources, but Ortberg's book is clearly presented from the Christian viewpoint. Those who follow this guidance can certainly experience greater well-being of the soul, but I believe it misses an element that is wholly essential to be fully Biblical. To be fully Biblical, it must be solidly anchored on the spiritual foundation of God Himself. Only then will it be "regardless of my circumstances". So, how/where can I find well-being for my soul regardless of my circumstances?

It is undeniable that woven throughout the Scriptures is the message that well-being of the soul comes from the God who created and nourishes our soul. It comes from living in harmony and closeness to Him. It comes from living life in His way, not in the way that *we invent*, which is actually, "the way of death." (Prov. 14:12) It is the way of Christ, as taught and modeled by Him. It is taking up His yoke and learning His ways, because in that path alone, we "find rest for our souls". (Matt 11:29)

As a disciple of Jesus, you will learn, in the most personal and practical way, that all good things come down from the Father above. You will learn this not just as a doctrine to believe by faith, but as a way of life—as a life principle to follow. Sometimes, that good way is abundance. Other times it is less than what you might prefer. Other times it might be deprivation or hardship. Sometimes it is lush green grass and quiet waters. Other times it is the valley of the shadow of death but safeguarded by your Shepherd. Most of the time, it is somewhere in between—just normal life, and that is where we tend to lose sight of Him.

The Father who provides all things for His children provides them for our enjoyment, not just for our endurance. Learn to truly enjoy the things that are enjoyable, then learn that even the hard times are laced with things to enjoy, all threads that can nourish the soul. The well-being of our souls comes from truly and freely enjoying all these things in the way that our Father in heaven meant for them. Enjoy them and enjoy the God who gives them as the Giver of every good gift! Delight yourself in the Lord! As you do this, you will learn to have a zest for life that is unsurpassed. You will have a blessed life! "Blessed are those…" (Matt 5: 3)

CHAPTER 24

LIVING IN GOD'S KINGDOM— THEN, NOW, AND THEN

Discipleship in the Kingdom of God

The amount of written material on the subject of the kingdom of God is huge. It is as if all those theologians, interpreters, teachers, preachers and authors were trying to rival John's words that if all the deeds of Jesus were written down, the whole world could not contain the books. (John 21:25) It is an important subject set forth in the Scriptures, and it is well worth the time and effort to gain at least a basic grasp of the subject. As with other subjects referred to in this book, it would be well beyond the scope to launch into a thorough treatment of the subject of the kingdom of God. However, it's importance and role in Biblical discipleship compels me to include certain elements which must not lie untouched. I have found it to be very helpful in grasping certain aspects of discipleship.

Regardless of which view or theology of the kingdom you may favor (if any), each of them generally recognizes that any kingdom has three common and indispensable elements. Any kingdom must have a ruler (such as a king/queen), subjects which are ruled (a.k.a. citizens/subjects) and a realm, (where that rule extends). For purposes of this book, I recommend a fourth element, which is *a culture* (social and behavioral customs and norms that reflect that rule, over those citizens, in that place). In other words, what would it be like to live under this ruler, under his/her law and in this place with the other citizens who live there with you?

Throughout the Old Testament, it is asserted that God is the Sovereign Ruler over all the heavens and the earth and everything in them. Yet in the book of Revelation, a time yet future is described as when, "The kingdom of the world has become the kingdom of our Lord and of His Christ..." (Rev. 11:15) This span seems confusing to most, but it need not be so.

As recognized by nearly all reputable commentators and teachers, the kingdom of God is, in fact, the overarching theme of the entire Scriptures. Within this overall theme is also a sub-theme about good and evil. How did evil ever arise in a universe created and controlled by a good God? Why? How did it affect the human race so powerfully? What is the ultimate destiny of evil and all those who perpetrated or joined it? As this theme progresses and expands through the Scriptures, it focuses more and more on that end of time when Christ returns and establishes His kingdom on earth. These passages predict very specific things or conditions that would be established as part this kingdom that will yet be established fully by God.

Without exception, these passages also declare that before this kingdom is instituted, a great judgment by the One True God will be carried out to include all Israel and all Gentiles. Even though all nations will be included, the primary focus is on Israel and her ancient neighbors. Even for those of Israel, all must "pass under the rod". (Ezek. 20:37) In Daniel, a specific but "obscured" timetable of "prophetic weeks" is set forth for all of these events. Within these passages is also woven the promise of a Messiah and Savior who will come to redeem Israel before the judgment falls.

When John the Baptist arrives as the "forerunner", his message is, "Repent, for the kingdom of heaven is at hand" (Matt 3:1). To the Jewish leaders and teachers, he warns, "…who warned you to flee from the wrath to come?" (Matt. 3:7) To those who thought they could simply come to participate in another official ritual to escape judgment, he warned, "Bear fruits in keeping with repentance". (Matt. 3:8) He further warned these Jewish leaders that they would find no safety from judgment and wrath in their claim that they were sons of Abraham. (Luke 3:7-8) Only the truly righteous will escape the judgment and be accepted into the kingdom of God. Jesus began His public ministry by declaring the same message as John the Baptist, "Repent for the kingdom of heaven is at hand." (Matt. 3:1, 4:17) This continued to be His message and focus for much of His earthly ministry.

Each theological viewpoint of "the kingdom of heaven" recommends a specific and differing meaning, both short-term and long-term. A popular and wide-spread theology in the Church drives a wedge between kingdom and Church, as being separate programs of God that must never be confused or overlapped. A careful consideration will lead us to a better understanding of the Scripture without creating conflicts or contradictions. This begins with the proclamations by John the Baptist and Jesus, "Repent, for the kingdom of God is at hand." (Matt. 3:1)

The literal meaning of the original Greek word for "at hand" is "has come near". There are a number of things that are essential to accurately grasp this offer that the kingdom "has come near":

1. It is in the perfect indicative verb form in the ancient Greek text. This is the verb tense that normally expresses completed action. There is no indication or implication that nearness of the kingdom of God is temporary, dependent on anything, nor will it be withdrawn. It won't disappear in a few days or weeks or years. It is as if Jesus was saying, "The door into the kingdom has been installed and opened for all who wish to enter."

2. "Near" can refer to time, as "it will happen soon". However, just as legitimately, it can also mean it is "close by", i.e. "It is located not far from here" or "it's readily available." If someone asked you to direct them to the closest gas station which was just down the street and around the corner, you might say, "Oh sure. Its real close by (near). Just keep on this street down to the corner, then turn left and go about two blocks down that street. It will be on the right side of the street. You can walk there if you need to." If you are waiting on a call to pick up a friend at the airport, you might say, "I need to keep the phone handy (near), in case he calls." If you are camping in the open in bear territory, you might tell your companion that you are going to keep your bear spray "handy" during the night, in other words keep it somewhere you can grab it quickly and easily—"keep it near".

3. None of this can mean anything like, "The kingdom of heaven has arrived. It is here right now." Nor can it mean, "The kingdom of God might come sometime soon, and will only be available for a short window of time. After that, it won't be available again for a long, long time". It also cannot mean, "The kingdom of God has been set up in heaven for eternity; and when you die, you will get to go there if you believe in Me."

It is quite clear from the pertinent Scriptures that there is some degree of overlap between the kingdom of God and the Church. Otherwise, several statements by Paul make no sense at all, such as:

- "...for the kingdom of God is not eating and drinking, but righteousness, and peace and joy in the Holy Spirit." (Rom. 14: 17)

Paul is speaking of the questions at hand about eating and drinking things that have been offered to idols. He is clearly alluding to the fact that Christians are in the kingdom of God.

- "The kingdom of God does not consist in word, but in power." (I Cor. 4:20)

Paul is speaking of those who have been attempting to arrogantly undermine his apostolic authority by criticizing certain aspects of his way of life and ministry. He is linking his gospel ministry with the kingdom of God.

- "...these are the only fellow-workers for the kingdom of God from the circumcision." (Col. 4:10-11)

Paul is speaking of Aristarchus, Mark and Justus who had labored with him in the work of the gospel and the care of the churches. He is not speaking of heaven or of an offer of the Messianic kingdom that is now withdrawn until the Second Coming.

Paul also says that the Gentile Christians have been made, "...fellow-citizens with the saints and members of the household of God." (Eph 2:19) Citizen is a term used of a country, or kingdom, not something unique and different as the Church or the Body of Christ. Paul is clearly stating that those in the Church are also citizens of the kingdom on an equal basis as "the saints".

It seems we have missed that, within John's message of wrath to come, his overall message was to, "...repent and be baptized for the forgiveness of sins". He clearly stated that, although many would be judged by God as, "trees to be cut down and thrown into the fire and, ... "chaff to be burned with unquenchable fire...", the overarching message is to "repent and be baptized for forgiveness of sins". He clearly declared that those who pass through the winnowing process of the coming "Greater One" would be gathered into His barn and not be consumed in the fires of the coming judgment.

Nowhere in the Old Testament is it stated, or implied, that baptism can forgive sins. The Law quite clearly states that "There is none righteous, no not one" (Ps. 14, 3-4, Rom. 3:10), and, "Without the shedding of blood, there is no forgiveness." (Heb. 9:22). John came as the forerunner of the One who would execute God's judgment and wrath. How could he proclaim that repentance and baptism would forgive sins? To this mix is added the fact that the Ark of the Covenant had never been found or returned to the Jewish temple after it disappeared in connection with the Babylonian captivity in approximately 587 BCE. The annual Day of Atonement was not possible during that entire time, including the time of John, the time of Jesus, and right up to and including now. When the high priest entered the Holy of Holies in Herod's temple, there was no Ark of the Covenant where the atoning blood was to be sprinkled. How did they observe the Day of Atonement all those intervening years? (Some scholars believe that within the Holy of Holies all those years was the original cornerstone of the old temple that had been destroyed, and that is where the blood was sprinkled each of those years.)

Upon this scene arrives Jesus. Much to our surprise, He begins His public ministry with the same declaration. "Repent, for the kingdom of God is at hand." However, when we look closely, we discover that His message takes on something new. To the message preached normally by John, He adds, "...believe the good news" (Mark 14-15, Matt. 4:23). How can a message of coming wrath and doom, from which few will escape, be considered as "good news"? The only possible answer that is demanded by the Scriptures is that the judgment and wrath are preceded by forgiveness of sin based on something the Law could not do. The good news is that forgiveness is available, now on a new basis. Forgiveness by grace! Throughout the gospels and the rest of the New Testament, this forgiveness by grace is proclaimed as being only through Jesus Christ—the Messiah, who comes first as, "...the Lamb of God who takes away the sin of the world. (John 1: 29)

All of the gospels clearly present the Kingdom of God as having two phases of implementation. First, the phase when God's grace and forgiveness is offered to the whole world, then the phase of wrath and judgment outpoured on the whole world who of those have not accepted His gracious offer. This is especially true of the Gospel of Luke. The most widely respected Dispensationalists acknowledge this and often refer to the first phase as "the mystery" phase. This first phase comes to be known as "the Church" —those who have been called out of the world and assembled unto Jesus Christ—those who have been "called out of judgement unto eternal life". (John 5:24) This is the emphasis of most of the New Testament. However, this does not deny that the Church is part of God's kingdom, as clearly demonstrated by the above Scriptures and others as well. Then how is the Church part of the kingdom, and therefore part of discipleship? This where it really gets good!

Moving to a New Country

Imagine your company transferred you to another country to work for them there. This has been a fairly common occurrence from time to time, as companies expand to international markets. To make the illustration clearer, let's say that your new location is a kingdom, ruled by a very benevolent, kind but strong king. All the citizens just love their king!

The country of your placement is significantly different than your home in many ways, yet not in ways that are oppressive or even disagreeable—just very different. This new country is much more uniform in their culture rather than a melting pot of culture like the United States. In order to properly represent your company, you must adapt, and join in with this new culture. You learn new things and new ways that you had not known before. Over time, you come to see that, in a great many ways, their culture is more enjoyable and fulfilling than your home culture. More and more you welcome it, surrendering your own culture. Eventually, you might even decide to emigrate permanently and become a citizen of the new country and its culture. This certainly has happened in our world, even in our own time.

Now, let's imagine that a high-ranking member of the royal family is selected to personally mentor and guide you into being part of this new culture. S/he is also very benevolent, kind and strong. This mentor guides you into more than superficially adapting to the new culture, but how to truly enter into it by how you think, how you feel, and how you instinctively respond. As you learn it at this far deeper level, you find it more and more likable and fulfilling. You start wishing you could have learned these things long ago. What a difference it might have made in you and in your life!

The Kingdom Invaded and Disrupted

Let's add another layer to the illustration. Let's say that, as you live in your new culture, you hear stories that centuries ago this kingdom had been attacked and invaded by an evil king next door. That evil king nearly destroyed all the good things in your new home. Slowly, over time, by both power and influence, he nearly wiped out the good culture and forced an evil culture on the people. The tragic result was that once the evil king was finally driven out and the country returned to its own people, most had forgotten who they really were and how they used to live. Only the wise old ones remembered. However, gradually, the wise ones were able to teach new generations who they really were and how to live in the joyous traditional culture, but the influences of the evil lingered on for a long time. Finally, it was accomplished, and the traditional culture once again prevailed, because it was so good that no one wanted to go back to evil.

A Tale of Two Kingdoms in the Same Space

Both of these illustrations tell the tale of humanity and the Church. Humanity was created as "good" and "very good", but evil attacked, invaded and destroyed much of what we were supposed to be. Now, we have a kingdom where both good and evil occupy the same space. Each one has a ruler, each one has an agenda to overcome and destroy the other, each one has its own citizens and participants who live by its principles and powers. Satan is an invader, trespasser, destroyer and usurper. He only knows how to kill, steal, destroy, lie and deceive. The citizens of the evil kingdom are his victims, but they have also become the perpetrators of his evil. Welcome to Stockholm!

The citizens of the good kingdom used to be citizens of the evil kingdom, but the good God chose to rescue them and return them to what they are supposed to be. Unfortunately, they find it difficult to learn. For many, they don't believe they can or even should. The habit of life is truly powerful! We have developed many who will tell us what we should know and believe about what we should be, but few indeed that will actually train us in fully doing it as our new home and lifestyle—our renewed culture. This requires discipleship! Discipleship trains and transforms us to be what we ought to be as citizens of the kingdom of God.

Unfortunately, evil has not yet been destroyed or expelled. It is still here and occupies the same space, side by side with the kingdom of God. Those who escape its control need much instruction to return to what they were supposed to be and can be once again. God is all powerful and this is His kingdom! He didn't leave. He can destroy evil anytime He wishes, and He promises that one day He will do so—forever. However, for now, He allows evil to share the space of His kingdom. Thus, two kingdoms in the same space. During this time, sincere Christians have the opportunity and privilege to learn how to live as a citizen of the ultimate kingdom of God, as we were meant to be. This is the foretaste of the ultimate kingdom where evil will be totally destroyed and only goodness will once again prevail.

As I ponder this "epic tale" over the years, I see two overarching purposes in this allowance by God. It displays two lessons across the universe and time that must be learned once and for all.

1.) Free will is a dangerous thing that can only be handled by a Being of infinite goodness and all those who willingly join their free will to the will of that Being.

2.) Evil never brings good. Not ever. It always produces sorrow and suffering—eventually. Those who live in this two-kingdom space are constantly confronted with, "Your ways and your deeds have brought these things to you. This is your evil! How bitter! How it has touched your heart" (Jer. 4:18) If they choose, God will rescue them and teach them differently—the way of goodness—the ancient way—the "Way of Christ."

The Third Kingdom

There is a third kingdom that is in play in this world. It is much like the "middle-of-the-road" described in Chapter 11. This is the kingdom of You, and what You want and what You prefer. The king of this kingdom is You. This is the only kingdom You have ever really known, and You think it is the only one that really exits.

When You become a Christian You accept Christ as Your Savior, allowing Him to enter Your kingdom—but only enough to save You from hell. If You take the next step, You accept Christ as Lord. You allow Him to live in Your kingdom with more rights over Your kingdom, but not too many. After all, it is Your kingdom!

You must recognize and embrace the knowledge that this third kingdom is merely a "shadow kingdom" of the evil kingdom. It isn't real at all! This kingdom came into existence when the original human pair chose to disobey God's command so that they might, "...become like God, knowing good and evil." (Gen. 3:5) This is the "middle-of-the road" kingdom. In this kingdom, You decide when You will do good and when You will do evil. This makes You your own god and your own king. This allows Satan to operate from the shadows, remaining invisible to your awareness. From there, he can play you, manipulate you, and deceive you into a destroyed life that eventually ends in sorrow, sadness, lack of fulfillment, and judgment from God.

Transfer of Kingdoms

Paul writes that, "He (God) has transferred us from the kingdom of Satan into the kingdom of His beloved Son (Christ)." (Col. 1:13, parentheses mine) Even though this Kingdom of God will ultimately be fulfilled in the Messianic Kingdom and in heaven, the Church is already its initial presence and expression here on earth. In this kingdom, Christ is Lord, and He will be back as our yet coming King. The kingdom has not been put on hold. Its first phase is in full effect. The message of free forgiveness and acceptance is being proclaimed throughout the world (salvation), and the citizens in this kingdom are being called and prepared for eternal life in the fulfilled kingdom (sanctification). Even though the King is not physically present, this kingdom has a culture of living in His commandments and teachings. This kingdom is, "within you." (Luke 17:21) Currently,

He rules not with the "rod of iron" but with the Shepherd's staff. He personally tutors each citizen to live in the culture of His kingdom, not to force unwelcome rules on you, but because His way is the very best way to live above all others! His kingdom is the very best kingdom you could ever wish to be part of, and He gives citizenship away—free! But along with citizenship is the expectation that you will live under the culture of His kingdom, and He will gladly teach and train you in these. They are new, and it takes time to learn them well.

In this kingdom, we learn to forgive—freely and wholeheartedly. This is what we do in the kingdom of God. In this kingdom, we learn to be kind—freely and wholeheartedly. This is what we do in the kingdom of God. In this kingdom, we learn to be gentle—freely and wholeheartedly. This is what we do in the kingdom of God. In this kingdom, we learn to be generous— freely and wholeheartedly. This is what we do in the kingdom of God. In this kingdom, we learn to interact and relate warmly, openly and sincerely. This is what we do in the kingdom of God. Etc. Etc. Etc. This culture is built by the King of this kingdom, and He invites us to learn it and enjoy its rich blessings.

No matter what particular theology of end times you prefer or adopt, a true Christian has faith vision of being there in the Kingdom of God, either on a renewed earth or in perfect heaven, or both. What kind of person do you see yourself to be in that perfect place? What kind of person do you think others will be? Will you be arguing and disputing over matters of doctrine, or position, or who is the greatest, or who should be chairperson of a committee? I doubt it. Will you be trying to figure out how to give the smallest amount so you can keep more for yourself? I doubt it. Will you be in a huff or a pout because you didn't get to choose the song for this week's worship service, or because you were not chosen to lead the worship team? I doubt it.

The church kingdom is like the warm-up for that ultimate perfect kingdom. It is like living on the great veranda of the mansion of heaven. From inside, you can savor the aroma of the most delectable dishes inside, and you even get to sample some on a regular basis. Inside the most wonderful worship imaginable is taking place, and you get to take part as you listen in from just beyond the door. All of this way of being and living is the "Way of Christ"— His way. In the church you learn the culture of the kingdom and you are called to be an avid student in that way. This world is not our home, and Christ wants you learn the culture of your future home—His kingdom. He wants to teach you as well as others who also on that same path.

By driving an artificial wedge between kingdom and church and by such neglect of Biblical discipleship, Christians have been deprived of so much of this, but it is possible. It was meant to be normal. Discipleship is the opportunity to learn the culture of the kingdom so that it sinks deep within you and becomes who you are. This is what we are supposed to be and do in the church, but until we fully embrace discipleship and true kingdom thinking and culture it will remain beyond our grasp. In one of the parables about serving, Jesus tells that the master gives "investment money" to servants and tells them, "Do business until I return." (Luke 19:13) Of course, the true Master is Christ. It is His kingdom and His culture and His business. We are here to do His bidding, not the other way 'round. His bidding was to make disciples! It's about time we got to His business, not ours!

CHAPTER 25

TOWARD A CHRISTIAN SPIRITUALITY

As mentioned in Chapter 11, it is extremely odd that Christianity has not taught Biblical spirituality. Unfortunately, it is not taught, and there is no encouragement or incentive to do so, other than the misguided and erroneous doctrines and practices of the charismatic church. Those who learn or develop Biblical spirituality typically do so outside the local church ministry. Sometimes this has been through the personal mentoring of a true disciple-maker, and other times it has been directly from Christ Himself. The outcome is a very visible and remarkable godliness, unhindered by the trappings of churchianity. It is glaringly obvious that except for those gemstones of exception out there, Christianity just does not get it. They don't make any real connection between what they hear, learn and do at church with any kind of daily spirituality.

If we simply hear the clear witness of Scripture, it is beyond doubt that Christianity was intended to be a spirituality. Above all other things it is a spirituality. It is the spirituality that is based solidly on the unshakable truth given by the One True Living God Who Really Exists—the God of the Bible. The reason sound doctrine is so important within Christianity is because it alone accurately teaches us this spirituality—how to truly know, love and obey the God of Abraham, Isaac, and Jacob—the God and Father of our Lord Jesus Christ.

When Paul writes to the Corinthian Christians, he told them that he could not give them mature truth, because mature truth could only be understood by those who are spiritual. (I Cor. 3:1-2) This leads to the inescapable conclusion that his letters to them did not include this mature truth. When he writes to the Ephesian and Colossian churches, he certainly writes mature truth, and he says he is praying for them to receive a spirit of, "…wisdom and revelation…" or "…spirit of wisdom and understanding…" so they can understand what he writes there. (Eph 1: 16-23, Col. 1:9-12) These Scriptures set forth what he referred to in I. Cor. 2:9-11—God's wisdom revealed and now declared to His church. Since the Western church is not spiritual, we still don't understand very well what Paul wrote in some of these sections. We can understand and explain the basic theology, but not the real meaning—not how to live in the reality.

> If we simply hear the clear witness of Scripture, it is beyond doubt that Christianity was intended to be a spirituality. Above all other things it is a spirituality.

Two generations ago, Lewis Sperry Chafer wrote, *He That Is Spiritual,* [49] but it is primarily a theology of the person and work of the Holy Spirit. It is a fine theology but gives little help to actually become spiritual. Subsequently, Francis A. Shaeffer wrote *True Spirituality* [50]. It is also largely an intellectual approach to the subject, providing solid theology as well as an intellectual framework. Chapters 5 and 6 especially present some understanding of Christian spirituality, but they focus on the "supernatural" aspects of the Christian faith, not using the terminology, concepts or experiences of "spirituality". Supernatural is still presented primarily as something to be believed by faith, not lived. It still falls short in actually tutoring and guiding individuals into a deep Christian spirituality. More importantly, spirituality does not demand "supernatural" at all. Spirituality teaches you to recognize and deeply love the "supernatural" that is all around us all the time, as well as its true source, power and purpose. We must do much better, and that will not happen until we learn to do discipleship much better! However, as alluded in Chapter 14, this requires that the disciple-maker is strongly spiritual to assure proper instruction and guidance to others in developing true spirituality.

Biblical spirituality is rather simple, and that is why it developed amongst simple people, like the ancient Celtic Christians of Ireland and Scotland. It is simply living fully and deeply all of normal life on the sole basis of really believing what God's Scriptures tell us is true. It is not based on imaginations, or traditions, or empty ceremonies or intellectual explanations, or churchianity. It is certainly not limited to only "the saints", or "the great ones" in the church, or as Paul put it, "those of reputation". (Gal. 2:2) It is to truly see, embrace, and interact with everything that exists based on its spiritual source (God) and its spiritual purpose (God's will). It is to truly see and live in the truth that, "All things are from Him and for Him and to Him". (Rom. 11:36) It is to rejoice in all that is good in all that exists, and to glorify and thank God for all of it. It is also to sorrow about all evil that has crept into what God created and intended as good.

Whenever possible, and in whatever small or large ways, true Biblical spirituality also seeks to limit or undo the evil that has crept in. It is to heal and save what can be healed or saved. The undoing is not by application of worldly power, or Papal armies, or by power of Church authority, but by the power of Truth, both in word and deed. The effort to undo, limit, heal and save is done in deliberate and conscious linking with God Himself who is seeking to do the same thing at all times. It is to be an ambassador for Christ, at all times and deliberately. It is to be a priest before God, at all times and deliberately. It is to "walk with God" (Gen. 3:22, 6:9) in all of life. God is not distant and not just a theological concept. He is all around you, but also within you through the Person of the Holy Spirit. Most of all, it is to do everything you do with a deliberate and fully aware connection to God in loving face-to-face fellowship. Biblical spirituality recognizes Him in everything and molds our thoughts, emotions, words, intentions and actions around that fact. This puts Him in the center of all of our lives, which is where He rightfully belongs. This is to be like Jesus, which every true disciple wants to be.

God is spirit. As a Christian, you have been made alive in spirit by the indwelling Holy Spirit sent by Christ. This can allow you to sense the presence of God at all times. Everything around you is not a spirit and does not have a spirit, but everything around you has a spiritual source (God) and a spiritual purpose (God's will). They do not exist by some accident of evolution. This includes all the things that are a delight to you and all the things that are a demand or stress upon you. Everything you do is *with Him* who is the Creator and Sustainer of all things. He deliberately included you in this reality He has made. He calls on you to be His agent, His ambassador, His priest—those who truly bear His image, His righteousness, His light. We seek to fulfill our Lord's directive, "Do (My) business until I come." (Luke 19:13, parenthesis mine) Our role is not as rulers, or as an occupying force, but as a vanguard. We are citizens left here to mind His kingdom and extend it until He returns to take it up fully Himself. We learn to be faithful citizens of a kingdom that has not yet fully come to the earth. The flaming torch of witness in this two-kingdom culture is the light that shines from you, as you seek to live out fully that, "The kingdom of God is within you." (Matt. 5:14, Luke 17:21) We learn to live in the fullness of all that is here, but in light of the greater fullness yet to come when He returns.

Living a Sacramental Life

The ancient Celtic Christians spoke of "thin places". These were certain "sacred places" where something special or significant had occurred to those that they considered to be very special and famous Christians who had led the way for them in Christ. Sometimes it was a vision from heaven, sometimes it was a miracle, sometimes it was direct intervention from God to provide for, or protect, His servants or His people, reminiscent of Old Testament experiences. They thought of these as places where God had "come near", breaking through the barrier between natural and supernatural. This mirrors the same error committed by famous Bible characters like Jacob, Gideon and others. (Gen 28: 10-19, Judges 6:11-25) When Jacob was fleeing his brother in the desert, he saw a ladder leading to heaven. Jacob's response the next morning was, "Surely the Lord is in this place, and I did not know it." (Gen. 28: 16) He then proceeded to set up a pillar and anoint it with oil to indicate it as a holy place. When God appeared to Gideon to instruct him in delivering Israel from their enemies and corruption, Gideon's response was to build an alter and offer a sacrifice, even though God had already departed.

When God did something dramatic in their world, the Celtic Christians thought that place was especially holy and powerful. Setting up stone pillars marked and commemorated these places and dramatic events. Sometimes they believed that, in these "thin places", there was a lingering open door from God for subsequent direct interventions for others in that same place. Sometimes, this prompted subsequent "pilgrimages" to these "special places", in order to seek the same kind of blessing or act of grace.

It is easy to reject this part of the Celtic Christian traditions as being superstitious and unscriptural. However, when rightly understood under the clear guidance of the Scriptures, a new and far greater reality bursts onto our awareness. According to the Scriptures, everywhere and everything is a sort of "thin place". There is no "barrier" between the natural and supernatural, and the supernatural is not only somewhere far off in heaven. God is omnipresent and the center of all things here on earth as well as in heaven. We read in Scripture that God visibly appeared in the holy of holies in the Jewish tabernacle and temple, but He did not stop being omnipresent in all other places. While visible in the temple, He was also present in all the places described by David in Ps. 139, and all other places as well. He was sitting on His throne in heaven, He was in the heavens declaring His glory, He was declaring His truth throughout the sky and universe, He was in Greece, and Russia, and Japan, and China, and America, declaring His power and glory as described in Rom. 1:20. He is still present in all those places, even though there is no longer any Jewish temple in Jerusalem. In those many places, He veils Himself from our normal senses (for our safety), but He is always there. All of His creation that surrounds us can be what you notice first, and that may draw you into recognizing His greater invisible presence whether surrounded by nature or not. In each and every one of those places He is doing huge lists of "wonderous works", most of which we still have not grasped. Each and every one of those places is a "thin place". If we were to set up commemorative stones, the landscape would be so covered with them we could not walk.

When rightly understood in light of Scripture, there is no need of any "open door", or any "door left slightly ajar" where God would manifest His presence or action in a way that we can perceive with our natural senses. The Living God does not need any such "open door" to do His sovereign working of all things for our good, and you do not need any such "open door" to sense His presence and action. How much do you really believe that "…God is working all things together for your good"? (Rom. 8:28) How many things are not included in "all things"? You only need to grasp and recognize, by faith, that God is always near/here. This is what Scripture tells us. This is living in true faith, as one who "sees what is unseen". This is what Jesus did and this is how His disciples are also called to live. A disciple robustly embraces this view. By this spiritual mind of Christ, we can realize that every moment, and everything happening in any moment, is a kind of "sacred moment", or "sacrament". Jesus said to doubting Thomas, "Blessed are they who did not see and yet believed" (John 20:29) The "hall of faith" in Hebrews chapter 11, tells us that Moses, "…endured as seeing Him who is unseen." (Heb 11:27) Moses had seen God in the burning bush. Later he would see Him on the banks of the Red

Sea, at the top of Mt. Sinai, and in the desert. However, Scripture does not say that God was visible to Moses as he left Egypt. Moses acted with certainty and commitment *as if he could see.*

Living in true faith is living with the same sense of ultimate reality that you would have if you could actually see the spiritual realities before you and around you with your physical eyes. But

> Living in true faith is living with the same sense of ultimate reality that you would have if you could actually see the spiritual realities before you and around you with your physical eyes.

you don't have to wait until you actually see with your physical eyes. You don't have to wait for some kind of vision, or angelic appearance, or miracle. You don't have to go out looking for a "thin place", hoping God might show up there with miracle in hand. This is about walking with God in the most common, everyday ways, even in a sandal repair shop, or baking bread, or even eating and drinking, but doing all these things to the glory of God. For all these "by faith" interactions with God, you can speak and act just as you would normally do, because to Him, all ways of communication are normal. He does not speak only in "heavenly language" or by some approved ceremony or ritual.

By living in vital, robust faith, you can walk with God every moment, in everything you do. As you live in each moment of your daily life, you can interact with Him, and you recognize and attribute every good thing as being from God who is there. You enjoy every good thing far more because you recognize it comes from His hand, just as if it had been delivered to you personally by an angel or a raven, or as if it had miraculously appeared there like manna. Thank and praise Him for every good thing and seek to hear from Him about the ultimate good purpose of both good and bad. Seek to hear His voice as He directs you to be His agent in bringing good out of the bad. This glorifies Him for everything. However, this should not be an "assumed" thought that is never present to your conscious mind. You can deliberately think about these matters in all things, and consistently express your recognition, thanks and praise for the God who is there.

The immediate and normal human reaction to this concept is to feel that God is intruding too much on your private life. However, the Scriptures clearly tell us that we do not have a private life away from God! Everything you are and everything you have belongs to God—even your very breath and even your soul! This inward conflict you feel is another struggle between the old nature and the new nature prompted by the indwelling Holy Spirit. It is like a wrestling match going on inside, but it is also a wrestling match between true discipleship and churchianity.

All too often, God does not prevail in this match. Like Jacob in the wilderness, He lets you win the struggle, for the moment, but it is always to your detriment and loss. (Gen. 32: 22-29) He will never force His way onto you. He waits for you to finally yield. Nevertheless, He doesn't give up. He will return with another training session on that very same matter at a later time. Every training session will set off the same old inner conflict until you finally yield. He is relentless, and that too is for your good.

How would your daily life and experience be changed if you were to really, really believe and act in complete consistency with the fact that God is everywhere all around you, that He is always acting toward you with complete grace, that every good gift is intentionally from Him, and He is always acting for your good? This is why we can, "give thanks in all things. (I. Thess. 5:18) This is why the apostles can accept arrest and threats by the Jewish leaders and then praise God for the privilege. (Acts 5:41) This is why Paul and Silas can accept arrest, beating, and sitting in stocks in a Philippian jail and sing songs of praise to God rather than bemoaning their situation and doubting that God loves them anymore. They could not yet see the earthquake that was about to happen that would set them free. They could not yet see or hear the cries of their jailer saying, "Sirs what must I do to be saved?" They could not yet see that the jailer and all his household would be saved through this severe trial they were going through! (Acts 16: 22-34) But they were living, "as if they could see" the spirituality of what was happening. This is not only for apostles, or great evangelists or missionaries or pastors or radio preachers. It is for every child of God who is walking as a disciple.

In order to glorify God in everything, even eating and drinking, you will simply live openly and naturally as if you could see the spiritual reality all around you and give all credit, praise, worship and honor to God who is behind it all. You don't need some special and anointed way from a celebrity preacher to respond to God. You don't need some special heavenly language. God speaks all languages and hears all thoughts and words, even before they come to your lips.

This will lead to a lot of time merely observing, pondering, meditating, and more importantly doing these things in open and free conversation with God about them. It also requires weaning off living a life of constant hurry, stress and tunnel vision to accomplish what seems pressing. As Dallas Willard has stated, "Ruthlessly eliminate hurry from your life. Hurry is the great enemy of spiritual life in our day." [51] If God is at the center of everything and everything is for His glory, what is more pressing than seeking Him and glorifying Him?

Biblical Spirituality in Worship

I have been in my share of committee meetings and group discussions on what should be included in "the worship service" of a church. Sometimes it is referred to as "the program for the Sunday morning service". The primary problem in all these discussions and considerations has been that there seems to be so little Scriptural commands or teaching on the subject. There are no passages that tell us what should be included in the "official worship service", not even in the "pastoral epistles". The brief pieces of information seem to imply that the Lord's Day gathering of the early church was a simple gathering for fellowship, teaching, prayer and singing. Over the centuries it morphed from those simple elements. As it increasingly Romanized, it became highly formal, ceremonial and rigid. As that happened, we lost what it means to "...worship in spirit and truth" (John 4: 23).

As the Evangelical church was born and flourished, we increasingly recognized that the highly formal, ceremonial and rigid that had been passed on to us was not satisfying the great cry of our hearts to worship in spirit and truth. The Spirit of Jesus cried out from within our hearts to move us back to something more akin to the simple fellowship, teaching, prayer and singing. For baby-boomers/Jesus freaks, that urge flowered out in "the Jesus music". (I urge you to see the recent film.) After a few years, this also led to great worship and praise gatherings, sometimes filling huge arenas and stadiums.

However, in all of this, both good and bad, it seems we did not really learn/relearn what it means to worship in spirit and truth. The evangelical church truly believes that they have a solid lock on the "truth" part by solid expository preaching. The Pentecostal/charismatic church truly believes that they have a solid lock on the "spirit" part by their doctrines and practices of the charismatic or sign gifts. Neither is the case.

The word "worship" means far more than "worth-ship" or "ascribing worth-ship". In almost all references throughout the Old Testament, it is one single Hebrew word. It means to completely prostrate yourself on the ground before someone of greatness to express your total awe, admiration, surrender and obedience to them. It is to get down on your hands and knees with your forehead to the ground to express complete obeisance toward the person before you.

Of course, with the deceitfulness of the human heart, this can easily be/become an empty gesture. Numerous Scriptures condemn ancient Israel because they "worshiped God in vain" (Isa 29:13, Mark 7:7). They come and bow down, but then they go away and do as they please, dishonoring God completely. It's pretense. It's superficial. It's a sham. Of course, this is not what God wants, and it is not what we want in God's church. Our Lord's teaching about worship does not require a body posture or position. It requires a position or posture of the heart without even implying a posture for the body, and without any reference to place or building or city or a particular ritual.

Worshipping in spirit is about what is going on in your spirit—the place where you are in touch with God when you are actually in touch with Him. He is Spirit, and to be in touch with Him in worship means in your spirit. When, in your spirit, you prostrate yourself before Him in recognition of His greatness and your expression of total awe, admiration, surrender and obedience you, are worshipping in spirit. Without this, no matter what the form, or ritual, or ceremony, or building, or place, or city, or powerful worship band, it is not worship in spirit. Paul declares that Christians, "...are those who worship in the Spirit of God..." (Phil 3:3). Worshipping in the spirit is deemed the normal for normal Christianity, not the exception and not a rarity. Only the new Christian, (the initiate or uninstructed) should have this gap in their spiritual experience and practice. But it was lost and never re-established on any widespread basis. Now, only a few know it truly. This has nothing to do with Pentecostal or charismatic doctrines or practices.

When worshipping in truth, it is based on two indispensable components. First, you must have a fundamental grasp of who this God really is—what He is really like—that He is one who totally deserves your worship. He is fully worthy of your worship, and He is the only One Who Is. Second, your worship must be "true". It must be deeply sincere and genuine, it is worship "in truth", i.e., truly worshipping, as described above. This is the kind of worshipper God seeks. It doesn't require any necessary form or ritual or ceremony or building or place or city or powerful worship band, etc., etc., etc. Listening to dynamic preaching is not worshipping in truth. Dynamic preaching may move you to worship in truth, but not vice-versa. It can be in a church, or in your bedroom, or in your study, or in a jail or in a pig pen. Thus, "If you can't worship in a pig pen, you know nothing

"If you can't worship in a pig pen, you know nothing about true worship".

about true worship". A disciple learns all of this as actual experience and consistent life practice. It is what your heart cries out for—a foretaste of heaven.

Biblical Spirituality in the Ordinances

In the Roman Church and its early off-springs, the official rituals (sacraments) of the Church were understood to be "physical symbols" that represent "spiritual realities", but few there be that can make any real sense out of that, because the Church has not taught Biblical spiritualty. They have only taught the intellectual, logical, and reasoning concepts that try to explain that "wholly other" that forms the "spiritual realities". Most Christians in liturgical churches have only gone through the motions because it is required and expected as part of being accepted by God and his Church. The Evangelical church does their own version of the same thing—all because Biblical spirituality has not been taught.

The Reformers labored to demonstrate that the "sacraments of the Church" do not convey salvation or God's actions for sanctification; but, as we are so prone to do, they went too far the other way. Turning the sacraments into "ordinances", then into nothing but empty symbols that are entirely unnecessary, has not held or returned the Church to Biblical spirituality. It has only further drained the ordinances of their deep meaning and power. Now they are only empty, meaningless rituals to most, and the manner in which we conduct baptism and the Lord's Supper supports this notion. This is the exact opposite of what they were intended to be when God gave them.

It is sadly obvious that water baptism has been so changed and distorted as to lose much of its meaning and power. This is not something you do for God. It is not a step in identifying with a local church, or a denomination, or with Christianity as a whole. It is something *God does to you*, through the hands of those who already know and serve Him. (See John 4:1-2) It is not a sacrament that saves you, but it is a sacrament that ushers you into the total *experience* of being born again, washed from your sins, immersed into Him to be raised from sin and death into a new life. It is undeniably clear in the New Testament that baptism was almost always given to new believers immediately after their sincere decision to trust Christ. There was no waiting period for weeks or months or years. There is no other explanation for the rapid development of the belief in baptismal regeneration. Water baptism is one of God's actions upon you to assure that your faith is not limited to "mental assent" or a "mental contract" with God. It makes your decision to trust Christ a "total-self experience". It drives the whole meaning deeply into your being, including your human body and consciousness. It should always be administered by those who fully believe in, and are committed to, Christ and His commands. Interestingly enough, it also ties the kingdom and the church together, because the church is an expression of Gods kingdom. When you join yourself to Christ, you also join yourself to His kingdom and His church.

Similarly, all the debates and arguments about the meaning of the Lord's Supper (the Eucharist) have been centered on the theological meaning. The theological meaning is important, but it has missed the main point of this being an actual experience of the presence of the Risen Savior within His church. When we partake, we can and should experience the same kind of experience as the first disciples in the upper room. In our hearts and in spirits, we are transported back into that upper room. Jesus stoops to wash our feet, shares supper with us, and then personally distributes the bread and wine as symbols of His body and blood which were about to be sacrificed as, "...the Lamb of God who takes away the sin of the world." (John 1:36). As He serves us, He speaks the words, "What I do tomorrow is for you, my dear child. Remember this from now on and remember that I did it *for you*." It is hardly an empty symbol which is entirely unnecessary and void of meaning. It is hardly something to complain about because, "It makes the service longer than usual, and we are in a hurry to meet our friends for lunch or get to the ball game." It is only empty to the carnal heart, to the legalistic heart, to the superficial heart. It can only be deeply meaningful if entered on the basis of the faith and spirituality of the participant. Disciples learn to embrace this fully.

Far better if the Reformers had stuck with the understanding that the mystical presence of the Lord's body and blood are present with the bread and wine. This mystical presence is just that—mystical. It cannot be explained with a few words of doctrine and theological terminology. Even the supposed distinction between "real presence" and "spiritual presence" is missing the point entirely. When properly understood, *spiritual presence is real presence*. It is the most real presence that is possible or available anywhere in the universe, and in any dimension, but it is intangible to our very limited physical senses and awareness. Luther's view that the spiritual reality is "under, over and around" the physical symbol was closer than we realize. We do not literally partake of the body and blood of the Lord "spiritually wrapped around" the physical bread and wine. But we are compelled to recognize and confess that, when we partake, "...in remembrance of Me", He intended a spiritual link to His previous words, "...he who eats My flesh and drinks My blood has eternal life…". (John 6:53) It is a New Covenant fulfillment of the Old Testament Passover. In the Old Covenant, the sacrificial blood was smeared on the doorposts and the flesh of the sacrificed lamb was eaten inside, as nourishment from God for the imminent journey from slavery to freedom. In the New Covenant, both the flesh (the bread) and the blood (the wine) of the sacrificed Lamb of God are consumed, to remember His sacrifice and to symbolically take His life into ourselves to strengthen us for the journey.

Christ was clearly referring to a spiritual nourishment, refreshing and union which can only be known and welcomed by those who are born of the Spirit. When mixed with a vital and living faith of a believer, the symbols are avenues, channels and tools for His sanctifying work in the believer. They were given by God as inspired actions to bring our focus into an actual spiritual presence and power when we partake by faith. It allows us to edge a little closer to the fully Biblical truth that, "…the cup of blessing that we bless is a sharing in the blood of Christ… the bread that we break is a sharing in the body of Christ" (not a reference to the Church). (I Cor 10:16, parenthesis mine) It establishes and strengthens our understanding that we are nurtured and refreshed by Him who gave His life that we might live. All of this can be known only by Biblical spirituality, but Biblical spirituality has not been taught, so spiritual experience is so minimal as to be nonexistent. Meanwhile, teaching that these are empty or outdated symbols that are unnecessary and with no real meaning or value, is outrageously faulty. Practicing them in a manner that rushes people through a meaningless ceremony is equally outrageous.

Missing the clear meaning of such passages is another symptom of "believing the Bible" but not understanding it's meaning or how to live in it = intellectual Christianity = churchianity. We must become spiritual to truly receive the wonderful blessing of the ordinances. We can learn to experience the spiritual presence of the Lord through His "symbols", because this is why He gave them! If pictures are worth a thousand words, better to use the pictures, not the one-thousand intellectual/theological words! But the pictures are seen and understood only by those who are spiritual, so we must teach Biblical spirituality!

Biblical Spirituality in Daily Life

This year, the fall colors in the trees and shrubs in our area were truly glorious, far beyond what is typical. It was just the right combination of temperatures and moisture to maximize the colorful foliage this year. Each day when I walked, it was a glorious experience as I watched all of this around me. Each day it developed and changed, eventually to fade away into the sleep of winter. As I walked, I did not limit my awareness to only the beauty and glory but also the living presence of the God who makes it all and dwells here. This is His garden, and He is here tending it. I rejoice in the beauty and glory, but most of all I rejoice in the God who is here in all of this. He brings me here to enjoy it with Him. This is a spiritual experience which is only available in Biblical spirituality.

Let's say you are making homemade chocolate-chip cookies. As you measure and add each ingredient, you are actively mindful for each ingredient and how it came to be available to you. You notice carefully the texture, the color, the aroma and how it adds to the overall appearance, aroma and taste of the cookies. You give thanks to God for each of these and you enjoy the process of making the cookies. As you sample a finger of the finished batter, you smile and your eyes light up at the taste. God smiles. You rejoice in God that He has provided such wonderful things for you to enjoy. You rejoice in knowing that He is right there with you as you make the cookies, and He is enjoying that you enjoy this. He has been planning this day with you for a long time. As you take each sheet of finished cookies from the oven you notice how they look and smell. What a delightful aroma, and God made it just for you (along with everyone else who chooses to partake of some). This is a spiritual experience which is only available in Biblical spirituality.

How about something even simpler, such as having a good drink of water? Although water is not supposed to have taste, anyone who has had good well water or real spring water knows it does. Beyond that, it has a sensation all its own, especially when you are thirsty. A nice big drink of water when you are tired and thirsty is a treat unto itself. Whether it is between innings of a long hot summer baseball game, or between wagon loads of hay on a sweltering July summer day, it is spectacular! Water is created by God (not evolution). It was created for you and all others who need it. He created you to enjoy the refreshing and satisfying drink of good water. (How does evolution explain that?) He did that deliberately for your enjoyment and blessing. As you are enjoying that nice big drink of good water, be fully mindful of it being a gift from a good God who likes to bless those He created. Look up to God and thank Him for this treat. Let your thankfulness come flowing up all the way out of your soul and express this fully to your loving Heavenly Father who gives this good gift. This is a spiritual experience which is only available in Biblical spirituality.

Let's say you wake up in the morning to find that, instead of the promised warm sunny day, it is chilly and a bit drizzly. (Whatever happened to good forecasting, huh?) Instead of chaffing and grumbling, you recognize and embrace that God is the one who determines the weather, and He has the complete right to make the weather what He chooses. After all, He is the Sovereign Lord of all creation. He is not silent, He is not absent, and He is not uninvolved. You recognize that many others may be rejoicing about the changed weather, for various reasons and purposes. It may even be an answer to prayer for some. You deliberately choose to gladly live in the weather that He chooses. He has a reason for it all, even if He did not ask your opinion or input. You rejoice in Him, in His sovereign gifts and purposes, and walk forward into the day with eager anticipation to discover the reasons that might have something to do with you. There usually is. God never has a single purpose in mind for anything He does. What good thing(s) has He planned for you in this "change of weather"? You go out of the door not chaffing and grousing, but in eager expectation of what God will bring to you in this day. This too is a spiritual experience which is only available in Biblical spirituality.

There are millions of examples and illustrations that could be described, and when you choose to walk in Biblical spirituality, you will experience more than you can count or write in your journal. It can be your consistent way of life as you walk with your Savior. You do not do these things in a mechanistic manner or merely by wrote or cultural norm. You do them as your true living experience, as you share each day with the God who gave it and implements it each day to bring you His blessings.

True Biblical discipleship teaches you true Biblical spirituality. This allows you to connect to the powerful process of living all of your life out of who you are in Christ. This cannot be duplicated or matched by anything else. The lack of it is the ultimate root of Christians who don't act much like Christ. It is also the root of believing that being a Christian is so hard! If you want to discover for yourself how easy, light and restful to the soul it can be to walk in obedience to Christ, all you need do is walk the path of true discipleship. You will be learning to be like Him! You will never want to go back!

CHAPTER 26

ENEMIES
WITHOUT AND WITHIN

As described in Chapter 4, moving back to the pathway where we were supposed to be may not be easy. We are likely to encounter enemies bent on preventing us from this journey. Most regrettable of all, those who oppose making this journey are likely to include some of our own Christian brothers and sisters, perhaps more than you would ever guess.

Years ago, God led me through a powerful spiritual exercise about forgiveness, related to Romans 4:25. It was a word picture that came vividly into my mind and awareness during prayer. It pictured our dear Lord being nailed to the cross. At first, you see this scene from the side view as you would in most movies. Then you see it as if you were looking through the eyes of Christ as He was being nailed to the cross. You look up at the Roman soldier who is nailing you. Then you see his face, angry and sneering as he nails you. Then you see the soldier's face more clearly, and he is you!

Now, imagine you determine to take the journey across that mountain pass to the true path of discipleship. After a while, you encounter enemies who furiously fight to obstruct and prevent your journey. As you draw nearer, and much to your great surprise, you begin to recognize some of these enemies. Eventually, you recognize some of them as good friends or fellow church members. Then suddenly, with even greater shock, you recognize that one of them is you! Now what will you do? Will you fight on to go forward, appealing to them to surrender their positions and join you? Some will join you, but some will still oppose and fight ferociously. Centuries of churchianity is that powerful and astounding.

I will never forget the interaction I had with one of my Bible college professors many years ago. He was a "guest professor" who briefly joined the faculty during a time of transition at the college. He was a well-known and popular pastor and preacher of a large Fundamentalist church in the area. The subject he taught was church administration. In the class, he firmly held and advocated the view of the "single-pastor-God's anointed–CEO" model for church leadership. I politely, but firmly, advocated the Scriptural model of elders in the local church as true co-pastors. He openly opposed this model. From time to time, I would stay over after class to further discuss some aspect of the subjects at hand. These were never unpleasant, but it was clear that we were both well entrenched. In one of those discussions, he shared with me, "I know that the Bible teaches elder-led local churches, but it doesn't work. It just never works." Of course, I went away absolutely stunned that such a view would be held by someone of his position and status.

After graduation, I went about seeking to teach the Scriptural truth of elder-lead local churches, and training men to fill these roles. Again, I learned that in the real world of churchianity, this professor was largely right. I had come from a church where it did work, and it was amazing to see; but, by and large, it doesn't work, and now I know why. It's because God's people have not been properly discipled for nineteen centuries! It's nearly impossible for un-discipled Christians to take up their proper role in church leadership and ministry. They don't know how, and no one is training them or even offering to do so! In a great number of evangelical churches, training for church leaders is about worldly leadership and administration issues, not being true under-shepherds under Christ. In most cases, they are simply an advisory board for the pastor(s). Properly training them would require full Biblical discipleship!

Pertinent to the focus of this book, accepting that discipleship is the primary focus of the Church will go down hard and change will not be easy. The churchianity model for churches is deeply entrenched, especially in Evangelical churches. This deeply entrenched churchianity is built on years of seeking to build large, apparently successful churches, with dynamic preaching, powerful worship bands, and lots of popular and fun church activities. Those who benefit from this model will fight ferociously to hold onto it. Most of these truly believe that this is the Scriptural model for the Church and abandoning is tantamount with violating the Scriptures. They do not yet see for themselves that this version is actually empty of the wonderful life that Christ Himself came to give. It is built on modern theory of marketing, not on the Scriptures. They genuinely believe that the wonderful new life can be achieved through churchianity, not realizing it is a mirage in the desert. "They keep seeking but will never find." (Matt 13: 14) It will never bring satisfaction of their hunger and thirst. It will never bring "restoration of my soul". (Ps 23: 3, paraphrase mine) I genuinely fear what God may have to do to His church to finally bring about obedience!

Most who oppose will do so on the basis of believing all the erroneous notions about discipleship and churchianity that are addressed in this book. They would easily assert that a strong program of discipleship as the primary purpose of the church "does not work". Becoming a Christian is supposed to be easy, based on cheap grace. Nothing should be included that interferes with it being easy, and now, fun! They truly believe that cheap grace and churchianity is the only way to get people to church and hold them there. Marketing theory trumps the Bible!

Believing that discipleship "doesn't work" stems from not knowing true, Biblical discipleship. They have never walked in that path with the Master. They will continue to believe this until they see correct discipleship truly implemented and see for themselves the tangible results of changed lives, open to full view. Once it is properly implemented, no one will want to go back. It's too good! Just like the cheap wine and the gas-station fast-food, once people taste the far superior blessings from Christ, no one wants the cheap stuff back. Once people experience true freedom, they never want to go back to slavery.

We must have the courage to face the truth that refusal of the path that Jesus has called us to is the height of foolishness and denial of the very Word of Christ. It automatically labels Jesus as a fool because He doesn't seem to know how to build a Church that actually "works". But churchianity can still build big churches with lots of excitement and church activities, based on personality, money and organization—for a while. Sooner or later, it withers, because it "has no root" (Matt 13:21).

Once again, the message of John the Baptist must ring in our ears, "Make straight the way of the Lord". (Luke 3:4) Let us be clear that John was not calling Israel to a massive highway reconstruction project to bring the Messiah to Jerusalem. "The way of the Lord" is spoken of throughout the Scriptures. It is the ancient path to which Jeremiah called Israel centuries before John the Baptist (Jer. 6:16). Throughout their history, Israel had made an absolute mess of what God had commanded them to do, throwing in a multitude of twists, turns, valleys and mountains well-mixed with disobedience and superficial faith. The call of Jeremiah, John the Baptist and many more was a call to do away with this twisted path and return to the true path. This is our only true path and our only true hope!

Now that you have read this book, you have a very important decision to make. Read again the summary in Chapter 3 of the promises given by Jesus Christ for those who follow Him. Ask yourself if you truly want the blessings He offered. He does keep His promises! The only way to consistently have these blessings in your life is to walk with the Master as a disciple. He calls out to you to join Him on this path. You will never want to go back! You have His word on it!

"I bow my knees before the Father and ask that He would grant you, according to the riches of His glory, to be strengthened with power through His Spirit in the inner man, so that Christ may dwell in your hearts through faith and that you, being rooted and grounded in love, may be able to comprehend with all the saints what is the breadth and length and height and depth, and to know the love of Christ which surpasses knowledge, and that you may be filled up to all the fulness of God." (Eph. 3:14-19). Amen.

Appendix 1

Grace by Faith Process for Personal Transformation Through Your Position in Christ

As you go about daily life, the Lord walks with you and actually rides around within you. This is His indwelling, and it is an absolute promise. It never changes or goes away. Any perceived difference is entirely on you and your focus, attentiveness and yieldedness. As you live out your life, numerous issues surface that reveal your consistent traits and characteristics. In each of these, the witness of the Lord will be present to guide you in whether those traits and characteristics are Christlike or not. You can perceive His witness which will either confirm that you lived out that moment and situation being like Him, or not. If not, His transformation is what is needed. His invitation will be, "Would you like to learn how to do that better? I can teach you if you submit to Me."

Following a simple process such as this may give you some practical direction and guidance:

1. In close consultation with the Lord, closely evaluate what your motive is in the transformation you seek. (James 4:3-6)

2. With the help of a good Bible concordance, other study materials and inquiry with other faithful believers, learn what the Scriptures say about this matter. (Heb. 4:12-13, John 6:63, Deut. 32:47)

3. Based on the Scriptures and the voice of the Holy Spirit, are you certain that the change you desire is right and pleasing to Him?

4. Each day, read, meditate and pray the key Scriptures on this matter until the Lord gives you permission to proceed.

5. Truly and fully repent before the Lord for the sinfulness that He has now shown you. Openly and humbly, confess this to the Lord. (I John 1:9) Then, ask the Lord to show you what parts of your old nature will have to die in order to have this aspect of transformation take place.

6. Take a faith posture in your mind and heart that Christ took this sin or weakness upon Himself to the cross and the grave; that when He arose from the grave, it was left there; that from His exalted place in heaven, He now seeks to flow this goodness into your life; by faith, receive it from Him into yourself. (This is just like when you accepted and received your salvation from Christ when you first believed. (Rom. 6:3-4, 8-11, Gal. 3:27, Col. 3:3)

7. Do you really, really believe that Christ can make this change, and that you will gladly embrace it as it comes?

8. Remind yourself of what blessings and freedom will come to you as this change is made. Will you welcome this? Will you openly give God all the glory when it happens?

9. Intentionally and faithfully pray that Christ will make this change. Don't give up until it is yours, or until the Lord tells you to move on.

10. Ask at least one other believer that you trust to pray for you in this matter and keep you mindful that you are seeking it from God. (This is not a time to discuss this matter, or for them to advise you on it.)
11. Praise God openly each time you see any small change/ improvement in this matter. Rejoice in God each step of the way!
12. Journal how the Lord leads you and speaks to you during this process. Don't be surprised or shocked that God shows you many things that may be part of entering this transformation in you. Journal those also.

Appendix 2

Key Scriptures About Discipleship

Believers/those who believed
Acts 2:44; 4:32; 5:14; 10: 45
I Tim. 4:12

Disciples
Acts 6: 1-2, 7; 9: 1, 19, 25-26, 38; 11:26; 13:52; 14:20-22, 28; 15: 10; 18:23, 27; Acts 20: 1, 30; 26: 28
I Peter 4:16

Brethren
Acts 11:1, 12, 29; 12: 17; 15: 1, 3, 23, 36; 16: 2, 40; 17: 6, 10, 14; 18: 18, 27; 20: 32; 21: 7, 17;
Romans 8:12; 12:1

The Way
Acts 9:2; 18:25-26; 19:9, 23; 22:4; 24:14, 22

The Saints
Acts 9:13, 32; 26:10
Romans 1: 7

I Cor. 1:2, 14:33
II Cor. 1:1
Eph. 1:1, 15

Church(es)
Acts 2:47; 5:11 8:1, 3; 11:22, 26; 15:3, 4, 22; 18:22; 20:17, 28
Romans 16: 1, 5
I Cor. 1:2; 4:17; 6:4; 10:32; 11:22; 12:28
Eph. 1:22; 3:10, 21

Christians
Acts 11: 26; 26:28
I Peter 4:16

BIBLIOGRAPHY

Adomnan of Iona, translated by Richard Sharpe. *Life of Columba*. London: Penguin Books, 1995

Allchin, A.M. and Esther De Waal. *Threshold of Light*. London: Darton, Longman and Todd, 1991

Anderson, Hans Christian. "The Emperor's New Clothes" in *Fairy Tales for Children*. public domain

Andrews, Alan, general editor. *The Kingdom Life*. Colorado Springs: NavPress, 2010

Archer, Gleason L. *The Encyclopedia of Bible Difficulties*. Grand Rapids, MI: Zondervan Publishing House, 1982

Arndt and Gingrich. *A Greek-English Lexicon of the New Testament and Other Early Christian Literature*. Chicago: The University of Chicago Press, 1957

Augustine of Hippo. *Confessions, Book 1*. as quoted in *Ancient Faith Bible*. China: Holman Bible Publishers, Nashville, TN, 2007

Barna Group, George Barna and David Kinnaman, general editors. *Churchless*. Carol Stream, IL: Tyndale Momentum, 2014

Barna, George. *Revolution*. Carol Stream, IL: Tyndale House Publishers, 2005

Batterson, Mark. *Wild Goose Chase*. Colorado Springs: Multnomah Books, 2008, Kindle edition

Blackaby, Henry and Claude V. King. *Experiencing God*. Nashville, TN: LifeWay Press,1999

Bonhoeffer, Dietrich. *The Cost of Discipleship*. New York, NY: Touchstone, 1995

Bradley, Jayson D. *Future-Proofing the Church*. MinistryAdvice, 2017, Kindle edition

Brother Lawrence and Father Joseph De Beaufort, updated and translated by Robert Elmer. *Practicing God's Presence*. Canada, NavPress, 2005

Bruce, Alexander Balmain, D.D. *The Training of the Twelve*. New Canaan, Connecticut: Keats Publishing, Inc., 1979

Bunyan, John. *Pilgrims' Progress*. Mineola, NY: Dover Publications, Inc., 2003

Campus Crusade For Christ, International, William Bright, editor. *Teacher's Manual for the Ten Basic Steps Toward Christian Maturity*. Arrowhead Springs, San Bernardino, CA: Campus Crusade For Christ, International, 1971

Carmichael, Alexander. *Carmina Gadelica, vol. 1.*, 2012, Kindle edition

Chafer, Lewis Sperry. *He That Is Spiritual*. Grand Rapids: Zondervan Publishing House, 1976

Chan, Francis, with Mark Beuving. *Multiply, Disciples Making Disciples*. Colorado Springs: David C. Cook, 2012

Cook, Michell and Diane. *Practicing God's Presence.* Bloomington, IN: Westbow Press, 2015, Kindle edition

Corey, Benjamin L. *Official Blog of Corey Benjamin.* GOOGLE, 10/10/15 www.patheos.com\blogs\former-lyfundie\10-reasons-why-people-leave-church, August 7, 2013,

Davies, Oliver, with Thomas O'Loughlin, Bernard McGinn, editor in chief. *Celtic Spirituality.* Mahwah, NJ: Paulist Press, 1999

Dennis, Jay. *The Jesus Habits.* Nashville: Broadman & Holman Publishers, 2005

De Sales, Francis St. *Introduction to the Devout Life.* Point Roberts, WA: Eremitical Press, 2009

De Waal, Esther. *The Celtic Way of Prayer.* New York: Doubleday, a division of Random House, Inc, 1997, Kindle edition

Deyoung, Kevin and Ted Kluck. *Why We're Not Emergent.* Chicago, IL: Moody Publishers, 2008

Duin, Julia. *Quitting Church.* Grand Rapids, MI: Baker Books, 2008

Earle, Mary C. *Celtic Christian Spirituality.* Great Britain, Skylight Paths Publishing, 2012

Earle, Mary C. and Sylvia Maddox. *Holy Companions.* Harrisburg, London, New York, Morehouse Publishing, 2004

Edersheim, Alfred. *The Life and Times of Jesus the Messiah.* Grand Rapids, MI, W. B. Eerdmans Publishing Co., 1971

Eims, Leroy. *The Lost Art of Disciple Making*. Grand Rapids, Michigan: Zondervan Publishing House, Colorado Springs, Colorado: NavPress, 1981

Fenelon, Francois de Saligna de la Mothe, translated and edited by Robert J. Edmonson CI and Hal M. Helms. *The Complete Fenelon*. Brewster, MA: Paraclete Press, 2014

Fenelon, Madame Guyon and Pere La Comb, edited by James W. Metcalf. *Spiritual Progress*. Chicago, IL, Letcetera Publishing, 2015 Kindle edition,

Garrison, Bruce. *A Guide to True Peace*. Shoals, IN: Kingsley Press, 1999, Kindle edition

Gaines, Donna. *Leaving Ordinary*. Nashville: Thomas Nelson, 2014

Gaultiere, Ph. D, Bill. *Your Best Life In Jesus' Easy Yoke*. Irvine, Soul Shepherding, Inc., 2016

Groeschel, Craig. *The Christian Atheist*. Grand Rapids: Zondervan, 2010

Guyon, Jeanne Marie Bouvier De La Motte. *Experiencing the Depths of Jesus Christ*. 2012, Kindle edition

Guyon, Jeanne Marie Bouvier De La Motte, translated by A. W. Marston. *Spiritual Torrents*. Edinburgh and London: Ballantyne and Company, 2012, Kindle edition

Guyon, Jeanne Marie Bouvier De La Motte, translated and re-arranged by P.L. Upham. *Letters of Madam Guyon*. 2012, Kindle edition

Haidt, Johnathon. *The Happiness Hypothesis*. New York: Basic Books a Member of Perseus Books Group, 2006

Hay, Alex Rattray. *The New Testament Order for Church and Missionary, Third Edition*. Netherlands: H.H. Blok, – Dieren (Gld)

Holladay, Tom. *The Relationship Principles of Jesus*. Grand Rapids, MI: Zondervan, 2010

Hollinger, Dennis P. Ph.D. "To Glorify or Enjoy Forever", published in *Knowing and Doing-A Teaching Quarterly for Discipleship of Heart and Mind*, by the C.S. Lewis Institute, Summer 2003, https://www.cslewisinstitute.org/ Knowing and Doing

Holman Bible Publishers. *Ancient Faith Bible*, China: Holman Bible Publishers, Nashville, TN, 2007.

Hull, Bill. *The Complete Book of Discipleship*. Colorado Springs: NavPress, 2006

Hull, Bill. *The Disciple Making Church*. Grand Rapids, MI: Fleming H. Revell, 1996

Hunter, George G. III. *The Celtic Way of Evangelism, revised and updated*. Nashville: Abingdon Press, 2012, Kindle edition

Husbands, Mark and Jeffrey P. Greenman, editors. *Ancient Faith for the Modern Church*. Downers Grove: Intervarsity Press, 2008

Huxley, Thomas Henry, quoted by R.H. Hutton, Clark University, in "Professor Huxley as a Machine", "The Spectator Archive", page 10, April 30, 1870, accessed on Google, March 9, 2022, https://mathcs.clarku.edu/huxley/comm/Hutton/Hut-Mach.html

Jethani, Skye. *The Divine Commodity: Discovering a Faith Beyond Consumer Christianity.* Grand Rapids, MI: Zondervan, 2009

Julian of Norwich, Father John-Julian, OJN. *The Complete Julian.* Brewster, MA: Paraclete Press, 2014

Law, William. *A Serious Call to a Devout and Holy Life.* Createspace Independent Publishers Platform, 2013, Kindle edition

Law, William. *The Power of the Spirit.* Fort Washington, PA: CLC Publications, 2009

Lightfoot, J.B., edited and compiled by J.R. Harmer. *The Apostolic Fathers.* Grand Rapids, MI: Baker Book House, 1973

Little, Paul. *"Know What You Believe".* Downer's Grove, IL: IVP Books, 2003

Little Paul. *"Know Why You Believe".* Downer's Grove, IL: IVP Books, 2008

Lynch, John, Bruce McNicol and Bill Thrall. *The Cure.* San Clemente: CrossSection, 2011

McDowell, William Fraser. *In The School of Christ.* New York and Cincinnati: The Abingdon Press, 1923

McIntosh, Kenneth. *Water From An Ancient Well.* New York: Anamcara Books, 2011

Moon, Gary W. *Apprenticeship with Jesus.* Grand Rapids: Baker Books, 2009

Morton, Scott. *Down to Earth Discipling.* Colorado Springs, Colorado: NavPress, 2003

Moulton, Rev. W.F. M.A. D.D. and Rev. A.S. Geden D.D., editors, revised by Rev. H.K. Moulton, M.A. *A Concordance to the Greek Testament*. Edinburgh, Great Britain: Morrison and Gibb, Limited, 1970

Nee, Watchman. *The Normal Christian Church Life*. Anaheim: Living Steam Ministry, 1994

Nee, Watchman. *The Normal Christian Life*. Carol Stream, IL: Tyndale Publishers, 1977

Newell, Phillip J. *Celtic Prayers From Iona*. New York: Paulist Press, 1997, Kindle edition

Newell, Phillip J. *Listening for the Heartbeat of God*. Mahwah, NJ: Paulist Press, 1997

O'Donohue, John. *Anam Cara*. New York, NY: HarperCollins Publishers, Inc, 2004

Ogden, Greg. *Discipleship Essentials, expanded edition*. Downers Grove: Intervarsity Press, 2007

Ogden, Greg. *Transforming Discipleship*. Downers Grove, IL: Intervarsity Press, 2003

Ortberg, John. *God Is Closer Than You Think*. Grand Rapids: Zondervan, 2005

Ortberg, John. *You Have a Soul- It Weighs Nothing But Means Everything*. Grand Rapids: Zondervan, 2014 Kindle edition

Ortberg, John. *Soul Keeping*. Grand Rapids, MI: Zondervan Press, 2014

Osborne, Larry. *Sticky Church*. Grand Rapids: Zondervan, 2008

Packard, Josh, PhD. and Ashleigh Hope. *Church Refugees.* Loveland: Group, 2015

Pentecost, J. Dwight. *Design for Discipleship.* Grand Rapids, Michigan: Zondervan Publishing House, 1981

Platt, David. *Radical–Taking Back Your Faith From the American Dream.* Colorado Springs: Multnomah Books, 2010

Platt, David. *Follow Me.* Carol Stream: Tyndale House Publishers, Inc, 2013

Putman, Jeff, and Bobby Harrington with Robert Coleman. *Real-life Discipleship.* Colorado Springs: NavPress, 2010

Putman, Jim and Bobby Harrington with Robert E. Coleman. *DiscipleShift.* Grand Rapids: Zondervan, 2013, Kindle edition

Rainer, Thom S. and Eric Geiger. *Simple Church.* Nashville, TN: B&H Publishing Group, 2006h.

Rees, Wilbur E. *$3.00 Worth of God.* Valley Forge, PA: Judson Press, 1971

Richards, Lawrence O. *A New Face For the Church.* Grand Rapids, MI: Zondervan Publishing House, 1970

Rippon, John. "How Firm a Foundation", in *Hymns of the Christian Life.* Camp Hill, PA: Christian Publications, 1978, no. 406

Schaff, Phillip, editor, revised by David S. Schaff. *The Creeds of Christendom, Vol. III.* Grand Rapids, MI: Baker Books, 2007, p. 676

Schaeffer, Francis A. *True Spirituality.* Wheaton, Tyndale House Publishers, 1972

Schultz, Thom and Joani. *Why Nobody Wants To Go To Church Anymore.* Loveland: Group, 2013

Sjogren, Steve. *Changing the World Through Kindness.* Ventura: Regal Books, 2005

Smith, James Bryan with Lynda Graybeal. *A Spiritual Formation Workbook*, revised edition. Englewood, CO: Harper One, 1999

Sparks, T. Austin. *Discipleship in the School of Christ.* Online library on Austin-Sparks.net, Kindle edition

Stanley, Charles. F. *Living the Extraordinary Life.* Nashville: Nelson Books, 2005

Swindoll, Charles R. *The Church Awakening, An Urgent Call for Renewal.* New York: Faithwords, Hachette Book Group, Inc, 2010

Tozer, A.W. *Delighting in God.* Bloomington: Bethany House Publishers, 2015

Tozer, A.W. *The Crucified Life.* Bloomington: Bethany House Publishers, 2014

Tozer, A.W. *The Pursuit of God,* (updated version). Abbotsford, WI: Aneko Press, 2015, Kindle edition

Watson, David. *Called and Committed.* Wheaton, IL: Harold Shaw Publishers,1982

Willard, Dallas. *Hearing God.* Downers Grove, IL: IVP Books, 2012

Willard, Dallas. *Renovation of the Heart.* Colorado Springs: NavPress, 2012

Willard, Dallas. *The Great Omission.* New York: HarperCollins Publishers, 2006

Willard, Dallas. *The Spirit of the Disciplines*. New York: HarperCollins e-books, 2009, Kindle edition

Willard, Dallas. *The Divine Conspiracy*. New York: HarperCollins Publishers Inc, 1998

Willis, Avery T, Jr. with Sherrie Willis Brown. *Master Life*. Nashville: B&H Publishing Group, 1998

Wuest, Kenneth S. LL.D., *Wuest's Word Studies From the Greek New Testament, Vol. 3*. Grand Rapids, MI: William B. Eerdmans Publishing Co., 1974

Wuest, Kenneth S. *The New Testament, an expanded Translation*. Grand Rapids, MI: Wm. B. Eerdmans Publishing Company, 1961

Wyrostek, Joe. *Disciples That Make Disciples*. Chicago: MPI Publishing, 2015 Kindle edition

Vine, W.E. M.A. *An Expository Dictionary of New Testament Words*. Old Tappan, New Jersey: Fleming H. Revell Company, 1966

Young, Sarah. *Jesus Calling*, Nashville, TN: Thomas Nelson, 2004

Endnotes

1   Dallas Willard, *The Great Omission* (New York: HarperCollins Publishers, 2006), p. xi-xii

2   Francis Chan with Mark Beuving, *Multiply, Disciples Making Disciples* (Colorado Springs, CO: David C. Cook, 2012) pp. 16-17. Used by permission of David C. Cook. May not be further reproduced. All rights reserved.

3   Dallas Willard, *The Great Omission* (New York: HarperCollins Publishers, 2006), p. xv

4   Unknown author, taken from a traditional hymn, "How Firm a Foundation", public domain

5   *Ancient Faith Bible* (China: Holman Bible Publishers, Nashville, TN, 2007).

6   John Bunyan, *Pilgrims' Progress* (Mineola, NY: Dover Publications, Inc., 2003)

7   Attributed to Albert Einstein, however sources do not agree on the specific source.

8   Dallas Willard, *The Great Omission* (New York: HarperCollins Publishers, 2006)

9   Skye Jethani, *The Divine Commodity: Discovering a Faith Beyond Consumer Christianity* (Grand Rapids,

MI: Zondervan, 2009), p. 11. Used by permission of HarperCollins Christian Publishing. www.harpercollinschristian.com

10 Chuck Swindoll, *The Church Awakening—An Urgent Call for Renewal"* (New York: Faithwords, Hachette Book Group Inc, 2010), p. 29

11 Brother Lawrence and Father Joseph De Beaufort, updated and translated by Robert Elmer, *Practicing God's Presence* (Canada, NavPress, 2005)

12 Paul Little, *"Know What You Believe"* (Downer's Grove, IL: IVP Books, 2003); *"Know Why You Believe"* (Downer's Grove, IL: IVP Books, 2008)

13 Dietrich Bonhoeffer, *The Cost of Discipleship*, translated from the German by R.H. Fuller, with revisions by Irmgard Booth. Copyright 1959 by SCM Press Ltd. Reprinted with permission of Scribner, a division of Simon & Schuster, Inc. All rights reserved. (New York, NY: Touchstone, 1995), p. 59

14 Alex Rattray Hay, *The New Testament Order for Church and Missionary, Third Edition* (Netherlands, H.H. Blok – Dieren (Gld))

15 Craig Groeschel, *The Christian Atheist* (Grand Rapids: Zondervan, 2010)

16 Hans Christian Anderson, "The Emperor's New Clothes" in *Fairy Tales Told for Children,* public domain

17 Barna Group, George Barna and David Kinnaman general editors, *Churchless* (USA, Tyndale Publishers, Inc., 2014), back cover. Used by permission of Tyndale House Publishers, Inc., all rights reserved.

[18] Dietrich Bonhoeffer, *The Cost of Discipleship*, p. 59

[19] William Fraser McDowell, *In the School of Christ*, p. 25, 159-160 (New York and Cincinnati: The Abingdon Press, 1923), public domain

[20] Gleason L. Archer, *Encyclopedia of Bible Difficulties* (Grand Rapids: Zondervan Publishing House, 1982), p 347-356

[21] Thomas Henry Huxley, "The Spectator Archive, page 10, April 30, 1870", quoted by R.H. Hutton, Clark University, in "Professor Huxley as a Machine", Google, March 9, 2022, https://mathcs.clarku.edu/huxley/comm/Hutton/Hut-Mach.html

[22] Arndt and Gingrich, *A Greek-English Lexicon of the New Testament and Other Early Christian Literature* (Chicago, USA: The University of Chicago Press, 1957), pp. 166-167, used by permission under their published Fair Use Guidelines.

[23] Arndt and Gingrich, *A Greek-English Lexicon of the New Testament and Other Early Christian Literature* (Chicago, USA: The University of Chicago Press, 1957), pp. 166-167, used by permission under their published Fair Use Guidelines.

[24] W.E. Vine, M.A, *An Expository Dictionary of New Testament Words* (Old Tappan, New Jersey: Fleming H. Revell Company, 1966), p. 162, used by permission under their published Fair Use Guidelines.

[25] Dallas Willard, *The Divine Conspiracy,* p. 35-59, 41, (New York: HarperCollins Publishers Inc, 1998)

[26] Blaise Pascal, public domain

27   Augustine of Hippo, *Confessions, Book 1*, public domain and quoted in *Ancient Faith Bible* (China: Holman Bible Publishers, Nashville, TN, 2007), p. 1135

28   Barna Group, George Barna and David Kinnaman general editors, *Churchless,* back cover. Content used by permission of Tyndale House Publishers, Inc., all rights reserved.

29   Barna Group, George Barna and David Kinnaman general editors, *Churchless,* p. 41.

30   Dietrich Bonhoeffer, *The Cost of Discipleship, p. 59*

31   This statement is not original with me, but there is no record of its source.

32   Chuck Swindoll speaking on James 1:22 on "Insight for Living" radio broadcast.

33   Dallas Willard, *The Divine Conspiracy,* pp. 35-59

34   Brother Lawrence and Father Joseph De Beaufort, *Practicing God's Presence*

35   Michell and Diane Cook, *Practicing God's Presence* (Bloomington, IN: Westbow Press, 2015, Kindle edition)

36   Sarah Young, *Jesus Calling* (Nashville, TN, Thomas Nelson, 2004)

37   Wilbur E. Rees, *$3.00 Worth of God (*Valley Forge, PA: Judson Press, 1971)

38   John Bunyan, *Pilgrim's Process,* public domain

39   Sources attribute this to several people, including Friederich Nietzsche and Anne Louise Germaine de Stael.

40 Kenneth S. Wuest, *Wuest's Word Studies From the Greek New Testament, Vol. 3.* (Grand Rapids, MI: William B. Eerdmans Publishing Co., 1974, p. 60-61

41 John O' Donohue, *Anam Cara, A Book of Celtic Wisdom.* (New York, New York: HarperCollins Publishers, Inc, 2004), pp.13-36

42 Kenneth S. Wuest,, *The New Testament, an expanded Translation* (Grand Rapids, MI: Wm. B. Eerdmans Publishing Company, 1961, used by permission under their published Fair Use Guidelines.

43 Phillip Schaff, editor, revised by David S. Schaff, *The Creeds of Christendom, Vol. III* (Grand Rapids, MI: Baker Books,2007), p. 676, used by permission under their published Fair Use Guidelines.

44 Henry T. Blackaby, and Claude V. King, *Experiencing God* (Nashville, TN: LifeWay Press,1999), pp. 19-20,

45 Brother Lawrence and Father Joseph De Beaufort, *Practicing God's Presence.*

46 Francis A. Schaffer, *He Is There and He Is Not Silent* (Wheaton, Il: Tyndale House Publishers, 1972), p. x., used by permission of Tyndale House Publishers, Inc., all rights reserved.

47 Dennis P. Hollinger, Ph.D, "To Glorify or Enjoy Forever", published in *Knowing and Doing-A Teaching Quarterly for Discipleship of Heart and Mind*, published by the C.S. Lewis Institute, Summer, 2003, Google, C. S. Lewis Institute, https://www.cslewisinstitute.org/ Knowing_and_Doing

48 John Ortberg, *Soul Keeping* (Grand Rapids, MI: Zondervan, 2014)

49   Lewis Sperry Chafer, D.D., LITT.D, *He That Is Spiritual* (Grand Rapids, MI: Zondervan, 1967)

50   Francis A. Shaeffer, *True Spirituality* (Wheaton, IL: Tyndale House, 1972)

51   Dallas Willard, as quoted, in *Soul Keeping* by John Ortberg (Grand Rapids, MI: Zondervan, 2014), p. 20. Used by permission of HarperCollins Christian Publishing. www.harpercollinschristian.com

Printed in the USA
CPSIA information can be obtained
at www.ICGtesting.com
LVHW020408140124
768650LV00016B/1090